Original title: *Ecos de la guerra entre México y los
Estados Unidos*
Copyright © 2004 by **Ediciones Tecolote**

Copyright © 2004 by **Krystyna M. Libura**,
Luis Gerardo Morales Moreno,
Jesús Velasco Márquez
Translation copyright © 2004 by **Mark Fried**
Copyright © 2004 by Groundwood Books

Published simultaneously in Spanish by Ediciones
Tecolote and under the Libros Tigrillo imprint as
Ecos de la guerra entre los Estados Unidos y México

Groundwood Books / Libros Tigrillo /
Douglas & McIntyre
720 Bathurst Street, Suite 500
Toronto, Ontario M5S 2R4
Distributed in the USA by Publishers Group West
1700 Fourth Street, Berkeley, CA 94710

Library and Archives Canada Cataloguing in Publication
Libura, Krystyna M.
Echoes of the Mexican-American War /
Krystyna M. Libura, Luis Gerardo Morales Moreno,
Jesús Velasco Márquez ; translated by Mark Fried.
Includes index.
ISBN 0-88899-555-5 (bound).
ISBN 0-88899-582-2 (pbk).
1. Mexican War, 1846-1848. 2. Mexican War, 1846-
1848--Sources. I. Morales Moreno, Luis Gerardo
II. Velasco Márquez, Jesús III. Fried, Mark IV. Title.

E404.L5213 2004   973.6'2   C2003-907319-X

Printed and bound in Mexico

THIS BOOK OWES MUCH
TO THE PASSION AND KNOWLEDGE OF COLLECTOR
ROBERTO L. MAYER

SPECIAL THANKS TO:
Mario A. Chávez Ch.
Joanne H. Hillefeld, Eva Márquez Romay
and Josefina Z. Vázquez Vera
for their cheerful and generous assistance;
Omar Lazcano Pérez
for his careful critical reading of the manuscript;
Vera and Roberto L. Mayer
for their heartfelt embrace of the project;
to the staff of all the museums and libraries consulted
for their professionalism and cordiality;

to our dear ones
Bárbara, Hanna and Mina;

and to Miles Davis, El Fatimí, Wojciech Kielar,
Astor Piazzolla, Alexandre Tansman,
and the inevitable Bach,
for keeping us company during the long hours.

Project director: **Ma. Cristina Urrutia**
Editor of text and graphics: **Krystyna M. Libura**
Graphics adviser: **Roberto L. Mayer**
Design and layout: **Krystyna M. Libura,
Mónica Solórzano Z.**

(A CONACULTA • FONCA

This publication was made possible thanks to the
generous support of the FONDO NACIONAL PARA LA
CULTURA Y LAS ARTES (FONCA), MÉXICO

Cover image: "General Wool's army marches toward
Monclova in Mexico," by Samuel Chamberlain,
The San Jacinto Museum of History, Houston.

ECHOES OF THE MEXICAN-AMERICAN WAR

Krystyna M. Libura

Luis Gerardo Morales Moreno

Jesús Velasco Márquez

Translated by Mark Fried

Groundwood Books / Douglas & McIntyre
Toronto Vancouver Berkeley

Echoes of the Mexican-American War *is divided into two parts: the first from the Mexican point of view, and the second from the American one. Each chapter has its equivalent in the other half of the book, and the symbol of a small cannon* indicates where connections between the documents and images of one part can be found in the other. The texts appear as they were originally written, except for some minor corrections for spelling and grammar and some editing to improve the flow where it seemed necessary.*

The dates used by the editors have been taken from the original documents, which were not always accurate.

Each chapter begins with an introduction to set the context for the documents to follow. Side notes throughout provide commentary and explanation for both images and text. Explanatory graphics are included for some of the battle scenes. The Mexican portion of the book includes contemporary maps depicting the deployment of forces and the territories in dispute. A key to the map symbols is shown below.

Battles

U.S. Campaigns

Mexican Campaigns

Uprisings

Occupations

Contents

Mexican Voices

Americans Viewed by a Liberal

Two Americas emerged on the American continent, one Hispanic-Latin and another Anglo-Saxon. The two battled to expand trade and to control the Atlantic trade routes. Both sought to imitate European models and to improve on them. Yet their cultural foundations were utterly distinct. The Spanish colonization of Meso-America and the Andes strove to inculcate Catholicism, while the Dutch and English colonization of the territory that is today the United States was thoroughly Protestant.

When Mexico's colonial ties with Spain ended in 1821, the country's intellectuals and politicians came face to face with the historical reality of a continent divided into two value systems: traditional Catholicism identified with the Spanish monarchy, and Anglo-American Protestantism marching toward political and material modernity.

Lorenzo de Zavala, along with other intellectuals of the time (1821–1836), viewed the United States of America as a political model worthy of imitation. The Americans had created a new version of European society—politically organized and stable, based on religious tolerance, individual citizens' rights and the right to unlimited private property—that offered its members prosperity in the broadest sense of the word.

THE TERRITORIES OF THE UNITED STATES AND MEXICO
AT THE BEGINNING OF THE NINETEENTH CENTURY.

*I*n *1819 Spain and the United States signed the Transcontinental Treaty, which defined the border between New Spain and its northern neighbor. Two years later, an independent Mexico inherited the territory of New Spain.*

This map compares the territories of the two countries at the moment of Mexican independence. The dotted lines indicate administrative divisions. In the United States, the eastern states are clearly delineated, but the huge territory to the west of the Mississippi is not yet settled. In Mexico, Texas and Coahuila are still united as one.

The United States of America:
An Example Worth Following

[Lorenzo de Zavala; *Viaje a los Estados Unidos del Norte de América...*]

...This book has no merit as far as originality is concerned... When I organized it, I added a number of observations arising from the circumstances or facts referred to. Nevertheless, the Mexican people, to whom I dedicate this book, ought to find it very useful. In it, they will find an accurate description of the people their legislators would like them to be. A hard-working people, active, thoughtful, circumspect, religious amid a multiplicity of denominations, tolerant, avaricious, free, proud and persevering.

The Mexican is easygoing, lazy, intolerant, generous to the point of extravagant, vain, combative, superstitious, ignorant and an enemy of all shackles. The North American works, the Mexican enjoys himself; the former spends as little as he can, the latter even what he doesn't have... In the States of North America everyone owns property and seeks to accumulate wealth; in Mexico the few who own property fail to care for it and some simply run it into the ground...

Hard Workers of the North

If I wished to create a nice work of art with engravings, of course I would carve beautiful panels representing steamships, workers clearing the land and laying out ties and steel for railroads, fields bathed by streams, cities crossed by navigable rivers, settlements that spring forth from the earth and work to improve it. I would include rooms filled with children of both sexes learning to read and write, workers and artisans with a hoe or a tool in one hand and a newspaper in the other, six thousand temples of many beliefs in which man can pray to the Creator however his heart dictates. In sum, peace and plenty bringing happiness to 15 million inhabitants. Such is the view I have of the United States of the North...

Lorenzo de Zavala was one of the foremost defenders of the independence of New Spain. For his conspiratorial activities against the Spanish regime, he was imprisoned in the fort at San Juan de Ulúa from 1814 to 1817. While in jail, he taught himself both English and medicine. Zavala wrote this essay after his second trip to the United States, which confirmed his idealization of U.S. society at the beginning of the 1830s. He clearly believed the U.S. political system embodied the progressive liberal ideals he sought for Mexico.

This scene painted around 1835–1840 shows the port of New York with the city's skyline in the background.

NEW YORKERS RELIGIOUSLY LITERATE

New York has nearly two hundred and twenty thousand inhabitants... In no town on the globe are there so many newspapers in proportion to the population as in the United States of the North. In New York, in 1831, there were twenty-eight newspapers, most of them quite sizeable. In every town of two thousand inhabitants, the first thing people do is put up a small church, build one or two buildings for schools, and set up a printing press...

IMPORTANCE OF EDUCATION
IN BUILDING A CITIZENRY

New York has more than three hundred schools, most of them free, in which nearly forty thousand children of both sexes study. Among those who populate the cities of the

United States, I haven't met a single man who doesn't know how to read, and very few who don't know how to write. Thus they read public decrees, they take part in issues of broad interest, and they create a mass of irresistible opinion...

AMERICAN COMMON SENSE

In no country of the world are there more commercial businesses or more ways of making money. Few talk of abstract questions or issues in which they have no material interest. An American will ask a Mexican if there are steamships, if there are factories, if there are mines, if money can be made easily in one state or another. A Mexican will ask what sort of government, what religion, what the customs are and if there are theaters in this place or that. Americans are essentially thrifty and hardworking...

This drawing from 1825 shows public works around City Hall in New York. The building at the center housed the American Museum.

A fascinating aspect of modern economic history is the Industrial Revolution in the United States. The decade of the 1830s wrought enormous changes in land transportation (railroads), grain markets and the textile industry, which transformed an agrarian society into an industrial power unparalleled in the Western Hemisphere. Between 1790 and 1815 the Americans became the neutral trading partner of warring European powers, in the process accumulating sufficient capital to finance the mechanization of the manufacturing sector.

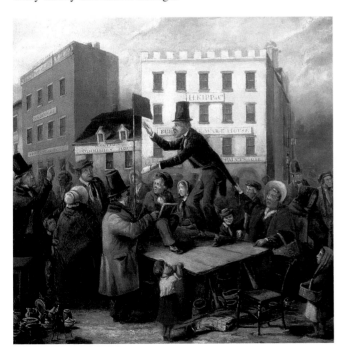

Auction in Chatham Square, New York City.

The allegory on the opposite page sums up Zavala's ideals. On the "Ladder of Fortune" morality and honesty are the struts that support the steps of industry, temperance, prudence, integrity, economy, punctuality, courage and persever- ance. These values lead to such golden fruit as God, riches, suc- cess, honor, happiness and a long life. In the background lurk temptations and vices, such as gambling and strikes, that make for an evil life.

SOCIAL OSTRACISM OF AFRICAN-AMERICANS

In the city of New York there are a considerable number of blacks and people of color, although happily, as in the other states of the North from Maryland on up, slavery is not per- mitted. Despite the emancipation of the African class and their children, there is a sort of social ostracism which excludes them from all political rights and even from doing normal business with the rest, in a way as if they had been excom- municated. This situation is rather unnatural in a country where the broadest principles of freedom are professed.

PRIVATE PROPERTY:
A PILLAR OF SOCIAL STABILITY

The United States...is today perhaps the nation least impe- riled by revolution. But its stability is due...to the unique circumstance that the vast majority of citizens are property owners. There is no doubt that this is one reason for the unswerving confidence of that fortunate nation, though not the only one. No question about social systems can be ex- plained by a single factor...

REPRESENTATIVE DEMOCRACY:
A POWERFUL INVENTION

In effect, the school of political thought in the United States is a complete system, a unique classic work, a discovery comparable to the printing press, to the compass, to steam power. It is a discovery that applies moral force to individual intelligence in order to set in motion the great machinery of society, which up to now has been more dragged than led, pulled along by artificial means. [Society is] a monstrous mosaic of fragments, a heterogeneous mixture, united by feudalism, superstition, caste privilege, legality, religiosity, and other unnatural elements; plus rubble from the deluge of

darkness that inundated the human genus for twelve centuries... Perhaps the most powerful argument to be made against the eternal declamations of absolutists and aristocrats is people's power in all its plenty, governing a wealthy, powerful nation and an immense territory, ruling it with wisdom, with moderation, with certitude, and seeing under its administration the unfolding of the elements of great territorial, industrial and commercial prosperity...

The city of Boston around 1846, as portrayed in a Mexican magazine.

Cultural Conflict during the Colonization of Texas

*I*ndependent Mexico inherited a territory of more than four million square kilometers and a population of approximately six million people, most of them in the Central Highlands and certain parts of the Central Lowlands, the West and the South. During the first few decades after independence, successive Mexican governments favored settling foreign immigrants on "abandoned" lands, in the belief that it would help agricultural development and achieve what was then termed racial improvement. This colonization policy completely excluded Indians even though they made up sixty percent of the population—in fact, they were considered an obstacle to progress.

During the decade from 1824 to 1834, the Mexican government offered nineteen land grants to some seven thousand settler families, most of them English-speaking Americans, although there were also a few Mexicans among them, including Miguel Ramos Arizpe who brought two hundred families to Texas, Lorenzo de Zavala who brought five hundred, and Vicente Filisola who brought six hundred.

Even so, the Mexican government grew apprehensive at reports of the growing American influence in Texas, especially when the expansionist designs of the U.S. government became evident.

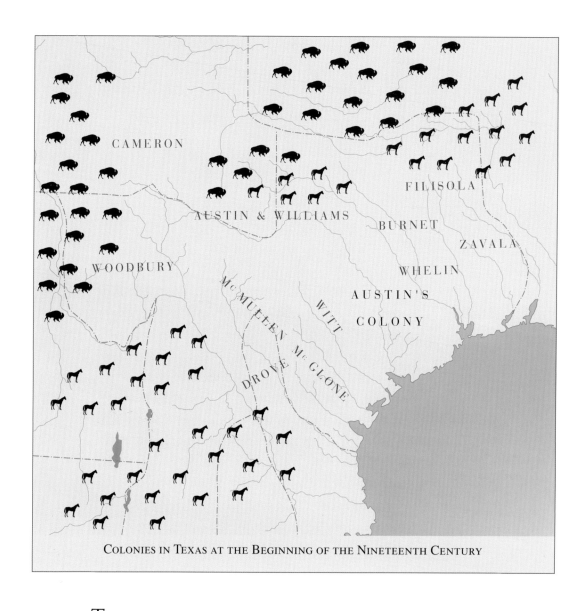

COLONIES IN TEXAS AT THE BEGINNING OF THE NINETEENTH CENTURY

*T*his chart of Mexican and American colonies in Texas, based on a map by Stephen Austin, shows the extent of American colonization. On his map Austin did not record a single Indian tribe, indicating instead regions of wild horses and buffalo—which is where the Indians who depended on those animals lived.

ZAVALA WARNS OF THE STRONG
AMERICAN INFLUENCE

[Lorenzo de Zavala, *Viaje a los Estados Unidos del Norte de América...*]

The influence of the United States on Mexico will become with time a force of opinion, of teaching, of instruction, all the more powerful insofar as it is solely moral, founded on its doctrines and lessons. But there is more. Ten thousand citizens of the United States move into Mexican territory every year... Along with their industriousness, these settlers and merchants bring their habits of freedom, thrift, hard work, their austere customs and religion, their individual independence and their republicanism...

Within a few years the Mexican Republic will be fashioned on a combination of the American system and Spanish customs and traditions...

The American system will obtain a complete though bloody victory...

[The North American colonists] will be incapable of submitting to the military regime and ecclesiastical government which unfortunately still hold sway in Mexican territory, despite the republican-democratic constitution. They will propose what institutions ought to govern the country, and they will want them to be not a trick or an illusion, but a reality. When a military boss tries to intervene in their civilian affairs, they will resist and they will win. They will form popular assemblies to take charge of public affairs, as is the custom in the United States and in England. They will build churches of various denominations to adore the Creator according to their beliefs. Religious practices are a social necessity, one of the prime consequences of human evil.

Will the Mexican government send a legion of soldiers to Texas to impose Article 3 of the Mexican Constitution, which prohibits practicing any other religion besides Catholicism?

El Colonol Norte Americano.

An ideal American settler, according to a Mexican calendar from the period.

Zavala's desire to reject what he considered a retrograde Spanish colonial heritage, and to build a Mexico along the lines of the U.S. political system, helps to explain his participation in the colonization of Texas. And when Texas rose up against Mexico, Zavala sided with the Texans.

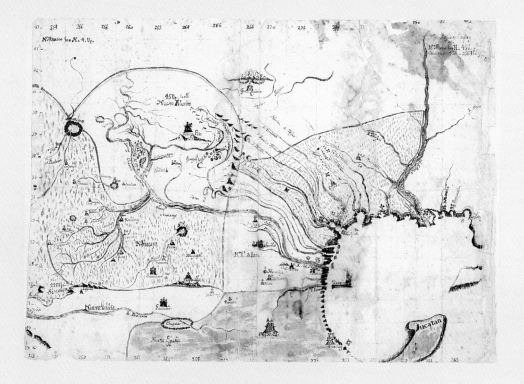

This unusual map, while not very precise, indicates the provinces of Texas, New Mexico and New Biscay, which formed part of the kingdoms of New Galicia and New Spain, and leaves no doubt that Texas was under Spanish dominion.

The dispute over the border can be traced back to the Transcontinental Treaty, also known as the Adams-Onís Treaty for the names of the negotiators who signed it on behalf of the U.S. and Spanish governments. In it, Spain ceded Florida in exchange for the United States renouncing its claim to Texas. The confirmation of that treaty after Mexico's independence in 1821 was subject to political pressure and diplomatic controversy. In 1828, a confirmation was signed, but the U.S. government postponed an exchange of ratifications until 1832. At the same time, a binational commission was set up to establish the precise location of the Texas border. A new border accord was ratified in April 1836, although by that date Texas had already declared its independence.

THE DIFFICULT TASK OF ESTABLISHING BORDERS

[Report by General Manuel Mier y Terán to the President of the Republic Guadalupe Victoria, 1828]

...Even when the treaty [of Adams Onís] is approved in the near future, its implementation by commissioners on either side will take several years: the task of establishing the borders of Louisiana when it belonged to Spain dragged on from 1726 until 1800, according to the American commissioner (Ellicot), and there is certainly no comparison between that plot of land and the immense one to be dealt with now. Thus we ought to plan on sixteen years of considerable labor to establish our borders from the Sabina River to the Southern Sea. Fortunately, the need is not so urgent along the entire boundary as it is at its extremes, particularly along the border with Texas, where every minute the number of North American settlers increases.

SCANTY MEXICAN PRESENCE
IN TEXAS

As one travels from Béjar to this town [Nacogdoches], the influence of Mexicans diminishes to the point where it seems to be practically nil. But where could such influence come from? Not from the population, because the proportion of Mexicans to foreigners is one to ten. Not from Mexican culture either, because precisely the opposite occurs; the Mexicans of this town form what is known everywhere as the common class, the poorest and the most ignorant... Neither are there any officials or judges. One paltry little man, not to put too fine a point on it, who calls himself the mayor, and a council that fails to meet even once in a lifetime, are all we have at the most crucial point on our border, where, from what I have seen in the short time I have been here, there are very serious developments in political and judicial affairs...

Mexico's rulers were slow to become aware of the dangers posed by the large influx of Americans into Texas. What tipped them off was the alarming proposal from Ambassador Joel R. Poinsett, ☞ p. 169, to purchase Texas, and the failed insurrection led by settler Haden Edwards. The Mexican government then sent a scientific and military expedition led by Gen. Manuel Mier y Terán, who wrote a detailed report on Texas's geography and the social and political climate in the period 1827-1832.

The first U.S. census in 1790 found 3.5 million people living in what was then the territory of the United States. By 1815 the Americans numbered 8.4 million. The five colonies of the American South (Maryland, Virginia, North Carolina, South Carolina and Georgia) had nearly two million inhabitants, while Texas's population was no more than two thousand.

PROBLEMS CAUSED BY THE ILLEGAL IMMIGRATION OF AMERICANS TO TEXAS

This state of affairs has given rise to an antipathy between Mexicans and foreigners, which is not the least of the burning issues I have found to report to you, and, if prudent actions are not taken in time, Texas will sink the entire [Mexican] federation... In the meantime, the arrival of new settlers is incessant; one first learns of them by discovering a plot of land already planted where they settled many months beforehand. The former inhabitants claim the property—based on a regulation title from the time of the Spanish government, of doubtful authenticity because the archives have been lost—and litigation begins in which the mayor has an opportunity to demand some sort of payment. In the towns that have no judges such cases are most numerous. This should be understood as the case in Nacogdoches and its immediate surroundings, since in more distant lands, particularly the ones that belong to the government, as far as we know the natural order carries on, which is to say that it is being settled without anyone being the wiser.

In 1772, San Antonio de Béjar had the largest population in Texas: sixteen families from the Canary Islands with their domestic servants, one priest and 22 soldiers.

DIFFERENT CLASSES OF SETTLERS

Besides the North Americans who settled in the time of the Spanish government, who number few, there are two classes of settlers. First, there are fugitives from our neighboring republic, many of them bearing a facial scar, which marks them as thieves and swindlers. They have settled between Nacogdoches and the Sabina River, and are ready to cross and re-cross the river as often as need be to put distance between themselves and the scene of their crimes; some have reformed themselves and spend their lives working the land.

The other class is made up of poor workers who don't have the four or five thousand pesos to buy a piece of land in the north. Out of a desire to own property, which is one of the virtues of our neighbors to the north, they have come to Texas. The colony of Austin is made up of such people. They are generally hardworking and honest and appreciative of the country; most of them own a slave or two.

[The] total population is such an incoherent mixture of unconnected parts that it is unlike any other in our entire federation. There are tribes of savages, numerous and peaceful, but armed and always ready for war, whose progress toward civilization will certainly be achieved through close vigilance by a careful and enlightened political authority. There are settlers come from another, more advanced nation, with more shrewdness than Mexicans but also more malice and irascibility. Among the foreigners there are all sorts: fugitive criminals, honest laborers, men prone to laziness and vice, hard workers, etc. They all carry their constitution in their pockets and claim the rights and the authorities and officials that it promises. Most of them own slaves and the slaves, having already sensed the favorable intent of Mexican laws regarding their pitiful state, are anxious to throw off their yoke, while the owners think they can keep it on them by making it all the heavier. The slave-owners perpetrate barbarities that are common where men live in relations so opposed to nature: they pull out their slaves' teeth, sick dogs on them to tear them to pieces, and even the most moderate among the owners whips his slaves until their flesh is flayed...

View of Galveston.
This city owes its name to the Spanish visitor, Bernardo de Gálvez, who founded it out of concern for the meager population of Texas.

Juan Nepomuceno Almonte, son of independence hero José María Morelos y Pavón, was commissioned in 1834 to demarcate the border between Mexico and the United States.

At the dawn of the nineteenth century, skilled Indian horsemen continually attacked the settlers who occupied their lands and disturbed the environment on which the tribes depended.

STRATEGIES OF THE SETTLERS TO ANNEX TEXAS TO THE UNITED STATES

[Report of Colonel Juan Nepomuceno Almonte, 1834]

Some of the American settlers, and these are the most moderate, say that the surest way to achieve the separation of that precious territory is first to set it up as a state, in order to acquire some degree of sovereignty over it; then they would declare it entirely independent of Mexico, and take advantage of the first stirrings that might occur in the interior to join the republic to the north. [Should this lead to war], they would declare themselves neutral and await the reaction, and if that doesn't work out, or if the civil war goes on too long, they would make a declaration to the entire world, explaining why they should break away from Mexico and join the United States of America...

STOP THE AMERICAN SETTLERS!

To my thinking we Mexicans would gain nothing by giving the foreigners more land and we must recognize that these American settlers could never unite with us... How could we expect a people, who would have to begin by learning our language, to love us and adapt to our customs, when the first thing they will do is study new ways and get involved in interests entirely opposed to our own, such as those of the Anglo-Americans... I, for one, would be of the opinion that, from now on, no one but Mexicans should be allowed onto empty lands, Mexicans from the laboring class who are as industrious as any foreigner... As soon as a campaign is waged against the savage Indians and they are taught a lesson, emigration to Texas will be easy to achieve... The government must be convinced that as long as no formal campaign is waged against those savage tribes, the unfortunate inhabitants of the border regions will be their victims...

A Star Is Born

Despite having been the world's foremost producer of silver, the Mexican state emerged from its colonial past utterly bankrupt, due to loans made to the Spanish crown by the viceroyalty of New Spain to the tune of thirty million pesos between 1790 and 1821, which the debtor never repaid.

To alleviate the crushing scarcity of liquid reserves, besides turning to private money-changers and British lenders, the first federalist governments sought to encourage private investment through colonization. When the financial situation reached the breaking point in the midst of political chaos on October 23, 1835, Congress promulgated a document called "The Basis for Reorganizing the Mexican Nation," which was given constitutional status. It set up a centralized governing system and buried the precepts of the federalist Constitution of 1824.

These measures consolidated political and military power in the capital city. No one imagined at the time that such a change would provide the Texas colonists with a legal pretext not only to reject the new centralized system, but, above all, to proclaim their independence from Mexico.

The Declaration of Independence of Texas was issued in the Texas town of Washington (later renamed Washington-on-the-Brazos) on March 2, 1836. That event would open the door to confrontation between Mexico and the United States of America.

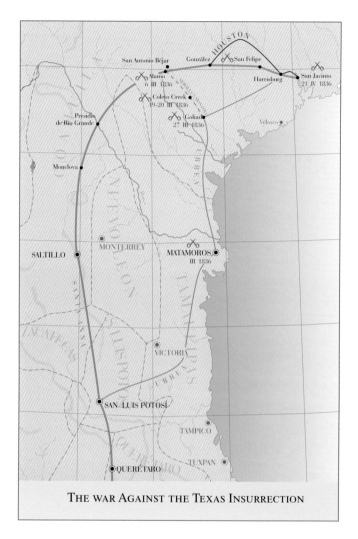

THE WAR AGAINST THE TEXAS INSURRECTION

In November 1835, Texans rose up against the centralized system of govern-
ment in force since the promulgation of "The Basis for Reorganizing the
Mexican Nation," and soon drove out the few Mexican soldiers stationed in
Texas. As constitutional president on leave and commander-in-chief of the
army, Gen. Antonio López de Santa Anna personally led what he believed
would be a brief punitive expedition. The army he commanded, made up of six
thousand men, was very poorly equipped and the forced march from San Luis
Potosí to Texas in the bitter February of 1836 exhausted his inexperienced sol-
diers. The campaign turned out to be disastrous for Mexico. This map shows
where the principal battles were fought.

THE AMERICANS WANT TEXAS

[Ramón Alcaraz et al., *Apuntes para la historia de la guerra...*]

The Mexican Republic, so favored by nature, so well endowed with the elements that make for a large and happy nation, has the misfortune (besides others not to be mentioned here) of being situated next door to a strong and enterprising people. Emancipated from the Spanish metropolis, lacking the experience that it could not acquire while its fate was in foreign hands, trapped for long years in the whirlwind of incessant revolutions, Mexico was an easy prey for anyone who would deploy a respectable force against it...

More than most of the Republic, Texas boasts the advantage of having at its heart beautiful and navigable rivers, perhaps the only boon lacking in nearly every other part of the privileged soil of our homeland. Texas has all the necessary elements to prosper as a nation in agriculture, industry, commerce and navigation...

The benefits to be had by possessing Texas encouraged the United States to procure it at any cost, despite the fact that the U.S. had no need of new acquisitions; its own lands were more than two-thirds unsettled, [but] it valued them little since they were not conducive to great progress in agriculture, due to the poor quality of the soil and the extreme and unpleasant temperatures in all seasons...

POPULATION GROWTH AS A STRATEGY FOR EXPANSION

As long as the province of Texas was under Spanish rule, the inordinate prudence and vigilance of the government maintained a strong barrier against the Americans' intent... In the year 1819, not long before the independence of Mexico, the Spanish government gave Moses Austin authorization to found a colony in Texas...

The emancipation of our Republic from the Spanish Crown opened the door wide to new immigrants. Foreigners

These texts are excerpts from Apuntes para la historia de la guerra entre México y los Estados Unidos *(Notes for the History of the War between Mexico and the United States). In 1848, a number of Mexican authors, including Guillermo Prieto, Manuel Payno, Ignacio Ramírez and Ramón Alcaraz, set about writing their version of the war. Alcaraz's book defends the thesis that the war and its consequences were due to the expansionist cravings of the "enemy next door," encouraged by political divisions within Mexico. The military defeat Mexico suffered gave rise to an incipient patriotic consciousness. Liberal intellectuals sought to record a version of the facts which would communicate historical awareness to the Mexican people.* Apuntes..., *along with* Recuerdos de la invasión norteamericana *(Memories of the American Invasion) by José María Roa Bárcena (1883), became an official history of the war reflecting the viewpoint of the vanquished.*

The Mexican Constitution of 1824 was inspired by the U.S. Constitution of 1789, providing equal representation in Congress of the nineteen states into which Mexico was divided. The country's magna carta was modified in 1835 by "The Basis for Reorganizing the Mexican Nation," which restricted the sovereignty of local legislatures and re-established power at the center. Governors of provinces were to be named by the president of the Republic. The Texans used this change as a pretext to rebel against a central government which, they claimed, was violating their legal and natural rights as citizens.

who set foot on our soil were welcomed with open arms, but the political inexperience of successive national governments turned a generous and eminently civilizing stance into a source of problems. And immigration, which ought to have provided hardworking hands for agriculture, and skilled workers for industry and commerce, led instead to the isolation of one of the most important states of the Republic...

Our intent is to demonstrate that the United States sought to take control of that territory no matter the cost; and to achieve it they sent their citizens, made sure their population would grow, and by the year '29 they had 20,000 settlers in a place where before there had been only 3,000. Bit by bit, they laid the groundwork for carrying out their plans, and in the end they took advantage of the first opportunity that presented itself in order to make their move...

JOSÉ MA. ROA BÁRCENA SUMS UP
THE TEXAS REBELLION

[José Ma. Roa Bárcena, *Recuerdos de la invasión norteamericana...*]

Interior view of the ruins of the Alamo.

The substitution of Mexico's federal system for a centralized one provided Texans with a pretext to launch the insurrection, to which they were already predisposed due to the Mexican government's prohibition on land sales, and to the hostilities the Texans had initiated against the line of forts set up by General Terán to control them. Our army, under the command of Santa Anna, opened the campaign in March of 1836, by advancing to the Bay of Espíritu Santo, in the dependency of Guadalupe and Matagorda. A command post was set up in Béjar, and from there two divisions were deployed, that of Ramírez y Sesma toward the Colorado River, and that of Gaona toward Nacogdoches; the rest of the forces finally set out under the command of Filisola to meet up with the first of those divisions in Austin, capital of the State of Texas. This campaign began under dismal portents: the Americans were

When the Mexican government learned that American mercenaries and volunteers were enlisting to support the Texas rebellion, it issued a decree on December 30, 1835, defining those foreigners as "pirates," meaning that they were criminals who lacked a country of citizenship and a flag. According to the rules of war at the time, "pirates" could be put to death.

In bitter fighting at the beginning of March 1836, Mexican troops captured the Alamo fort in San Antonio Béjar. Following orders from the Mexican government, Santa Anna did not accept the surrender of the fort's defenders and had hundreds of them shot. During the military conflict of 1846–1848, "Remember the Alamo" became an American battle cry to show no mercy.

Map of San Antonio Béjar and the Alamo fort, drawn for Gen. Vicente Filisola.

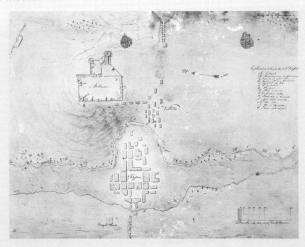

Ruins of the Alamo, exterior.

On March 2, 1836, in Washington (on-the-Brazos), the declaration of independence of Texas was solemnly proclaimed. When Santa Anna learned of this sobering news, he hastened to put down the rebellious Texans, but did so in a careless and overconfident manner. On April 21, 1836, in the battle of San Jacinto, the Mexican Army was surprised in its own encampment at four in the afternoon and was defeated in less than an hour. Santa Anna managed to escape, but was caught the following day.

Playing card from a deck depicting the life of Santa Anna, which shows his defeat in San Jacinto.

the ones standing firm, and several of our victories were besmirched by appalling executions and undeniable atrocities. With Austin and Harrisburg occupied then abandoned by our army, we continued searching for the Texan sent by Houston who on April 21 attacked and defeated Santa Anna on the banks of the San Jacinto. Our leader captured, the troops retreated to Matamoros. Texas was irretrievably lost...

Santa-Anna derrotado en S.Jacinto 1836.

THE CAPTURED PRESIDENT WRITES TO FILISOLA

God and Liberty
San Jacinto Camp, April 22, 1836
Most Excellent Division General Don Vicente Filisola

Most Excellent Sir. The division fighting short-handed with me late yesterday had an unfortunate encounter, and as a result, I am now a prisoner of war held by the other side, despite having taken all possible precautions; in that regard, I caution Your Excellency to order General Gaona to march back to Béjar to await instructions, which Your Excellency should verify with the troops you have at your disposal; as well, General Urrea should retreat with his division to Guadalupe Victoria, since an armistice has been agreed with General Houston; and certain negotiations underway will bring the war to a definitive conclusion... I hope that Your Excellency will fulfill these measures to the letter, informing me as soon as you have begun to carry them out.

MILITARY OPERATIONS ACCORDING TO VICENTE FILISOLA

God and Liberty
Guadalupe Victoria, May 14, 1836
Most Excellent Sir
Secretary to the Office of War and Navy

Most Excellent Sir. Our army captured Fort Alamo, defeated and destroyed most of what the enemy called line forces, capturing a considerable number of artillery, rifles and munitions, and crossed three raging rivers; and despite hunger and exposure, remained inspired by an ardent yearning to defend the integrity of our fatherland; a bit more equanimity would have undoubtedly rewarded their heroic effort and suffering.

On the afternoon of the 23rd [of April] I was concluding the operation of transporting across the river the division with whom General Gaona ought to have marched to Nacogdoches, when a soldier from the fort approached me with a note, written in pencil, from Colonel Don Mariano García, first aide of Guerrero, in which he informed me of the unfortunate occurrence [the capture of Santa Anna] on the 21st in the afternoon. A short while later a few stragglers arrived, and among them was the captain from Tampico Regiment, Don Miguel Aguirre, wounded in action with a musket ball in the thigh, who said that defeat was unequivocal and that the survival of the president was at best doubtful. This news caused me to suspend the river crossing at once...

Informed of Santa Anna's capture, the Mexican Congress formally removed his authority to negotiate, given that he was a "prisoner of war." Nevertheless, during his captivity, Santa Anna signed two treaties (one secret, the other public) in Velasco between May 8 and May 14. In them he accepted the retreat of Mexico's troops, recognized the independence of Texas and, what's more, acknowledged the Río Grande (or Bravo) as the border. These treaties, however, never acquired legal standing.

The document presented here describes how the second-in-command of the Mexican Army, General Vicente Filisola, who was not only a former Texas colonist but Santa Anna's god-brother, accepted the orders of the imprisoned president to move Mexico's forces south of the Río Grande (or Bravo), despite the fact that the border recognized by the Mexican and U.S. governments was the Nueces River.

THE FATIGUE OF THE SOLDIER...

This cynical cartoon from a Mexican newspaper depicts the misuse of funds appropriated for the war in Texas. Officers are busy trying to pull something from a large container marked "For the war in Texas," while in the background two soldiers, one Mexican and one Texan, go at each other with their fists, since neither has any other weapons. No other comment is needed on the deplorable state of the Mexican Army.

The army, as I already said, is in rags, its weaponry ruined, all the munitions in a miserable state, the horses and mules

extremely overworked; we have no surgeon, not even a medicine kit; we are threatened with an epidemic due to the season and the innumerable travails the army has suffered, and if such a misfortune occurs, the men will die without the least relief, disheartened and abandoned, without even the solace of spiritual assistance, since we have not a single chaplain to say mass. The immense bulk of our convoy is incredible; the army takes up three times as many cargo mules as it should. Because of poor organization and disorderly administration ever since we left Saltillo, the convoy is simply immense, with twice as many to be fed as carry weapons; because, I repeat, the single-minded goal was to make headway and nothing more. So we need to reorganize, rest and train, since most of the recruits barely know how to carry a rifle on their shoulders...

THE PRICE OF A PRESIDENT'S LIFE

God and Liberty
Camp on the right bank of the Nueces River
May 31, 1836
Vicente Filisola

All in all, Your Excellency, despite all the considerations I have presented, the one that most tormented my soul was another: the President of the Republic, the illustrious Mexican General Santa Anna was being held prisoner, he had saved his life by offering to pull the army out and leave the settlers free of it. He gave the order to that effect, in particular insinuating to me that upon this retreat depended his life and that of seven hundred gallant Mexicans: if I took the offensive, even winning the battle, they would kill him and the rest; and if I lost, the Republic would lose more than a battle but the President himself along with so many other brave souls who certainly would not have been pardoned by these bloodthirsty adventurers; and if I remained on the defensive, besides producing the same results, I would be exposed to other losses, as obvious as they would be inevitable. The step that had to be taken was, thus, clearly, to continue with the retreat that I had begun...

This cartoon depicts generals Santa Anna and Martín Perfecto de Cos, surrendering their swords to Samuel Houston after the battle of San Jacinto. Santa Anna says to the Texan leader, "I consent to being your prisoner, Your Excellency!!! No Alamo for me!!" He is pleading to be spared the fate that he himself imposed on the defenders of the Alamo. Houston, armed with a musket, answers, "You two are bloodstained villains who deserve to be shot to set an example. Remember the Alamo and Fannin!" (Fannin was Goliad's defender, who, a few days after the battle, was captured and shot along with many other prisoners.) Despite the cartoon's implications, which reflected the feelings of many Texans about Santa Anna, Samuel Houston never considered executing him. Rather, Houston seized the opportunity to oblige him to sign the Velasco treaties which benefited Texas's cause.

HOUSTON, SANTA ANNA, AND COS.

Mexican historiography has commonly represented Santa Anna as a despicable politician, while novelists and writers considered him a tragicomic character who embodied the chaotic political life of post-independence Mexico.

Born in Jalapa in 1794, he embraced a military career from his youth. In 1829 he earned a name for himself by defeating at Tampico the Spanish expeditionary force that sought to reconquer Mexico.

Santa-Anna se pronuncia contra el ministerio del vice-presidente Bustamante 1832.

His devastating defeat at San Jacinto in 1836 and his horrendous conduct of the war against the United States in 1846–1848 were his most serious setbacks, and unfortunately they also brought significant losses to Mexico. Nevertheless, he served eleven terms as president, the last one in 1853–1855, at the end of which he was sent into exile for the third time, on this occasion for twenty years. He died in 1876 in Mexico City.

These images summing up the life of Santa Anna appeared on calendars. Given his great popularity, they also circulated as a deck of playing cards.

Santa-Anna se pronuncia contra la federación. 1834.

Santa-Anna derrotado en S. Jacinto 1836.

Santa-Anna se pronuncia contra Iturbide. 1822.

Santa-Anna se pronuncia en Perote. 1828.

Santa-Anna se pronuncia contra la administración de Bustamante. 1841.

Santa-Anna es arrojado de la presidencia y desterrado. 1844.

Santa-Anna vuelve á la República 1846.

Santa-Anna se retira del Campo de la Angostura. 1847.

Santa-Anna es derrotado en cerro-gordo. 1847.

Santa-Anna abandona á Valencia en Padierna y se retira á México. 1847.

Santa-Anna deja escapar la ocasion de derrotar á los Americanos. 8 de Setiembre de 1847.

Santa-Anna abandona la ciudad la noche del 13 de Setiembre de 1847.

Santa-Anna sale de la República. 1847.

Santa-Anna desembarca en Veracruz y vuelve á ser presidente de México 1º de Abril de 1853.

Santa-Anna vuelve derrotado del sur y pasa por el arco de triunfo. 16 de Marzo de 1854.

Santa-Anna sale para Morelia para batir á los pronunciados. 30 de Marzo de 1855.

Santa-Anna sale con una expedicion para el sur 16 de Marzo de 1854.

Votacion para que se perpetúe en el mando Santa-Anna. 1º de Diciembre de 1854.

Santa-Anna se embarca en Veracruz el 18 de Agosto de 1855.

With the defeat of the Mexican Army at the battle of San Jacinto, the independence of the Republic of Texas became inevitable — and the country lasted nine years. Texans soon ratified a new constitution, legalized slavery and elected Samuel Houston president. The transfer of power was reflected immediately in the place-names of the new country. In the first year of independence, a settlement near the battlefield where the Mexicans lost the war was renamed Houston in honor of the Texas commander-in-chief. Even so, the names of many cities in the United States reflect their Spanish or Mexican Catholic roots, such as San Antonio, Texas.

A daguerreotype of Samuel Houston and a vista of the city that carries his name, published in a Mexican magazine in 1847.

IV   The Scar of Texas

During its nine years of independent life, Texas posed a serious problem for the Mexican government, given the constant threat that the United States would incorporate it into the American Union. In addition, the Mexican government faced claims presented by the U.S. government on behalf of its citizens for damages and harm suffered. The indemnifications sought totaled eight million pesos in 1839, with another million added on after Mexico sent a punitive expedition to try to recover Texas in 1841–1842. Despite Mexico's intention to meet U.S. demands, these claims became another pretext for diplomatic strife between the countries.

On the road to violent confrontation, the U.S. Senate, driven by the American craving for expansion, approved the annexation of Texas on March 1, 1845. The Mexican government had indicated as early as 1843 that such a measure would be considered a provocation leading to war. Even so, in May 1845, Mexico tried to negotiate with Texas, offering diplomatic recognition in return for a promise not to become part of or subject to any other country. The negotiations failed categorically and the Texas legislature ratified the country's annexation to the United States on July 4.

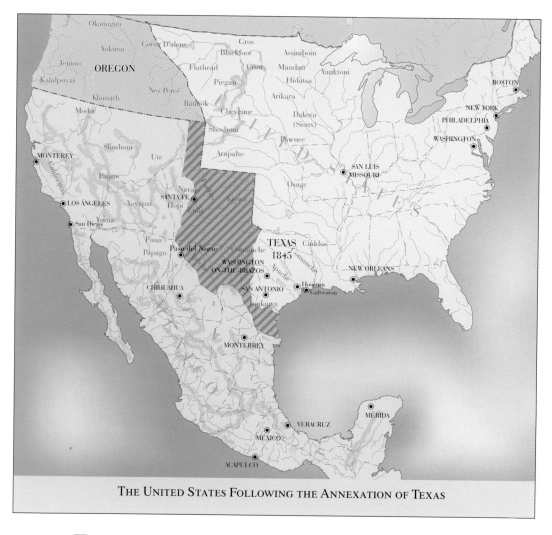

THE UNITED STATES FOLLOWING THE ANNEXATION OF TEXAS

*T*he map above shows the changes induced by the annexation of the young
Republic of Texas to the United States in 1845. Texas claimed much more territory than it occupied at the time and than had ever belonged to it historically. The disputed territory is marked in red.

These lands, still practically untouched by settlers, were inhabited as they
had been for centuries by Indian tribes. The governments of both countries
viewed the Indians as a serious threat to national integration.

Mexico Protests the U.S. Attempt
to Annex Texas

[Letter from José María Bocanegra to Waddy Thompson]

This document, written by Mexico's Foreign Relations Minister José María Bocanegra to American Minister Plenipotentiary Waddy Thompson, sums up the position of the Mexican government regarding the proposed annexation of Texas to the United States.

August 23, 1843

...The Mexican government has collected sufficient evidence, published extensively in the American press, that in the next session of the United States congress a proposal will be submitted to annex the so-called Republic of Texas, and although His Excellency the president still expects that so prudent an authority will reject such unjust designs, such a clear attack on the rights of the Mexican nation and on that territory, he sends this message which he requests Your Excellency Mr. Thompson to please transmit to your government: that Mexico will consider that accord to incorporate Texas into the territory of the United States as a declaration of war against the Mexican Republic, sufficing confirmation of this occurring for war to be then declared, leaving it to the civilized world to judge the cause of the Mexican people in a struggle they have been far from provoking.

The colonists of Texas, generously welcomed by the Mexican nation, entered that territory and later rebelled under different pretexts, but with the known intent of stealing the territory from its legitimate owner...and if now a party in Texas promotes its incorporation into the United States, it is because they understand the territory's evident incapacity to form and constitute an independent nation without effecting change in its status or acquiring authorization to separate from the motherland. Based on this profound conviction, His Excellency the provisional president is obliged to forestall an aggression without precedent in the annals of the world, and if it becomes indispensable for the Mexican nation to court the disasters of war in order to defend her unassailable rights, she will call on God, and she will fight in defense of justice...

MEXICO PROTESTS THE TREATY OF ANNEXATION

[Diplomatic note from José María Bocanegra to Benjamin E. Green, U.S. chargé d'affaires]

May 30, 1844

The above-named Minister of Foreign Relations and Interior has had the honor of receiving the note which the chargé d'affaires of the United States had addressed to him...in which he communicates the arrival of an official messenger...with the objective of informing the officials of this Republic that the executive of those States has signed and sent to the Senate a treaty to incorporate Texas into the United States.... A treaty which notoriously and without question dispossesses Mexico of a territory which properly and legally belongs to it...

[The] above-named has express orders from the president of the Republic to posit in the most conclusive and explicit way that Mexico has not renounced, nor ought it renounce, and consequently will not renounce or in any way cede all or any of its rights...that [Mexico's] firm and constant determination has been and remains that of maintaining the integrity and dignity of the nation. That on this occasion so opportune for repeating [Mexico's] protests they are offered here expressed as if pointedly face to face in particular that of August 23, 1843, in the words that Mexico will consider as a declaration of war against the Mexican Republic the approval of that accord to incorporate Texas into the territory of the United States.

THE THREAT OF ANNEXATION

[Ramón Alcaraz et al., *Apuntes para la historia de la guerra...*]

On April 12, 1844, the president of the United States signed a treaty with Texas regarding the addition of that territory to the Union. This treaty was not ratified by the Senate, leaving suspended for the moment the usurpation that was later achieved by a different route. But the simple fact that this business was even attempted constituted a new affront to Mexico... The American minister Mr. Shannon, either because he truly believed that war was positively about to begin, or because he sought a pretext to oblige Mexico to declare war on the United States, making us appear as the aggressors, sent a diplomatic note declaring in the name of his government that their policy had always favored incorporating Texas into the American Union, and that the aggression Mexico was threatening against that province would be considered an attack against themselves... Therein lies the confession, of inestimable value to us, that the plan to take over that part of our territory had been pursued relentlessly by all the political parties and nearly all the administrations of the North American republic over a period of twenty years...

CHANGES IN THE MEXICAN GOVERNMENT BRING CHANGES TO ITS TEXAS POLICY

As the year 1844 came to an end, a new revolution toppled the government of General Santa Anna, which was being run on an interim basis by General Canalizo, placing D. José Joaquín Herrera in charge...

The view that what General Santa Anna had sought [by naming an interim ruler] was to keep all power in his own hands, spread throughout the Republic; such that the people, who detested his oppression, rose up against him, overthrew him and gave victory to the party later known by the name of the Decembristas.

The policy adopted by the Decembristas diverged sharply from that followed by previous administrations. [The Decembristas] worked from the beginning under the clear understanding that the Province of Texas had been lost forever in 1836; that it was crazy to think that our eagles could find victory on the other side of the Sabina; that what we needed were negotiations, and not a war of any sort... [T]he main

At this difficult moment José Joaquín de Herrera, who had been minister of war in 1833–1834, assumed the presidency. Widely known as an honest man, Herrera was president on two occasions: 1844–1845 and 1848–1851. His moderate stance on the annexation of Texas by the United States is subject to a number of interpretations, but fundamentally he viewed the annexation as a diplomatic provocation intended to lure Mexico into the abyss of war, which in the end is what occurred.

Santa-Anna es arrojado de la presidencia y desterrado. 1844.

This playing card from a deck that depicts the life of Santa Anna 🔫 pp. 36–37, shows his departure for Cuba in 1844, where he spent two years in exile.

idea that dominated the Decembrista government's thinking was that the independence of Texas in any case was preferable to its annexation by the United States...

From the political parties there arose a furious outcry against this new approach: imputations of weakness, of perfidy, of treason stained the reputation of government officials. They clamored for war, declaring it to be the only means to save the nation's honor...

This cartoon from the newspaper La Voz del Pueblo *on the horrendous consequences of the loss of Texas depicts invasion as a lurking beast of the Apocalypse.*

The Debate on the American Threat

*T*he American threat obliged Mexico's numerous political factions to sharpen their stance on what future they desired for the country. At the beginning of 1846 they debated in the Mexico City press and in pamphlets whether political stability would be best served by a constitutional monarchy in keeping with the Iguala Plan of 1821 or a continuation of the republican model secured by the Constitution of 1824.

The Iguala Plan was a political compromise intended to unite the different groups struggling for Mexico's independence; it proposed setting up a representative monarchy headed by a prince of the Bourbon dynasty. When the plan was rejected by the Spanish monarch, Fernando VII, military and political leader Agustín de Iturbide proclaimed himself Emperor of Mexico in 1822. Congress, in turn, rejected this move and Iturbide was overthrown, leading to the proclamation of the first federal republic in 1824. In 1835, however, the federal system was abandoned in favor of a centralized government, which remained in place until the middle of 1846.

It should be no surprise that so many changes in so short a time spawned raging political debates. The most serious of these filled the pages of the newspapers El Tiempo *and* El Republicano, *where the relative merits of the monarchic and republican systems were discussed.*

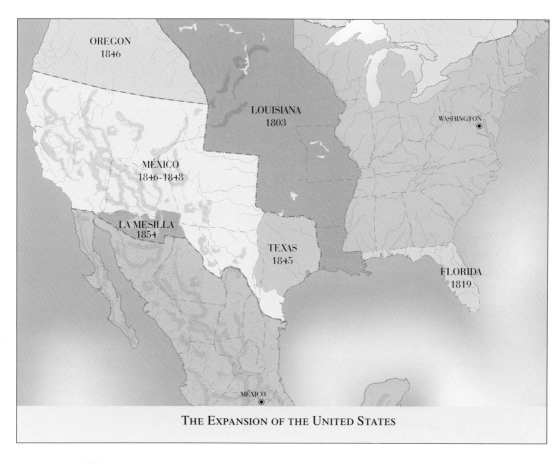

OREGON
1846

LOUISIANA
1803

WASHINGTON

MÉXICO
1846-1848

LA MESILLA
1854

TEXAS
1845

FLORIDA
1819

MÉXICO

THE EXPANSION OF THE UNITED STATES

*T*his map shows the astonishing territorial expansion of the United States during the first half of the nineteenth century.

In 1803 the country bought Louisiana from France. Given that this territory once belonged to Spain, the deal was cause for some misunderstanding since many Americans believed the purchase included Texas. Spain later ceded Florida in return for the United States renouncing its claims on Texas.

In 1845 Texas was annexed by its northern neighbor. Victory in the war against Mexico three years later gave the United States the enormous territory of the states of New Mexico, Arizona, Colorado and Upper California (which at the time included Utah). What's more, during those same years the United States negotiated an accord with Great Britain to obtain the Oregon country in 1846.

Over a period of less than fifty years, the Americans spread their country across the continent, right up to the Pacific Ocean.

THE FAILURE OF THE IGUALA PLAN

["Nuestra profesión de fe," *El Tiempo*, No. 19, February 12, 1846]

We believe that our independence was a great and glorious event, a necessary and inevitable one... Thus, sooner or later, independence had to take place; ten years of cruel wars could not achieve it, but a seven-month military march in 1821 was sufficient for the words spoken in Iguala to become the country's rallying cry. Why? Because the guarantees in that plan reconciled all discrepancies, united all views; because the clerics, the army, the people saw that a future of glory and prosperity for their fatherland would be assured... But the Iguala Plan was not carried out. Iturbide wanted to found a dynasty for his own benefit; and that empire, without foundations, without legitimacy, without respect for time and traditions, collapsed into ruins with the first revolutionary thrust...

THE THREAT OF AMERICAN IDEOLOGY

The United States then began to build in Mexico another sort of empire; their books and their ideas, the blandishments of their representatives and the deceptive allure of their prosperity dragged our innocent trust down new and dangerous roads. In the end, republican ideas gained control of the nation and found expression in the government. That's when we set off down the ruinous path on which we travel still...

...We believed that the shortest path to guaranteed political freedom was to throw ourselves into the arms of the United States, to slavishly imitate its institutions and to follow with precision its perfidious advice. Thus the absurd constitution of 1824 was drawn up, and the American representative [Joel Poinsett] in the name of liberty founded secret societies that tyrannized and undermined the country...

El Tiempo was the journalistic organ of the conservatives. Mexican historians use the term conservative to refer to the intellectual, social and political groups who promoted the establishment of a monarchic system and defended the interests of the Church. Strictly speaking, only as of 1845 did the conservatives oppose the establishment of an Anglo-American influenced republican system, considering it to be a threat to Mexico's Catholic identity and culture.

This document relied primarily on the pen of Lucas Alamán, considered by historians as the most lucid representative of conservative thought and an outstanding historian of Mexico since Independence. He doggedly defended Mexico's independence before the Courts of Cádiz in 1820, and occupied high posts in several governments until his death in 1853. A vastly cultured man, he founded the first cultural and economic institutions of the young nation, including the National Archives, the National Museum and the Bank of Credit.

DOMESTIC INSTABILITY AND THE LOSS OF TEXAS

Presidents and Congresses collapsed thanks to bloody revolutions. Civil war in the countryside, disorder in the cities was from then on nearly our normal state of affairs; meanwhile the barbaric Indians dared to assail our territory at will and the United States stole Texas and prepared to usurp California...

ANALYSIS OF THE REPUBLICAN EXPERIENCE

What do we see now? What is our situation inside the country and overseas? A disorganized administration, a fortune lost, enormous debts that consume us, income mortgaged to our creditors, soldiers begging from money-lenders for bare subsistence, public servants abandoned, justice neglected, barbarians pushing back the frontiers of civilization. Yucatan emancipated, the United States occupying our territory, and all this without a navy to defend our coasts and without the necessary resources for our valiant army to expel the impudent invaders from the soil of the fatherland...

We believe that this panorama points us not only toward ruin, the collapse of morals, anarchy, but toward the complete dissolution of the nation and the loss of our territory, our name, our independence...

THE CONSERVATIVE STANCE

For all this, we repeat, we believe that our Republic has been a costly experiment, a harsh lesson, but it can be remedied. Now, if we are asked what we want, what we desire, let us say it frankly.

We want a representative monarchy; we want the unity of the nation; we want order alongside political and civic freedom; we want Mexico's territory intact; we want, in sum, all the promises and guarantees of the Iguala Plan, to set our glorious independence on firm foundations...

We want a governmental system in which legislative bodies are elected and royal power is hereditary, to guarantee political freedom and the existing order...

We want, as in all the monarchies of Europe, that the only aristocracy should be one based on merit...

Yes, we want a strong and vigorous army that will cover itself with laurels nobly defending its country... We want proper and dignified support for the Catholic beliefs of our fathers, not the continuous threat posed to Church properties by anarchy. We were born in the bosom of the Church, and we do not wish to see the cathedrals of our religion converted into sectarian temples scandalized by religious quarrels. And in place of the nation's flag, we do not wish to see flying from our towers the detested colors of the Stars and Stripes.

We want a representative monarchy that can protect the distant provinces as well as those nearby, defend them from the savages who ravage them, and extend the frontiers of civilization that are now retreating in the face of barbarism... We want a stable government which by inspiring confidence in Europe offers us foreign alliances for our battle with the United States if that country persists in destroying our nationality.

Conservatives by conviction and character, we ask for protection for all the interests that have been created, no matter their origin. To believe that bringing a royal-blooded prince to Mexico to set up a dynasty means relying on foreigners is insanity. That could have been the case three centuries ago, but not today and certainly not under a representative government...

This cartoon depicts Mexico as a sinking ship amid the waves that carry the names of the territories claimed by the United States: Texas, New Mexico, etc.

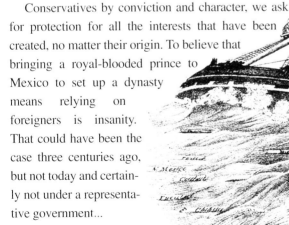

El Republicano was the journalistic organ of the liberals. During the nineteenth century liberalism was associated with democracy, constitutional rule, republican ideas and the expansion of the market economy. After Independence, radical liberals staunchly opposed New Spain's monarchic tradition and adopted a radical anti-clerical stance.

THE MISSION OF THE AMERICAN CONTINENT

["Al Tiempo," *El Republicano*, March 28, 1846]

All parts [of the American continent] ought to form a whole by means of a coalition, rather than through subordination. Climate, customs, products, locales, languages differ across the American republics; each ought to be a separate people so as to develop its respective character, and within such development and progress there should be harmony to show the New World to the Old. To reduce the Americas to a single republic would be as difficult as reducing Europe to a single monarchy.

THE RISKS OF U.S. EXPANSION

This is the principle that the Anglo-Americans ignore, confused as they are by their outsized ambitions they forget the indications of nature and aspire to universal domination of this continent. For the American republics to merge with that of the United States, either they would have to be forcibly subjected or they would have to join up voluntarily... Would the Anglo-Americans abandon their customs to adopt ours? Would we abandon ours to take up theirs?....

MESSAGE TO THE UNITED STATES

Our intention has been to make the United States aware of its own interests, and that those interests would not be well served by usurping the territory of the American republics, rather by offering them fraternal protection for two ends: so they may be free from attacks by Europe, and so they may progress. Both of these favor the United States.

 The Inevitable
Conflagration

In a period of twenty-five years the neighborly relationship Mexico enjoyed with the United States, which had begun under the best of omens and with the grandest of expectations, changed radically. In both countries, eloquent manifestations of admiration and respect gave way to mistrust and hostile confrontation. The annexation of Texas by the United States led Mexico to break off diplomatic relations, since such an act violated the border treaties signed by the two countries in 1828 and 1836. Even so, the Mexican government expressed a willingness to negotiate Texas's annexation should the U.S. government send an envoy for that purpose. U.S. President James K. Polk, however, named John Slidell not as envoy but as minister plenipotentiary to discuss a number of matters, including claims for damages to U.S. citizens, the Texas border and the purchase of New Mexico and California. Mexico took this presumption of normal diplomatic relations as an insult and refused to receive Slidell.

These diplomatic maneuvers were backed up by U.S. troop deployments and the threatening presence of warships off the port of Veracruz.

As war approached, Mexicans remained absorbed in domestic political struggles, which proved an impediment to drawing up an effective strategy for military defense.

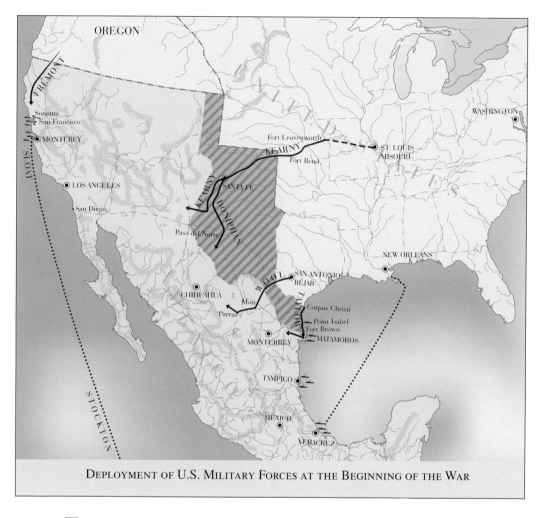

DEPLOYMENT OF U.S. MILITARY FORCES AT THE BEGINNING OF THE WAR

The United States deployed its initial offensive in four directions:
- *General Taylor moved his troops from Corpus Christi to Matamoros, and then on to Monterrey and Saltillo.*
- *General Wool left San Antonio Béjar heading toward Chihuahua.*
- *Kearny's troops left Leavenworth for Santa Fe, where they split, with Kearny leading half of them to California while the other half, under Doniphan, headed for Chihuahua.*
- *Mexico's main ports were blockaded: Commodore Sloat kept watch on the California coast while an apparently exploratory expedition led by Fremont approached California with orders to incite the settlers to rise up in an insurrection.*

THE CASE OF MR. SLIDELL

[Ramón Alcaraz et al., *Apuntes para la historia de la guerra...*]

On October 13, 1845, the U.S. consul, Mr. Black, sent a private letter to Don Manuel de la Peña y Peña, our minister of foreign affairs, which transcribed part of a communication from his country's secretary of state, in which he proposed that an envoy vested with full powers to settle all matters in dispute between the two governments be received. The Mexican agreed, on the condition that the naval force visible from Veracruz be pulled back, and offering to receive the envoy to settle peaceably the current disagreement.

Negotiations began anew in December 1845 and the envoy, Mr. John Slidell, arrived in Mexico, but from the start there was the difficulty that his government wanted him received as a minister plenipotentiary, general or extraordinary, and ours was only willing to accept him as an ad hoc commissioner for the Texas question. The foundation interview on December 16 of that year brought to the surface the evident difference between the two statuses. To admit Mr. Slidell as an ordinary envoy to settle the Texas question would have led to him dealing at the same time with other issues more appropriately suited to a plenipotentiary exercising his functions on behalf of a government with whom all relations were peaceful. To admit Slidell as he wished would have been tantamount to re-establishing diplomatic relations between the two countries without Mexico having had any of its concerns addressed; Mexico would have tied its own hands in the war, and the United States would have attained all the consequent advantages for its trade and interests...

In accordance with this analysis, the administration of General Herrera presented the situation to the envoy and refused to receive him. Mr. Slidell insisted that he ought to do so in the same terms as his government, but ours stood firm and refused.

New officials took to the political stage in the first days of 1846, elevated to power by another revolution. General Paredes announced his opposition to Herrera in San Luis [Potosí]... Then Mr. Slidell renewed his campaign in consideration that although his previous petition had been resolutely discarded this time it would be addressed by different officials and perhaps he might find them more disposed to agree.

He brought the matter once again to the governing council, and it repeated the reasons put forth on the previous occasion. The council went further, concluding with a renewal of the declaration that Slidell could only be admitted as an ad hoc plenipotentiary for the Texas question. The government explained this to the envoy, who could only ask for his passport and leave the country.

This painting shows Corpus Christi,  *p. 208, a small town at the mouth of the Nueces River on the Gulf of Mexico occupied by U.S. troops, whose tents can be seen in the distance. Published in 1846 in the magazine* Revista Científica y Literaria, *this image accompanied an article that ended with the following concern: "The Americans rush to our border like hungry nomadic wolves, and we do not know what will be the fate of our unlucky country."*

THE MACHINERY OF WAR
STARTS ROLLING

[José María Roa Bárcena, *Recuerdos de la invasión norteamericana...*]

Taylor, who had been encamped at Corpus Christi since August 1845, received orders at the beginning of 1846 to march toward the Rio Grande (Bravo), which the United States planned to establish as its border.

THE BORDER PRETEXT

[Ramón Alcaraz et al., *Apuntes para la historia de la guerra...*]

To explain the occupation of Mexican territory by General Taylor's troops, the United States [Congress] came up with the novel idea that the borders of Texas extended all the way to the Río Bravo del Norte [Rio Grande].

DEFENDERS OF THE BORDER

Ever since the wretched Texas campaign of '36, a more or less numerous contingent of our army had always been posted along the border, and on several occasions over the following years they fought Texans and adventurers who pursued a cause as unjust as it was fortunate. Those valiant soldiers engaged in such an honorable endeavor remained there in a state of near abandonment, separated from their families and relations due to the negligence of our governments. Their return home was continually postponed in repeated pronouncements and they felt themselves truly forgotten, while promotions and postings were plentiful for those whose only claim to them was favoritism, corruption, or having distinguished themselves in domestic trouble-making.

The government of General Herrera knew that peace between the two republics who ought to have been sisters was coming to an end, and he ordered reinforcements to the Northern Army so that our side could undertake at least the indispensable preparations for a war that was practically certain to take place...

Mariano Paredes y Arrillaga was forty-eight years old when he became president in 1846. His rise occurred thanks to the forced resignation of the constitutional president, José Joaquín de Herrera. Paredes sympathized with the plans of certain political groups to bring a Spanish monarch to re-establish political stability. The defeats Mexico suffered in the North undercut his prestige among the officer corps, and they overthrew him in another coup in the middle of the summer of 1846. His place was taken by General José Mariano Salas.

DIVIDED AGAINST THE ENEMY

Everything pointed toward an impending clash of armies. The government again sent orders for Paredes to get underway, deploying the division he commanded to its destination, but rather than do his duty to the fatherland that general rebelled openly against the government and its institutions, and backed by a few men as infamous as he, proclaimed an anarchic platform and marched on Mexico City to secure the triumph of his revolution...

The treasonous pronouncement General Paredes made in San Luis will ensure him a shameful notoriety.

On March 25, 1846, the first of Taylor's troops reached Frontón de Santa Isabel, located north of the mouth of the Rio Grande on the Gulf of Mexico, near Matamoros. The Mexicans who lived there set fire to their own homes and fled. The Americans then used the place as a supply base. This illustration depicts the arrival of Taylor's army at Frontón Bay.

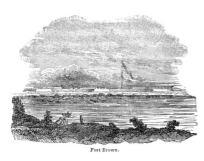

Fort Brown.

As of March 28, 1846, Taylor's army set up camp in Fort Texas, across from the city of Matamoros. The Americans were in constant communication with Frontón de Santa Isabel, another military base on the coast. The first two battles, at Palo Alto and Resaca, took place precisely halfway between the two bases. Fort Texas was later rebaptized Fort Brown, in honor of Major Jacob Brown who died defending it. Today the fort lies within the city limits of Brownsville.

GENERAL TAYLOR'S CAMPAIGN BEGINS

While the troops sent to the border were instead marching back to the capital and the small Northern Army remained therefore abandoned to its own resources, on January 15, 1846, the enemy troops under General Taylor received orders from their government to advance, indicating how convenient it would be to occupy the point known by the name Frontón de Santa Isabel... The enemy occupied that point, and immediately made contact with their maritime forces. They left a small detachment there, ordered several fortifications to be rapidly thrown up and continued straightaway toward the city of Matamoros, across from which they arrived on March 28...

At dawn on the 28th, the entire population was on the rooftops of the highest houses and buildings, awaiting with curiosity the arrival of the enemy...

At two in the afternoon several officers holding white flags appeared on the opposite side of the river, signaling that a commission should be named on our side to confer with their leaders. Mejía sent General Díaz de la Vega, who disembarked on the left bank of the Bravo, and in that very instant the enemy raised the flag of the Stars and Stripes. The anger that this sight prompted in the Mexicans was indescribable: for the first time that banner was waved arrogantly before our troops, as if taking possession of what by all rights belonged to us...

The soldiers of the Northern Army chafed under the enemy's insult. Raging, they called for combat, begged their general to allow them to avenge the outrage. General Mejía, unable to satisfy them, sought to calm their patriotic fervor, having been instructed not to risk battle unless victory was probable, or unless the North American army crossed the river, in which case they ought to be resisted with all our might, no matter the cost. At the talks that Díaz de la Vega held with General Worth nothing of import occurred. Our representative stated that the march of the enemy army constituted a true act of hostility; that despite their calling it an occupation, their advance to this point had to be considered an armed invasion, and thus our commanding general would act appropriately in fulfilling his duty...

General Mariano Arista led only two battles as commander-in-chief of the Northern Army. Because of the disastrous defeats in Palo Alto and Resaca, he was replaced by General Francisco Mejía, who was later replaced by General Pedro Ampudia, ☞ p. 70, Arista, however, remained in politics and became president in 1851.

MILITARY DISCORD

The news that Ampudia was going to become the commander of the army was received with disappointment in Matamoros by the many people with whom he was at loggerheads, as well as by some acting out of base self-interest and by others who judged him incapable of taking on the difficult task he had been handed and bringing it to a glorious outcome. They wrote, mostly by unofficial means, to the president, telling him of the dismal consequences for the nation if another person was not named in place of Ampudia, and they indicated that General Arista would be best suited...

The plan that General Ampudia had conceived consisted of crossing the river and crushing the enemy. The action was to begin on April 15 but did not, because the night before he received from the supreme government an order informing him that General Arista had been named commander in chief, leaving him second in command. This was the result of the aforementioned letters from the officers, which

John Phillips, an Englishman who visited Matamoros before the war, sketched this panoramic view of the city from the north bank of the Rio Grande (Bravo). The American soldiers must have contemplated a similar scene during the weeks they remained in Fort Texas across from Matamoros. They later wrote that women would wash clothes at the very spot where they would swim in the afternoons.

But both sides continued their preparations for combat. Once the Americans had established their fort, they scouted the surroundings on reconnaissance expeditions. The Mexicans, besides increasing their troop strength to five thousand, sought to encourage desertion among the enemy troops, especially those of Irish origin, appealing to their common religion and offering them land. They won the adherence of more than two hundred, p. 135.

convinced the president to accede to their desires, but the president committed the grave error of sowing the germ of discord in the army by leaving two bitter rivals in command.

NOW THERE IS NO ALTERNATIVE TO WAR

On March 21, 1846, General Paredes declared that, because peace was no longer able to achieve the nation's prerogatives and independence, Mexico would move to defend its territory, while the national congress considered whether to declare war on the United States. Congress did not go that far, limiting itself to issuing a decree on July 6 which authorized the government, in simple defense of the Republic, to repel the attacks perpetrated against several of her provinces, and to inform friendly nations of the reasons that obliged her to defend her rights, meeting force with force...

MANIFESTO OF GENERAL PAREDES

[Manifesto of President Mariano Paredes, March 21, 1846.]

I must confess that war between two or more nations is one of the most grievous and serious evils that can afflict them, and that today civilization instinctively seeks to avoid the disasters war brings and seeks instead progress in industry and commerce and closer ties under the aegis of universal peace. Yet peace must be compatible with the maintenance of the prerogatives and independence of nations, who feel compelled to meet force with force when all means of compromise and conciliation have been lost.

Having been dispossessed, by the direct actions of the highest authorities of our neighboring republic, of the rich expanse of Texas that has always belonged to the Mexican Republic, and having discovered plans by the same to take over several other of our border or frontier departments, the Mexican nation had to protest, did protest, and now I, in her name, solemnly protest that Mexico will not recognize the

American flag planted in the soil of Texas, that Mexico will defend its invaded possessions and will never, ever allow further conquests, further incursions by the government of the United States of America.

It does not fall to me to declare war, and the august congress of the nation, once it gathers, will consider all relevant aspects of the conflict in which we find ourselves, and which our magnanimous and suffering people has had no part in provoking...

No Recourse but to Deter Armed Invasion with Armed Defense

[Decree of the Mexican Congress, July 2, 1846]

Mariano Paredes y Arrillaga, division general and interim president of the Mexican Republic, to all her inhabitants, be it known:

That the extraordinary session of the national congress has decreed the following:

Article 1. The government, based on our natural right to defend the nation, will repel the aggression initiated and sustained by the United States of America against the Mexican Republic, invading her and launching hostilities in several Departments of her territory...

This painting of American officers keeping watch on the Mexican Army is the work of American soldier Samuel Chamberlain. Unfortunately, no one among the Mexican troops recorded battle scenes. Because Mexican iconographic material is so scarce, the Mexican texts in this book are illustrated with American artwork.

VII

Contemporaries blamed Mexico's defeats on infighting among the military leaders and their ineptitude, as well as on the political ambitions of both liberals and conservatives.

While the Americans advanced in a disciplined manner, fulfilling over ten months a well-designed military strategy, the groups leading Mexico were distracted by unrelenting infighting. What's more, political disputes debilitated the state governments of Sonora, Coahuila and Chihuahua, and the country faced difficult economic straits. All this helps to explain why much of the resistance against the invading army was waged not by soldiers, but by large groups of civilians armed only with fervent patriotism.

Through a three-pronged attack (led by Taylor-Wool, Kearny-Doniphan and Stockton-Kearny), the Americans covered nearly the entire north of the country. Of the northern campaigns, the most important was certainly Taylor's.

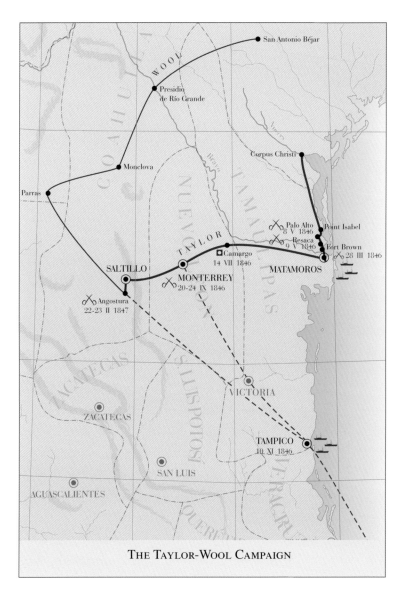

THE TAYLOR-WOOL CAMPAIGN

*T*his map shows the route followed by General Taylor and the principal battles he fought, all of them victorious. It also indicates the movements of the
troops under General Wool. Wool's objective was to reach Chihuahua, yet due
to the rugged unfamiliar terrain, which made it impossible to transport
artillery, he changed direction and met up with Taylor in Saltillo in time to
help him at the Battle of La Angostura. While Wool's troops faced no major battles on their long march, they fought many skirmishes with guerrillas.

PALO ALTO:
FIRST BATTLE AND FIRST DEFEAT

[Ramón Alcaraz et al., *Apuntes para la historia de la guerra...*]

Not until the 8th [of May] was it positively confirmed by scouts that the enemy numbering nearly 3,000 men, with plenty of artillery and an infinite number of wagons, was on its way from Frontón de Santa Isabel to its entrenched encampment across from Matamoros. The commanding general, once assured that this movement was underway, prepared to wage the battle he had hankered after for so many days. Our cavalry set out at ten in the morning for the broad plain at Palo Alto. The infantry did so at noon, and found the former already in sight of the enemy...

For the first time, the sons of two distinct races were to measure their strength, apparently fated by the Supreme Being to destroy one another in defense of the rights of their respective nations on the new continent as in the old. One side pursued a perfidious land-grab entrusted to them by an unjust government; the other defended a sacred cause for which sacrificing one's life is truly glorious...

Our batteries opened fire, and the enemy's superior artillery, situated at six hundred yards from our lines, answered immediately...

The firefight was destructive and lethal: the enemy, whose principal objective was to get through to their entrenched camp across from Matamoros, relied on the tactic of setting fire to the grass along their front lines, so the dense smoke that arose would hide their movements...

The North Americans' artillery, vastly superior in number to our own, wreaked horrendous damage on the ranks of the Mexican Army. Soldiers succumbed, not as victims in a combat in which they could kill as well as be killed, not enveloped in the bewildering bravado provoked by the heat of battle, rather in a deadly predicament which rendered them helpless. The battle went on for hours and

A Mexican lancer.

2ᵈ Dragoons.   H. 8ᵗʰ Infantry.   6 Duncan's Art.   F 4ᵗʰ Infantry   E 2 18 pound.

Angelo Paldi, a soldier of Italian origin and a musician in the American infantry, took part in the bloody battles of Palo Alto, p. 220-221, and Resaca; he made on-site sketches of each. This detailed drawing includes descriptive identifications and shows the distribution of military forces during the battle of Palo Alto. On the left are five supply wagons, and the grass is burning between the two armies. On the far right are the Mexican lancers under the command of Anastasio Torrejón.

hours under these dismal conditions, with losses rising by the minute. The troops, tired of dying so uselessly, screamed for a bayonet attack on the enemy, because what they wanted was to get in close and sacrifice themselves the way brave men should. At that moment it began to grow dark...

NIGHTFALL ENDS THE FIGHTING, BUT NOT THE SUFFERING

Fortunately, the Americans did not take advantage of or even notice the disorder among our forces, because night had already descended. Believing a more serious and dangerous attack was in the offing, they retreated...

The fire continued to spread: its sinister glow lit up the camp where shortly before cannons boomed, and in which now nothing was heard but the pitiful moans of our wounded. Since most of them were wounded by cannonballs, they were horribly mutilated. The sight of them was deeply saddening and their misfortune extreme. They were deprived

LO ALTO,

even of first aid, since the medic who carried the dispensaries had disappeared at the first shot and no one knew where he had left them. There was no choice but to send a few of the wounded to Matamoros in the wagons that had carried food, and to leave the rest abandoned on the battlefield on May 9...

The dead were buried the very night of the battle. This lithograph shows two Americans collecting the body of a soldier, while an officer pays him his last respects.

RESACA: GENERAL ARISTA'S MISTAKE

Following the lost battle at Palo Alto, Arista moved his encampment to a thicket of scrub oak very close to Resaca, thinking that the natural barrier would help his army against the enemy's lethal artillery. Reading about battles of the past, we rarely think of the importance of the physical characteristics of the battlefield. The dense thicket made it impossible to control the deployment of forces. The fighting was very chaotic and ended with the dramatic retreat of the Mexican cavalry, as can be seen in the distance on the extreme left.

The troops set off at six in the morning on the road to Matamoros, in sight of the enemy who made no move to deter them. At ten o'clock they arrived at a spot known by the name of Resaca de Guerrero, where the commander decided to lie in wait for General Taylor in order to attack him anew... The enemy advanced on our troops at four-thirty and opened fire. The commanding general, warned of what was happening, insisted on waiting, calling that attack a mere skirmish, and he retired confidently to his tent after speaking with General Díaz de la Vega, on whom he bestowed the honor of leading the action...

The enemy artillery devastated our ranks, and their dragoons reached our batteries, which fell under their control...

General Arista, who learned of the American successes,

Genl Taylor's Staff

DE LA PALMA,
6.

but was still under the sway of a regrettable delusion, did not believe this was a full battle... [The] enemy continued advancing... Our soldiers broke ranks, fleeing through the thicket; the most horrendous confusion reigned on the battlefield, and everything pointed toward the painful defeat of our forces.

The violence of the defeat obliged the commanding general, who had remained in his tent writing, to realize at last—unfortunately, too late!—that his assessment had been erroneous...

There was, therefore, nothing to do but retreat, as occurred in the best possible order, without allowing the enemy to follow within range and take advantage of their victory. Thus concluded the defeat of Resaca...

General de la Vega, on whom Arista so generously bestowed command, was captured in the attack by Major May, a moment that was portrayed in several American lithographs.

General Arista's personal tent was ransacked by the Americans. Besides valuable possessions, including a silver dining set (this sort of luxury was enjoyed by certain generals in the war), the invaders found a much more important prize: a map. The Americans realized this was a key factor for deploying their own troops, since they lacked a topographic map of the lands they were about to conquer. The legend of the 1847 map shown here explains that it is based on General Arista's own chart; the map details not only the main cities and roads, but also hamlets and mule paths.

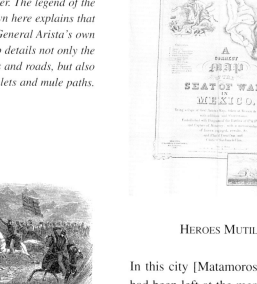

Americans entering Arista's camp.

The Americans invade General Arista's encampment.

HEROES MUTILATED, GENERALS PUNISHED

In this city [Matamoros] more than four hundred wounded had been left at the mercy of the enemy. Among them were some who, knowing of the army's retreat, abandoned the hospitals and followed, dragging themselves along the ground and leaving a trail of blood. These unfortunate souls preferred the worst of suffering to remaining unprotected in a town where they feared cruel treatment at the hands of the victors. Also left behind in the city were all the supplies of the commanders and officers, and most of the boxes and stores for the troops. Five artillery pieces were left in place; the many munitions that did not fit into the wagons were thrown into the river or completely ruined so they would not fall into the hands of the Americans, who took possession of Matamoros on the 18th [of May]...

In addition, the army lacked all sorts of food supplies and for much of the way no water was to be found, and its lack was what must have caused the soldiers the greatest suffering...

News of our disaster, spreading throughout the Republic with the speed that always characterizes bad news, demolished people's inflated hopes of victory. The supreme government, whose inflexible orders had contributed quite effectively to the fatal outcome now being lamented, wished to pin all responsibility on General Arista. He was relieved of his command of the army and subjected to an inquiry into his conduct. On June 3, the order to remove him was received in Linares, by virtue of which General D. Francisco Mejía was placed in command...

After winning the battles of Resaca and Palo Alto, which took place in the so-called "disputed territories," the U.S. Army crossed the Rio Grande. The operation was not easy, due to the strong current; soldiers had to take care not to get their weapons wet, as can be seen in this drawing from the hand of Samuel Chamberlain p. 220,, *a soldier who crossed the river under General Wool's command.*

Pedro Ampudia was born in Cuba and arrived in Mexico in 1821 when he was 18 years old. In 1829 he fought against the Spanish in the port of Tampico, when Spain made a vain attempt to reconquer its former colony, and in 1842 he took part in Mexico's failed attempt to recover Texas. Afterward, the Mexican government put him in charge of a military campaign to put down a rebellion in Yucatan, where in 1841 the citizens had seceded from Mexico. Ampudia earned a reputation for brutality when he crushed an 1844 insurrection in Tabasco and ordered the principal leaders shot and their throats slashed. As a result of that event, he was removed from his post, but soon reappeared as commander-in-chief of the Northern Army at the beginning of the war. In June 1846 he replaced Francisco Mejía in command of the defense of Monterrey.

MONTERREY AWAITING BATTLE

Monterrey is one of the loveliest cities of the Republic, and the capital of the border region...

After the misfortunes along the Río Bravo, the whirlwind of war drew near and the city's inhabitants foresaw a dire and painful conflict... Families that up to then had not fled now hurriedly abandoned their homes with terror in their faces. Shedding tears for their kin, young girls walked with the tremulous step of the elderly, doting fathers carried their children in their arms...

The lonesome aspect of a city awaiting battle can be understood by those of us who have seen it, but it is beyond all description...

THE ENEMY ACROSS FROM MONTERREY

At nine in the morning on the 19th [of September] our advance troops, exchanging shots with the enemy, pulled back into the fortified plaza and the enemy appeared directly before them. The general call rang out; troops ran to their weapons.

The enemy columns advanced near the Citadel, where they faced cannon fire, but did not reply...retreating immediately to the woods of Santo Domingo...where they set up their headquarters…

WORTH CUTS OFF THE ROAD TO SALTILLO

On the morning of the 20th, we learned that during the night a squad of enemy cavalry had approached the hill of the Bishop's Palace...

It was afternoon: an enemy column (General Worth's) was seen moving with several wagons and artillery, taking the Topo road. That movement was a clear sign that they sought to take control of the road to Saltillo and cut off all our communications with the interior of the country...

The following day at six in the morning, the enemy column with six artillery began marching; our cavalry threw themselves into the fight...the charge set off, led by... Don Mariano Moret. Fifty dragoons following him lay suddenly dead; alone and wounded, his lance broken, he attacked boldly, waving his sword and chasing the Americans right back to their artillery, then he calmly retreated. The enemy had to respect his daring, and did not shoot a single shot at him in his retreat... In this combat the cavalry was cut down...

And owners of the road to Saltillo, the Americans rapidly attacked the weak detachment on the hills across from the Bishop's Palace, winning two artillery pieces and raising their winning banner over our fort on Federation Hill...

ATTACK ON TENERÍA

The rude, sustained, desperate clash began in the redoubt of Tenería, whose small garrison with only four cannon was augmented by the soldiers' heroic fervor.

HEROIC WOMEN INCARNATE THE FATHERLAND

A Mexican soldier placing the bayonet on his rifle.

At ten in the morning, the enemy occupied positions abandoned the night before. At eleven, they drove forcefully toward the east; the firefight spread and seethed even in the homes around the main plaza. Just then, sublime as the heroines of Sparta and Rome, and as beautiful as the protective goddesses sculpted by the Greeks, a young woman, Doña María Josefa Zozaya, appeared amid the soldiers fighting on the roof of the home of Sr. Garza Flores. She gave them courage and passed them munitions; she showed them how to face down danger. The beauty and elegance of this girl inspired them anew: they had to triumph to gain her admiration, or die before her eyes to deserve her smile. She was a lovely personification of the fatherland itself; she was the beautiful ideal of heroism with all its charms, with all its tender allure!

This view of the battle of Monterrey, drawn by an enlisted man, Stephen G. Hill, shows the city's defensive fortifications and (1) General Taylor's plan to take capture from the east, the northeast and the west. From left to right we can see the following lines:

- *In the first line, General Quitman and his volunteers from Mississippi and Tennessee attack the fortified hill called La Tenería (2). Amid the smoke the Mexican flag can be seen. East of the city there is heavy fighting, as indicated by the clouds of smoke.*

- *The second line is headed to the city center. Near the cathedral (3), dense smoke indicates fierce street combat (4).*
- *The third line shows Worth's assault on the western part of the city. On the edge are two fortified hills (5) called Federation and Independence, and beyond stands the Bishop's Palace (6). Worth's troops,* *p. 228–229,* *are engaged in a skirmish with the Mexican cavalry (7).*
- *A raging fire is consuming the Citadel (8), which the Americans later renamed Black Fort due to its massive walls. This fort defended the northern approach to the city. In the foreground are the mortars (9). On the south, in the background of the picture, the city is protected by the Sierra Madre mountains and the (unseen) Santa Catarina River. This portrayal should be compared to that drawn by Carl Nebel,* *p. 225–227.*

When depicted from a distance, vicious bloody combat is only delicately hinted at by clouds of rising white smoke. This lithograph, in contrast, shows a close-up of the ferocious hand-to-hand fighting that occurred on the streets of Monterrey. Amid the crowd a priest wielding a cross can be seen. From the rooftops of homes transformed into forts, people throw stones.

Toward the City Center

A broad column with an artillery piece descended...from the hill of the Bishop's Palace...

The winding streets along which the invaders came kept them from using the artillery; nevertheless, the fight was on, with both sides fighting fiercely. The enemy began entering houses and thus penetrated up to our trenches. Their daring provoked the anger of our troops, who, disdaining a fight from behind cover, audaciously climbed the parapets and goaded the enemy, obviously risking death. The enemy, colder, more cautious and more skilled, kept up a treacherous fire along the gutters and embrasures of the houses...

THE BITTER TASTE OF CAPITULATION

At three o'clock in the morning Captain-promoted-to-Colonel D. Francisco R. Moreno rode off to Taylor's camp to seek talks...

General Taylor suspended hostilities, on condition that our troops evacuate the area and pledge not to take up arms against the United States in the future...

When the inhabitants of Monterrey saw the last Mexican forces leave, they could not resign themselves to staying among the enemy, and a large crowd of them, abandoning their homes and businesses, carrying their children and followed by their women, marched off behind the troops. Monterrey had become an enormous cemetery. The unburied bodies, the dead and rotting animals, the empty streets, everything gave the city a frightful appearance...

Ampudia was able to achieve a favorable cease-fire because the exhausted Americans knew that the Mexicans still had sufficient resources to prolong the defense of the city. The circumstances obliged Taylor to make two decisions that were later criticized severely, p. 233: he allowed the Mexican troops to retreat with all their armament, and he suspended hostilities for two months.

This lithograph shows General Ampudia facing Taylor; the caption sums up Article IV of the Capitulation Agreement: "That the citadel of Monterrey be evacuated by the Mexicans, and occupied by the American forces tomorrow morning at 10 o'clock."

Gen.ˡ Ampudia treating for the CAPITULATION OF MONTEREY, with Gen.ˡ Taylor, 24.ᵗʰ Sept. 1846.

Art. IV. That the citadel of Monterey be evacuated by the Mexican, and occupied by the American forces to-morrow morning at 10 O'Clock.

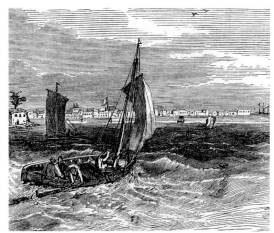

On November 10, 1846, without firing a shot, U.S. troops occupied Tampico, the largest city in the state of Tamaulipas and Mexico's second most important port on the Gulf of Mexico (after Veracruz). All the U.S. forces from the north reconnoitered in Tampico and from there they were transferred to Wolves Island, across from Veracruz. During the entire war the invading army maintained Tampico as a military base. That was where the reinforcements arrived to rescue Taylor in the north, and Scott on his approach to Mexico City from the east.

RETREAT FROM TAMPICO: ANOTHER CRUCIAL STRATEGIC ERROR

After taking Monterrey, the government of the United States approved General Scott's plan to change the base of operations, moving the theater of war from the north to the east. Meanwhile, General Santa Anna, who had been in San Luis mobilizing the army that he would lead to La Angostura, gave the order to the commander of the fort in Tampico to abandon the city without wasting a moment, thus handing the enemy a strategic point that it was anxious to take by force, given its importance in the new plan for their future operations...

On November 10, four hundred to five hundred Americans disembarked in Tampico and peacefully took possession of the key to the capital of the Mexican Republic, which our lack of expertise without a doubt handed them on a platter...

WHY TAMPICO WAS IMPORTANT

The government of the Republic had considered the defense of the fort at Tampico to be essential, and had renewed its fortifications and sent reinforcements for its garrison. The reasons for this were utterly clear, since if the enemy changed its base of operations and moved the theater of war to the east, as it soon did, Tampico would naturally become one of the most coveted points, not because it was considered to be the gateway to the interior of the country, but because it was an indispensable point of support for the success of their operations in Veracruz. Tampico would become the hub of their efforts; without Tampico, the entire contingent in the Gulf would have lacked fresh supplies or a place to transfer their wounded and to repair damages and breakage...

In the decade of the 1820s, the use of steam engines revolutionized transportation. For the first time in its history, the U.S. military used steamships
to transport its troops, supplies, weapons and reinforcements. The U.S.
Navy also blockaded ports and attacked cities. Naval squadrons played an
enormously important role in Taylor's campaign in the north, Scott's in
the east, Stockton's in California and Perry's in Tabasco.

It is worth recalling that the Mexican Navy was practically nonexistent. During the period 1840–1843, the government of Yucatan decided to
separate from the rest of Mexico until the country returned to a federal
system. Yucatan signed a friendship treaty with the independent republic of
Texas and, as a consequence, Texan ships began to patrol the peninsula's
waters. To put down the Yucatan rebels, the Mexican government bought
two steamships in England, the Guadalupe and the Moctezuma, as well as
another in New York called the Regenerador. These, plus two schooners
and two brigantines, made up the entire Mexican fleet. By 1846 the Mexican government had sold the Guadalupe and the Moctezuma to private
parties and the rest of the boats were quickly destroyed in the Gulf of
Mexico, due to the numerical and technological superiority of the U.S.
naval fleet. For the defense of the Pacific, the government had only two
schooners, the Anáhuac and the Sonorense, which were similarly unable
to stop the American conquest of the Californias.

Mexico's defeats in the Northeast weakened the position of President Mariano Paredes, who on August 4, 1846, was deposed by federalist liberals. They demanded the re-establishment of the federal system and the return of Santa Anna to power.

To satisfy their demands, Santa Anna, who was living in exile in Cuba, entered into secret negotiations with intermediaries of President Polk, in order to strike a deal for his return. He promised to bring the war to a conclusion favorable to the United States on the condition that they allow him safe passage through their naval blockade to Veracruz. President Polk agreed, but Santa Anna, once in Mexico, set about preparing to defend the country. He marched to San Luis Potosí where he brought together approximately eighteen thousand soldiers. He led them from there to Angostura, a debatable decision from a military standpoint, but not so illogical given the fact that General Taylor at that point was weakened: half of his troops (among them the best regiments) had been transferred to Veracruz, where a new front under the command of General Scott was to be opened.

Santa-Anna vuelve á la República.1846.

Santa-Anna se retira del Campo de la Angostura. 1847.

PASS IN THE SIERRA MADRE

LA ANGOSTURA: A STRATEGIC DIVERSION

...and if in the North we faced an army division that harassed us all the way to San Luis, this was only evidence of the astuteness of the United States, since by doing so it occupied our attention while actually being engaged in making a change that we ought to have noted if we were to avoid the dismal consequences it brought. Considering things from this standpoint, the battle of La Angostura was for us, in effect, the loss of the capital, and thus it would have been even had we won a resounding victory in that struggle...

General Santa Anna, after a stay of three months in San Luis, decided to head off in search of the enemy, who had advanced to Aguanueva... The army began to move out on January 28, the day that all the artillery with its wagons and war material departed...

No one can be blamed for the Mexican Army's inexperience; it was a result of history. The first professional army had been created only in 1783. At the time of the war against the United States the Mexican Army was made up of about 23,000 poorly equipped men, who had to fight an enemy of 45,000 soldiers. Besides, the Mexicans were at a technological disadvantage. They carried English single-shot flintlock rifles, while the American horsemen carried seven-shot Colt revolvers.

This little-known sepia drawing shows Mexican soldiers with women. Mexican soldiers usually brought their wives along with them, and they often brought along their children. In other words, the entire family went to war—on foot. There are many accounts of desperate women searching for their husbands among the dead and wounded and also of the important role women played when their husbands survived: they were the ones who tended their wounds, mended their clothes and prepared their food.

THE PROUD MEXICAN ARMY

[Manuel Balbontín, *La invasión americana 1846–1848. Apuntes del subteniente de artillería Manuel Balbontín*]

As is well known, the Mexican Army was created by conscription. In other words, those passersby in the street who due to their humble status fail to resist the violence done to them are taken by force. Transferred to the barracks, they are forced under the corporal's rod to learn a minimum of indispensable skills, how to handle a gun, and a few maneuvers. Neither rickets nor a large family nor being depraved excludes one from service, and amid the multitude of unlucky souls who are uprooted from their homes, usually the largest contingent are of indigenous background. Their pay is insufficient and infrequent.

Therefore, in the army that marched on La Angostura that day were battalions who wrapped their bodies with a few worn frock coats, who lacked blankets and hats to stay warm, and whose shakos were made of palm leaves lined with calico. The food given to our soldiers consists of a ration not always unspoilt or sufficient, the cost of which is charged to each individual at a *real* a day. But during a campaign, where resources and time for cooking meals are lacking, owing to the long days forced on our troops, each soldier is provided with a piece of raw meat, a few tortillas or a handful of corn...

Our army does not have its own wagons for transporting munitions, supplies, etc. When the troops march, they requisition supply mules or merchants' wagons of different sizes and build.

The weaponry for our infantry consists of old English flintlock rifles of nineteen half-drachm caliber. The cavalry, which could not be anything but light, is armed in part with sabers and flintlock pistols and most of them also with lances. The artillery cannot compete with the enemy's in either reach or mobility. There are no batteries of wagons with appropriate munitions to supply them during battle, and this service is provided by mule with a thousand inconveniences.

TAYLOR IN BUENA VISTA

[José María Roa Bárcena, *Recuerdos de la invasión norteamericana...*]

The road goes nearly direct from south to north, from San Luis to Saltillo, then leaves behind the ports or passes of Agua Nueva, Piñones and El Carnero and continues down the center of a valley formed by two ranges of the Sierra Madre mountains, which narrows at a place called El Paso or La Angostura, between two points known as La Encantada and Buena Vista. This is where Taylor centered his defense....

The theater of battle in the American plan of attack looked like a gigantic octopus, whose tentacles were the hills and gulches extending out from one or the other line of mountains, perpendicular to the road and cutting it in not a few places.

A Camp Kitchen.

The American encampment at Agua Nueva, near Buena Vista. Samuel Chamberlain made this drawing of the encampment showing the tents where the soldiers lived, the line of sentries guarding the camp, and on the right the transport wagons ready to roll. A few houses can also be seen. One day before Santa Anna reached Agua Nueva, Taylor burned the houses and moved to the hacienda at Buena Vista.

General Wool on the battlefield.

Mexico in a Tight Spot at La Angostura

The entire [Mexican] Army had concentrated in La Encarnación, where the first troops halted to await those coming behind. According to the count that was made there of the troops, there were 14,000 men in all companies. Thus, even before meeting the enemy, there had already been a loss of 4,000, between the dead, the ill, the exhausted and the deserters. But those who remained felt rejuvenated by the very nearness of the enemy....

At one o'clock on the 21st [of February] the troops ate their rations and filled their canteens with water; then they departed for the port of Carnero... Although General Santa Anna ordered the women who followed the troops not to go beyond La Encarnación, the order was not obeyed, and a large number of them marched on, forming a new army...

It did not take long to reach the enemy on the battlefield known by the name of La Angostura... Each hill was defended by an artillery battery, ready to kill those who sought to take it, and the lay of the land presented huge obstacles for an attack, clearly demonstrating that even if Mexico's arms were able to obtain a victory it would not come without considerable losses...

A captured Mexican deserter is questioned by the Americans. Desertions were a serious problem for the Mexican Army, made up as it was by conscripts. In the fighting at La Angostura some nine thousand soldiers fled the battlefield.

Fierce fighting continued all day; night was closing in and the result was still uncertain. The light corps fought with daring; the rest of the army, mere spectators to the action, anxiously watched the firefights and swung back and forth between doubt and hope. At the last minute, the Americans gave in, their soldiers retreated, and our own crowned the hill so tenaciously defended and so intrepidly won. The rest of the night was spent bivouacked across from the enemy. It was raining and bitterly cold. Since building fires was prohibited, not a single light could be seen in the encampment...

The 23rd dawned...

The battle resumed on the hill won the night before...

Artillery fire caused considerable losses on each side; all shots hit home due to the close proximity of one side to the other, ranging from but a hill's breadth to point blank. The Americans, who at one point had dreamed of victory, were crushed and retreated, leaving the battlefield littered with the bodies of the gallant souls who on both sides fell in this bloody struggle...

The fact is that our weapons defeated the Americans in each encounter, but we were unable to turn success on the battlefield to our favor. There were three partial victories, but no complete triumph...

Our soldiers displayed a bravery deserving of a better fate. They threw themselves fearlessly on the enemy, breaching gulches, climbing hills, leaping on the American batteries that were demolishing their ranks. And when they fell mortally wounded, they cried, "Long live the Republic," and breathed their last...

Samuel Chamberlain, who spent the night on the battlefield, made this drawing with the following description: "It was a cold night, with clouds scudding across the moon, which threw a weird light on the dismal scene. The ground was strewn with ghastly corpses, most of which had been stripped by our foes. A picket line of Mexican Lancers, mounted on white horses, was stationed not over two hundred yards in my front..." Chamberlain confesses that the liquor another soldier offered him from his canteen helped him bear what was truly unbearable.

Between 1845 and 1846, the Mexican Army had only twenty-three thousand men. These troops suffered losses from combat as well as from disease and hunger, not to mention desertions.

MISERABLE DEATH

The wounded numbered eight hundred, and not all of them could be taken away in the few means of transport at hand. A large number of them thus had to be left to their unfortunate fate. Those men abandoned in the middle of the desert, lying in their own blood, shaking with cold, suffering from a ravaging thirst and without medicines, blankets or food, saw their comrades march off, taking with them their lives, their hope, and watched with livid faces lit by the horrendous calm of desperation. They saw the coyotes and dogs approach, observed them waiting for the moment when they could begin their frightful banquet...

Thus it was that even though the battlefield was not more than four leagues from Agua Nueva, not until after ten o'clock at night did the troops begin to reach that spot. The hacienda, to which the Americans had set fire on their retreat, was still burning when our troops returned. On one side of the road lay a muddy swamp, into which the soldiers dying of thirst threw themselves. But the water, rather than bring relief, only opened their graves, since as soon as they drank it they died amid horrible convulsions. The few wounded who had managed to drag themselves that far, and many who arrived exhausted but without a scratch, died in that way. Their blood was mixed with the mud of the swamp, making the drink even more insufferable. Nevertheless, there was no other water to calm the ravaging thirst of the troops, and there were those who brought that filthy, disgusting and toxic brew to their lips.

Soon the sight of the bodies, the death rattle of the dying, the moans of the wounded, the cursing of everyone piled new afflictions onto their spirits, already weighed down by so much suffering...

After the battle of La Angostura (Buena Vista), the last of the great battles in northeast Mexico, the American troops had to continue fighting against Mexican guerrillas, p. 121, *who attacked supply lines, small groups of soldiers, and enemy message carriers in order to disrupt communications. This painting records one of the most spectacular assaults on an American convoy. The attack, led by the famous guerrilla of the North, Antonio Canales, took place on February 22, the very day of the Battle of La Angostura (Buena Vista).*

The wagons carried essentials for the troops and ammunition for the weaponry. During this attack, according to Samuel Chamberlain who painted this watercolor, one hundred and thirty wagons were destroyed.

As can be seen, the lasso was a common weapon among the guerrillas. Though simple, rope was a very effective weapon, much feared by marauders, that is, by those American soldiers who left the troops in search of pillage or women or simply due to exhaustion.

According to Santa Anna's dispatch, the retreat was ordered because of the utter lack of supplies and the need to attend to the wounded and to repair [the weaponry] and relieve the soldiers.

IMPROVISATION IN THE EAST

[Ramón Alcaraz et al., *Apuntes para la historia de la guerra...*]

While...these events occurred, an American army under the orders of General Winfield Scott, recently named commander of all the forces of the United States, disembarked near Veracruz and attacked the fort, which had to surrender...

General Santa Anna...prepared to leave the capital and gave the order for the two regiments coming from San Luis to turn off at Zumpango on the road to Veracruz before entering Mexico City.

CERRO GORDO, A NEW BATTLEFRONT

A position beyond Jalapa known as Cerro Gordo was chosen as the spot to await the invading army. It was well-known at the time of the insurrection and was viewed by scientific men as an excellent point to make the best defense. At that site...the regiments from the north arrived after marching double-time... The marches had been horrendous, the days long; they had suffered hunger, thirst, cold, wind, illnesses, disease and misery. They had crossed the desert twice in two and a half months with no rest. And in that long chain of suffering, the first link was a bloody battle in the north, the last a disastrous defeat in the east...

Rarely does one think of what forced marches really meant for troops dressed in uniforms of wool and leather. In those days there were no waterproof materials to make marching under the rain less arduous. Regarding shoes, several accounts describe conscripted Mexican soldiers wearing only their own sandals.

The Invasion
of the Northwest

*T*he northern part of Mexico at the time was sparsely populated and in poor communication with the rest of the country. Despite geographic isolation from the country's capital, the North was hardly destitute and life there was certainly not uneventful. Many of the population centers, it should be recalled, such as Guanajuato, San Luis Potosí, Zacatecas, Durango and Chihuahua, came into being because of nearby mines of precious metals. From Guadalajara and Zacatecas to Santa Fe and Saltillo, small regional markets of all sorts emerged, primarily agricultural, manufacturing and mining.

The environment of the North was harsh, particularly the desert habitat and the hostile population of "savage or barbarian Indians," which obliged the region's settlers to struggle to survive.

The territories of Chihuahua and New Mexico were less prepared than the northeast to defend themselves at the time of the U.S. invasion. Since the region's military leaders had been named by politicians from central Mexico, they were unable to exercise authority with the local population. Yet the invasion was resisted tenaciously by mobilized civilians and presidial troops, that is, regiments made up of prisoners taken from jail. The inhabitants of Taos, New Mexico, also waged a significant insurrection in which Mexicans and Pueblo Indians formed an alliance.

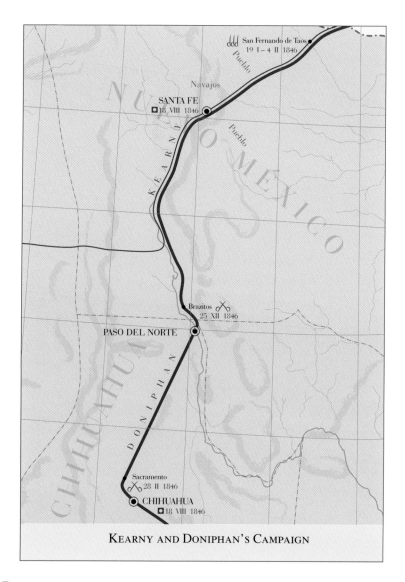

San Fernando de Taos
19 I – 4 II 1846

Navajos

SANTA FE
18 VIII 1846

Pueblo

Pueblo

NUEVO MÉXICO

KEARNY

DONIPHAN

CHIHUAHUA

Brazitos
25 XII 1846

PASO DEL NORTE

Sacramento
28 II 1846

CHIHUAHUA
18 VIII 1846

KEARNY AND DONIPHAN'S CAMPAIGN

*I*n Fort Leavenworth (Kansas) Colonel Stephen W. Kearny assembled the troops of the Western Army who would go on to conquer New Mexico and California. At the beginning of July 1846, the army left the fort and headed for Santa Fe by the old trade route. Once they occupied that city, Kearny left for California on September 25. Doniphan marched toward Chihuahua on November 20, along the trade route that came from Missouri. Once emptied of many of the invading soldiers, Santa Fe was the scene of a rebellion against the invasion, which was snuffed out on February 5, 1847.

THE NORTH AMERICANS' STRATEGY

[José María Roa Bárcena, *Recuerdos de la invasión norteamericana...*]

As I mentioned in the dispatch on general news of this campaign, besides the Army's Bravo Division under Taylor, the United States organized two others: the Central Division under the command of General Wool, and the Western Division led by General Kearnay or Kearny...

The Western Division under Kearnay [sic], out of Missouri and numbering 2,000 men, crossed into New Mexico in August of 1846. Having declared the territory to be part of the North American Union and having appointed their own provisional authorities in it, Kearnay and 300 dragoons set out from Santa Fe at the end of September bound for California. But upon receiving word that Colonel Fremont had already occupied its key outposts, he ordered most of his own forces to remain in New Mexico, and the rest to accompany him as an escort to Upper California, where he went, arriving in San Diego and later moving to Los Angeles and Monterey...

This watercolor by Samuel Chamberlain shows the U.S. Army on the move. Mounted sentries keep an eye on the long line of troops and wagons transporting munitions, food and tents. As always, there is a soldier with a drum. On the horizon lightning flashes. In many of their letters, soldiers complained about the rains that soaked them to the bone. Another interesting detail in this painting are the two Comanches observing the movement of the troops from a hiding place in the brush..

From the moment Mexico's Independence was proclaimed, the country's political leaders turned their backs on the Indians, considering them incapable of embracing the notions of prosperity or national integration. Similarly, during the war they refused to acknowledge the "barbarian Indians" of the North, who should have been their natural allies against the Americans.

DONIPHAN'S MARCH TO EL PASO

After an expedition from October to December 1846 among the Navajo (with whom he signed a peace treaty), Colonel Doniphan approached El Paso [Paso del Norte] with 856 men but no artillery, since it had not kept up with him... A detachment of 500 Mexican soldiers was sent off to meet the enemy; they advanced to El Paso, where they were joined by a few pickets from presidial companies, increasing their numbers to 1,200 men with four artillery pieces...

THE INTERNAL ENEMY
AND DEFENSE AGAINST THE INVADER

[Ramón Alcaraz et al., *Apuntes para la historia de la guerra...*]

Skilled at warfare, encouraged and protected by the North Americans, the savage tribes that inhabit the deserts on our borders with the United States had long been the vanguard of the invasion which has now penetrated all the way to the capital of the Republic. By sowing discord in our nascent society, and using the barbarians to devastate our border regions, the invaders prepared the terrain that would later lead them to our palaces...

The fatal names of Palo Alto, La Resaca, Monterey and New Mexico were etched one after another in our history; and Chihuahua, aware that it would soon come under threat from an American expeditionary force which had turned up in the northern part of the state, raised its voice more energetically and despairingly than ever, imploring the government of the federation for aid, not to save itself but to defend our national independence...

CHIHUAHUA ALONE

Trías, who was in charge of the government, decided to make a stand, and he bet everything on the patriotism of loyal citizens. Chihuahua lacked all the indispensable elements for organizing a force prepared to go into action—no artillery, no weaponry, no disciplined troops, and above all no resources—yet it faced the combined crisis of the new threat and the ongoing war with the barbarians. But sheer force of will, energetic determination to overcome all obstacles in order to resist the enemy, was more than enough to mount a defense that had seemed all but impossible...

A BAD BUGLE CALL DECIDES THE FATE OF EL PASO

As soon as our forces dig in...the Americans form three battle lines. Our infantry fires the first shots, gaining ground and breaking up into groups of riflemen, as the cannons blast away... The enemy fires... Ponce then calls for an all-out attack and that bugle—unheard of!—well or poorly played by the bugler, maliciously or mistakenly interpreted by the cavalry, calls out the signal for retreat!...

The Americans, unaware of the error, fortified the position where they had been attacked, and were so concerned with securing themselves that they left their horses entirely unattended, and these were collected by some ranchers who found them wandering in the countryside. But to complete our misfortune, the Americans' unwarranted fear turned into triumphant rejoicing the next day when a commission from the El Paso mayor's office presented itself to request guarantees for the civilian population that had been so notoriously abandoned [when the bugle sounded the retreat]. That same day, December 26, the odious American flag was raised in the town square. This sad event was the final news of the dismal year 1846...

Military Post, El Paso.

El Paso was the first important town on Doniphan's long route. To reach it, his army had to march more than 300 kilometers. Fifty kilometers before El Paso, where the Brazitos River meets the Rio Grande (Bravo), they were ambushed by a troop of inexperienced and untrained Mexican soldiers, who, despite having the advantage of surprise, ended up losing what became known as the Battle of Brazitos.

BATTLE OF SACRAMENTO

Because very few Mexican images of the battles of 1846–1848 have been preserved, ☞ p. 222, the majority of the lithographs in this book present the perspective of the victors. Generally they depict American troops on the offensive in the foreground, with Mexican soldiers enveloped in decorative plumes of smoke. There is practically no pictorial evidence of Mexico's military actions. The lithograph on the opposite page, taken from Álbum Pintoresco de la República Mexicana*, is an exception and carries the following inscription: "Battle of Sacramento, formidable attack by Mexican lancers against the U.S. Army, February 28, 1847." It is one of a handful of images that depict Mexicans fighting against the invaders' artillery, or show American soldiers retreating, confused, wounded or dead.*

Colonel Doniphan, commander of the American expedition, was making preparations in El Paso to advance on Chihuahua, and at last he began his march, taking with him several prisoners he had taken in that town, all individuals who had distinguished themselves in their hatred for the invaders.

General Heredia, in consultation with Trías, selected Sacramento, seven leagues from Chihuahua along the road to New Mexico, as the place to raise fortifications and resist the enemy if they were not stopped before reaching that point...

At the foot of the line of fortifications that cut across the road lay a sort of rise that was difficult to climb, making the position more advantageous; it rose slowly northward from there to the top of the hill where [the soldiers] awaited the enemy. The enemy did turn up at that point between two and three in the afternoon on the 28th [of December], marching directly on our positions with all their troops, numbering more than thirteen hundred men...

The first shots from their batteries produced a ripple effect: our cavalry, composed mostly of soldiers who had never before heard the roar of a cannon, sat there without undertaking any maneuvers, and was unable to withstand for long such withering fire without giving way; the undulations of their battle lines signaled a disorder that several officers tried in vain to rein in... Disorder built to a climax. The troops fled in all directions...

Left abandoned on the battlefield were our wounded and our dead, except for Captain Rosales (whose body was carried to Chihuahua by a grenadier of his battalion), as were the supplies, the money and nearly all the munitions, of which only a few loads could be taken out through the mountains...

AWAITING THE ENEMY

That night was horrendous for all of Chihuahua. In the city where people envisioning victory had been enthusiastically preparing a triumphal celebration, the sound of the afternoon's cannon fire caused acute distress. And when news arrived of the disaster that had occurred, terror swept through the population. Many, many families took to the roads just as they were, without any preparations, exposing themselves to the likelihood of being dismembered by the savages...

FALL OF CHIHUAHUA

[José María Roa Bárcena, *Recuerdos de la invasión norteamericana...*]

On the night of February 28, a crowd of families fled Chihuahua heading for the chaparral, and on the first of March, Colonel Doniphan and his troops occupied the city. In private letters published at the time, I read that large stores of corn were confiscated, that for lack of firewood the soldiers cut down the trees in the main square, and that at the funeral for one of their leaders killed in the action at Sacramento, a mob of [American] soldiers desecrated the parish church...

Government authorities in Chihuahua did what they could to deter the advance of Doniphan's army with the meager weaponry they had on hand to fight the Indians. They moved quickly to cast new cannon, rebuild rifles and improvise a national guard. They also sought loans but never obtained them. Despite their efforts, the Mexicans were defeated at Sacramento as a result of the inexperience of their troops, who had never before heard the roar of a cannon.

INVASION OF NEW MEXICO

In New Mexico, after the state was invaded by the Western Division, most of those troops, as was noted, stayed behind to occupy the capital Santa Fe and a few other localities. Invasion there soon became conquest, with the invader organizing authorities and finding support for them among some local sons who more or less voluntarily let themselves be used. But in general the population was against them, and the resistance, passive at first, soon became conspiratorial and openly hostile, and was put down in military operations with much bloodshed...

CRUSHING OF THE POPULAR INSURRECTION OF TAOS

The first indications of the uprising appeared in the northern part of the state, and the invaders blamed those unhappy with their rule for the widespread killing of North Americans and of Mexican officials and employees who worked under the U.S. flag. The murder of the governor and several other North Americans and nationals in San Fernando de Taos, Arroyo Hondo and Río Colorado lent credence to such allegations. These events coincided with the reorganization of the Mexican forces, made up entirely of volunteers, to attack Santa Fe, the state capital. The [American] military commander, Price, using most of his troops, advanced on his opponents near San Fernando de Taos. He defeated them successively in La Cañada, outside La Hoya, and in Puebla de Taos. He killed the principal leaders of the uprising, or chased them into flight, and he continued ruling without opposition in this part of our country, which from then on was irrevocably lost to Mexico...

 Defense
of the Californias

In light of the documentary evidence, the war in the Northwest of Mexico was truly a war of conquest. The territory was not implicated in the disputes regarding the Texas border, yet it held great strategic importance for the United States, given that the California coast would offer the country access to the Pacific. In addition, by conquering California the United States could achieve greater domestic political equilibrium between the abolitionist states of the North and the slaveholder states of the South.

The links between the Californias and the rest of Mexico were practically nonexistent and political relations were uneasy. In 1836 the region rose up against the centralized system, and in 1845 did so for a second time, overthrowing a governor imposed by Santa Anna. Despite these problems, the region continued attracting settlers, who soon took over the few trade routes in place between New Mexico, Arizona, Chihuahua, Durango and Zacatecas. Among the settlers were plenty of American adventurers, poachers, ruffians, vagrants, traders, businessmen, smugglers and mercenaries.

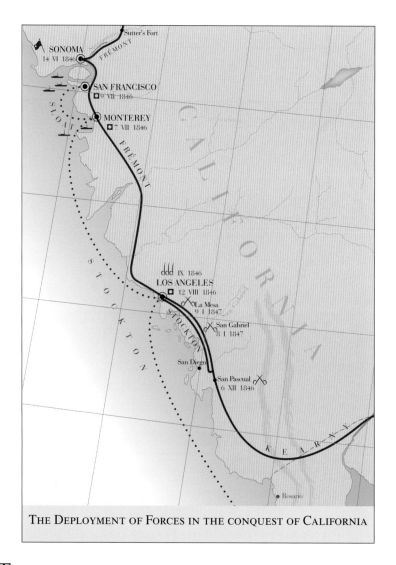

THE DEPLOYMENT OF FORCES IN THE CONQUEST OF CALIFORNIA

*T*he key personalities in the conquest of California were General Kearny, Colonel Fremont and Commodore Stockton.

Kearny arrived by land following the trade route from Santa Fe, Fremont along a trail he found during his supposed scientific expedition, and Stockton by sea all the way around Cape Horn.

After firing on the coast, Commodore Stockton ordered his sailors ashore to subdue the Mexican resistance and to assist Kearny, whose troops had arrived from Santa Fe exhausted.

By the decade of the 1840s, the California territory was inhabited by some seven thousand Mexicans. During those same years a massive migration of Americans began.

This image, which depicts an Indian attack on a wagon train of American migrants, appeared in Revista Científico Literaria with the following commentary: "In the English theaters of the United States, public lectures on the Californias are offered, and the enthusiasm of settlers and adventurers is large. He who writes these lines has seen them traveling in long caravans made up of over sixty wagons with three hundred or more migrants. Is it not probable that California will face the same fate as Texas?" Because many Mexicans wondered the same thing, the government issued a document, reproduced above, to promote Catholic Irish immigration to the ports of San Francisco, Monterey and Santa Barbara.

Fremont planting the American flag on the Rocky Mountains. The colonel made several expeditions to California seeking the shortest route to the Pacific. Though said to be solely scientific, the expeditions seem to have had other purposes. Upon reaching California, Fremont urged the American settlers to rise up and declare independence. Independence was in fact declared on June 14, 1846, in Sonoma after the rebels captured the commander for northern California, Mariano Guadalupe Vallejo.

COL. FREMONT
PLANTING THE AMERICAN STANDARD ON THE ROCKY MOUNTAINS.

THE EPHEMERAL BEAR REPUBLIC

[Ramón Alcaraz et al., *Apuntes para la historia de la guerra...*]

About a year before the war broke out, a band of adventurers from the United States spread across the vast Californias territory, awaiting only the signal from emissaries of that government to launch a war of conquest...

In the month of February 1846, Captain Fremont, a U.S. Army engineer, entered Mexican territory with a unit of mounted riflemen, under the pretext of a scientific commission. He sought and obtained permission from the commanding general, then-Lieutenant Colonel D. José Castro, to travel about the country.

Three months later (on May 14) that same unit and its commander launched a surprise attack and took over the important base at Sonoma, gaining control of all the artillery, weaponry, etc. stored there. The adventurers sprinkled along the banks of the Sacramento River joined up with that unit and, then numbering four hundred men, they proclaimed by themselves and to themselves the independence of the Californias, raising a flesh-colored flag featuring a bear and a star...

The flag of the Bear Republic, drawn by William L. Todd on June 14, 1846, in Sonoma, was destroyed in the earthquake of 1890. Fortunately, the negative of a photograph survived. The star offers an allusion to the "lone star" of Texas, since the "California Republic" sought to follow Texas's lead: declare independence and then seek annexation to the United States.

Two images of Russian settlements on the Pacific coast.

In the period 1820–1840, the intensive exploitation of natural resources, especially the fur trade, and the development of manufacturing fueled important economic growth along the Pacific coast of North America, where the interests of Mexicans, Americans, British and Russians all crossed paths. American politicians feared British expansion toward California, and they were jealous of Russian whalers and trappers who frequented the waters and lands from Alaska to California.

The Mexican government at the time sought to integrate the economy of its northern frontier with that of the rest of the country. With the intention of supporting Mexican industry, and in light of the near extermination of beaver and otter, the government outlawed fur trapping by foreigners throughout California and even in Texas. From that moment on, smuggling mushroomed.

As of July 1845, the U.S. Pacific Squadron was in place and ready to attack the California coast. Commodore Sloat occupied the port of Monterey on July 7, 1846, in his only important action in the war. He was then replaced by Stockton, who took nine months to arrive since he had to circle South America—an illustration of why the United States wanted direct access to the Pacific.

FALL OF THE PORT OF MONTEREY

On July 7 of the same year, the American squadron took possession of the undefended port of Monterey and their commander, in the name of their government, demanded that the [Mexican] commanding general surrender all the bases and forts in the state...

Thus, the occupation of all the towns of the northern part of the Californias was accomplished.

The American squadron under Commodore Stockton occupying the Monterey coast.

CAPTURE OF LOS ANGELES

Last August 7 an American squadron led by Commodore Stockton anchored off the port of San Pedro, nine leagues from Los Angeles. Four hundred men immediately disembarked with some artillery and, along with Captain Fremont's forces, occupied the city on the 15th of that month. The political and military authorities, deeming it imprudent to have the partially armed populace resist the invaders, dispersed their forces and left for the state of Sonora... In this way, the occupation of Upper California was accomplished without the least resistance. Most of the American forces [were] under Commodore Stockton, who was named governor of the territory... A proclamation from the American governor announced that the country would be ruled by the military.

CIVILIAN RESISTANCE

Meanwhile, patriotic fire glowed in the hearts of the majority of citizens. Hatred of the invaders spread...

Early on the morning of September 23, 1846, part of the population of the city of Los Angeles, led by Auxiliary Captain D. Cérvulo Varela, though poorly armed, attacked the barracks housing the Americans. Having been forewarned, they soon managed to repel the attack. However, the event was sufficient to intimidate the Americans, who did not venture to take their defense beyond the fort itself... From that moment on, men, women and children came from all over to unite against their common enemy, bringing with them whatever weapons they had on hand. The women were models of bravery and patriotism: some of them brought their sons, even the little ones, to take up arms; others spied on the enemy; still others carried rifles, powder and shot, which they'd buried for safekeeping, across enemy checkpoints to the patriotic camp. In sum, everyone proclaimed

At the time of the invasion, the governor of California was Pío de Jesús Pico, who had been named by President Herrera. Pío Pico and military commander José M. Castro led an assault to recapture the city of Los Angeles. On September 30, 1846, they took control of the city and forced Stockton to retreat to San Diego. Los Angeles remained in Mexican hands until the beginning of 1847.

the freedom and independence of their fatherland in the heart of a city occupied by the enemy...

On September 27, 28 and 29, they continued military operations against the fort, with the result that on the 30th, the American forces capitulated and abandoned it...

On October 6, an enemy warship docked at the port of San Pedro to rescue the defeated troops, who were on board a merchant ship. The following day they disembarked and began marching toward the city of Los Angeles in a column of five hundred men, made up of the defeated riflemen plus some line infantrymen and sailors...

At dawn on the 8th the enemy began marching in a tight column, deploying their guerrillas to the right and left to try to surround the Mexican cavalry, who had taken up combat positions on either side of the road in support of their artillery. Shooting broke out here and there, with the Mexican artillery so well aimed that it caused terrible damage to the enemy column. After an hour of very lively fire, the column was driven with considerable losses all the way back to the port, where they immediately re-embarked, leaving the battlefield littered with their abandoned possessions, including their flag...

All of the towns of the south, from San Luis Obispo, Santa Barbara and Los Angeles up to San Diego, were occupied by the Mexican forces: the nation's flag was raised and local officials reinstated... Since keeping supplies of food or animals and other means of transport for land mobility from the enemy was indispensable, a portion of the troops marched on San Diego and, along with a company of local citizens who had taken up arms, they laid siege to the fort to keep the enemy from sending out shipments of supplies. This operation had the happiest of outcomes, as the enemy was obliged to obtain supplies from Baja California, making use of their smaller boats...

This drawing by artilleryman Meyers, *p. 254, depicts one of the Californian lancers who fought against the American troops.*

SAN PASCUAL:
GENERAL KEARNY'S FIRST BATTLE

At the end of the month of November, a company of three hundred Americans with three artillery pieces under the command of General Kearny entered the Californias by the Sonora road, having come from New Mexico...wishing to keep them from joining the enemy forces occupying San Diego, the commander general ordered a hundred horses under squadron commander D. Andres Pico to march like mad...to harass Kearny's regiment and fight them if the opportunity arose. At dawn on December 6, in an attempt to drive away the troops laying siege to the fort and get inside, General Kearny (who had received relief from the fort) clashed with troops under Commander Pico, who made a false retreat then resumed his attack on the enemy cavalry with such ferocity that he managed to scatter them completely, killing over forty and wounding more than eighty, among them General Kearny...

DIVIDED AGAIN

The [American] prisoners of war being held in the city of Los Angeles, whose

In a period of six months, from June 5, 1846, when Kearny departed from Leavenworth, Kansas, to December 6, when he arrived in California, the American officer, 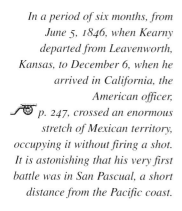 *p. 247, crossed an enormous stretch of Mexican territory, occupying it without firing a shot. It is astonishing that his very first battle was in San Pascual, a short distance from the Pacific coast.*

transfer to the state of Sonora had been arranged by the commander general, sought to block the transfer however they might. They managed to seduce a few civilians and soldiers with false offers and threats, drawing them into a conspiracy to overthrow the governor and the commander general. Fighting broke out on the eve of December 3. Although order was restored in forty-eight hours, a large portion of the troops was unavoidably dispersed, some for having taken part in the conspiracy, others as a result of the ensuing disorder... Thus, the road from San Diego to Los Angeles was cleared for the enemy. At the beginning of the month of December, Captain Fremont, with a company of seven hundred mounted riflemen and four light artillery pieces, together with the troops of the base at San Diego, began moving from the northern towns toward the city of Los Angeles, with the fort of Santa Barbara soon falling into their hands.

...AND DEFINITIVELY CONQUERED

On January 8, 1847, there was a very hotly contested battle between the two sides three leagues outside the city of Los Angeles. It ended at dusk with the battlefield occupied by the Americans, after they managed to push the Mexican cavalry back and cause them some losses.

On the 9th, the Mexicans again charged the enemy, although with no more success than the previous day, since they lacked munitions and weapons; numbering three hundred men, they were twice repulsed by withering fire from the American troops. Nevertheless, the enemy was held at a distance of a league outside the city. This was the final attempt by the sons of the Californias to defend the freedom and independence of their fatherland...

On January 10, the city of Los Angeles was occupied by American troops, and for Mexico the loss of that rich, vast and beautiful part of her territory was complete...

The only battle in northern California took place on January 2, 1847, near the Santa Clara mission, which was then being used as an American garrison. During the fighting, which lasted for two hours, the Americans suffered only one loss: a cannon which sank into the mud. The Santa Clara mission can be seen on the left, evidence of the Spanish evangelical work in California.

 *Invasion
from the East*

*B*y February 1847, U.S. military strategy had succeeded in conquering northern Mexico. American forces were occupying the coveted territories of the Californias and New Mexico, and they controlled Chihuahua, Coahuila, Nuevo León and Tamaulipas as well. However, Mexico's tenacious resistance forced the United States to change strategy and open a campaign in the East, from Veracruz to Mexico City.

Even though the port of Veracruz had been blockaded for months by naval forces, the initiation of new hostilities on this front took the Mexican government by surprise. Mexico's economic situation by then had worsened, primarily due to the collapse of revenue caused by the blockade of customs in Veracruz, and to domestic political conflicts. In an attempt to cover the steep cost of the war, the government, led in Santa Anna's absence by Vice President Valentín Gómez Farías, confiscated Church properties and obtained Congressional authorization to sell them off. The measure provoked an armed uprising in the capital city, which then obliged Santa Anna to return there to reassume his presidential duties and suspend the decree issued by his vice president—events which made timely assistance to Veracruz impossible.

The eastern campaign achieved its intended objective: the Americans captured Mexico City and obliged the Mexican government to negotiate a surrender.

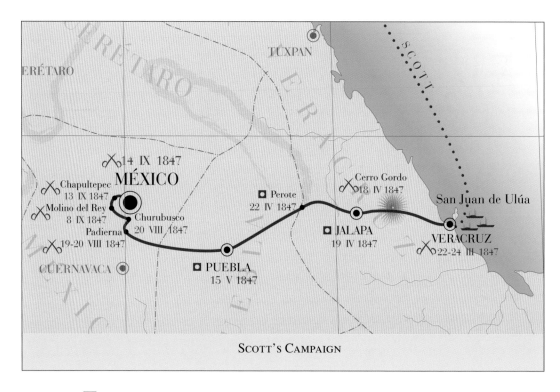

*T*he port of Veracruz was blockaded from the very beginning of the war. However, the massive transfer of U.S. forces to that city began on March 5, 1847, when half of Taylor's troops joined with Scott's for the first attack in the east. Scott disembarked at a beach near the city four days later.

This map shows the principal battles fought by Scott and indicates the places occupied by his troops. In all of those locations the invaders set up a military base to protect their rearguard and ensure lines of communication with the port, where reinforcements arrived constantly.

At the beginning of the campaign two large battles took place: at Veracruz and at Cerro Gordo. Meeting no more resistance, Scott's army marched on to the Valley of Mexico. There, near the capital city, they fought several fierce battles. Today all the battlefields are part of Mexico City. An estimated fifteen thousand men took part in the assault on the city.

The map does not register the many skirmishes with Mexican guerrillas who persistently attacked the American rearguard.

The Purpose of the Eastern Campaign

[Ramón Alcaraz et al., *Apuntes para la historia de la guerra...*]

...The U.S. government's primary objective in taking Veracruz ought to have been to bring the war to a close. However, the occupation of that city suddenly brought the American army much closer to the capital, and afforded it a smoother and easier path to get there.

But this plain and simple calculation... did not merit the attention of the men in charge of saving our country. And far from reinforcing our defenses on that side, General Santa Anna, upon his return from exile, ordered a number of soldiers wearied by immense suffering and loss, to march to Mexico City...

This picture shows the defenses of Mexico's oldest and most important port, Veracruz, protected by twelve forts on the walls surrounding it, and by Fort San Juan de Ulúa on the sea side. The port also had natural defenses: hurricanes known as "nortes," and an unhealthy climate which spread malaria, yellow fever and diarrhea, biological weapons which in this war were much more effective than Mexico's antiquated cannons.

To strengthen the regular army, as of August 1846 the Mexican government began setting up National Guard or Civil Militia units made up of volunteers from the middle and upper sectors of society: public servants, traders, craftsmen, professionals and landowners. The regiments and battalions took on the names of national heros or events like "Hidalgo" or "Independence" and, though formed to defend the country, they also sought to defend the interests of the groups they represented. One group of Civil Militias in Mexico City revolted at the very moment when their support was needed to defend Veracruz. On February 27, 1847, when the government tried to send them off to fight the war, three thousand of them mutinied. Poor people nicknamed these young renegades the "Polkos" because they were well-off and had a reputation for attending parties where they danced the latest craze, the Polka.

Historians agree that the uprising was manipulated by the Catholic hierarchy in order to overthrow Vice President Valentín Gómez Farías, who had tried to finance the war by seizing Church assets. For a month the city was the scene of confrontations between the "Polkos" and militias loyal to the government. The rioting ended when Santa Anna returned to the capital, but the Polkos Revolt brought divisions within Mexican society into full view.

Two scenes of the rebellion in the streets of Mexico City: the image above depicts a barricade near the church of La Profesa; the one at left shows a movable parapet thrown together with whatever material the rebels had at hand.

THE POLKOS REVOLT LEAVES VERACRUZ TO ITS FATE

And in those days of bitterness, Veracruz heard the shocking news that a civil war had broken out in the capital of the Republic, and that the government could not spare a single man or peso on its behalf... This terrible and woeful news reached the city on the 4th of March...

BOMBARDMENT OF THE CITY BRINGS INDESCRIBABLE HORROR

On March 22 at two in the afternoon, the enemy general demands that the city surrender within two hours. The response is negative, and as vigorous and dignified as would

On March 9, 1847, Scott's troops disembarked near Veracruz. They began their spectacular land and sea assault on the fortified city on March 26.

This lithograph is one of very few to depict the suffering of the civilian population during the bombardment, which destroyed houses and killed women and children. During the siege many more civilians died than soldiers, and all sources (including American ones) confirm the inordinate anguish and personal tragedy they suffered.

be expected from Veracruz. At four in the afternoon, a shell explodes on the parade ground, another in the Post Office. The battle is joined. God save the Republic.

The shooting continues without a break from that moment on: mortars, howitzers, cannon, batteries from smaller ships that have drawn near Callawadda, everything targeting the city center...

Instantly the horrors of a fort under bombardment begin... While a wounded man is being operated on, a shell explodes and plunges the room into darkness; when the lamps are relit, the patient is found torn to pieces and many more are wounded or dead. Scenes of agony and blood follow one after the other, which we must decline to describe to avoid a litany of horrors...

SURRENDER

March 25 was a terrible day that the city will never forget... Negotiations with the enemy began that day...leading to surrender on the 27th. General Landero was aware that, among other difficulties, there was but three hours' worth of munitions left, and that the only food on hand was what the municipal government had put aside for the civilian population. At a pre-dawn war council, he was obliged to decide to end the battle that was going so clearly against us. His decision calmed an anxious public, but provoked disgust among the troops... The Veracruz National Guard, which ...was part of a reserve force, declared that they would not surrender; word got around... However, the dismal truth of the reasons for capitulating overcame their disgust and calmed their anger. General Morales—what a hero of Veracruz—ensured his own glory alongside that of the garrison, by departing with the chief of the National Guard in a small boat, so as not to surrender...

FEAR FINALLY TAKES HOLD ON THE CAPITAL

The occupation of Veracruz by the American army sounded the first alarm for the capital of the Republic. Up to then, the notion that the United States would raise its flag over the palace of the Moctezumas was considered preposterous, but upon seeing the invaders already in possession of such an important base... and upon contemplating the impotence of the capital itself, weakened as it was by the most scandalous of revolutions, a presentiment of misfortune sowed terror and discouragement, the eternal precursors of the country's great disasters...

Cerro Gordo: A Poor Choice

When Engineers Officer Lieutenant Colonel D. Manuel Robles retreated from Veracruz, where his name had become so well respected, he was ordered by General Canalizo to undertake a tour of reconnaissance of positions in Cerro Gordo, and naturally he said he found them advantageous for harassing the invading army on its way to Jalapa, but not the best spot to stop them in their tracks, and certainly not a place for a decisive victory. He based this opinion primarily on the fact that the road could be cut off by the enemy in the rearguard, and that the best one could hope for in a head-on attack was to drive them back, but then they would surely regroup in the heights of Palo Gacho. He added that the lack of water in Cerro Gordo also made the situation quite unfavorable for our troops, and he believed a better place for the attack would be Corral Falso, a position that did not present these drawbacks. Despite his cautions, sadly vindicated by the outcome, General Canalizo, by express orders of General Santa Anna, sent Lieutenant Colonel Robles to Cerro Gordo to begin building fortifications...

On the battlefield, the dying were put out of their misery.

Fatal Defeat

At dawn on the 18th [of April], the roar of enemy cannon resounded in the countryside chillingly announcing the battle... The enemy blasted grapeshot, shells and all sorts of projectiles without respite, and these landed on the hill, on the road, and even beyond our encampment... The rifle fire was as intense as the ardor of the battle. Beating its wings over a bloodied field set aflame at certain points by enemy projectiles, death circled horribly above the clouds of smoke that enveloped thousands of men engaged in cruel battle. Our soldiers fell by the dozen in the midst of that confusion, as did the enemy troops, but they were instantly replaced by others who seemed to be their exact replicas...

The illustration above depicts the two high points fortified by the Mexicans at Cerro Gordo. On the far right is Telégrafo Hill, the higher and better defended of the two; next to it is Atalaya Hill, insufficiently fortified despite the warnings given to Santa Anna. Precisely for this reason, General Twiggs decided to attack Atalaya first, opening a path to the base of Telégrafo Hill. In the detail below the soldiers can be seen chopping down trees. During the night the Americans hauled three artillery batteries to the summit of Atalaya Hill, a task that would have required some five hundred men, in order to attack Telégrafo from that height, p. 269.

On the summit of the hill, a crowd of Americans in a dense column of smoke could be seen lit by the reddish glow of their musketry directed at the enormous mass of men scrambling in retreat down the steep hillside... That horrible spectacle was like the violent eruption of a volcano belching lava and ash from its breast. Amid the smoke and fire, on the blue strip formed by the Americans on the summit of Telégrafo Hill, our abandoned flag still waved. But all too soon on that same flag-pole but on its other side, the starred banner was raised, and for an instant the two of them fluttered together, before ours finally came down, violently tugged off amid the hooting and jubilant gunfire of the victors and the pitiful wails and confused cries of the vanquished...

General Santa Anna, accompanied by several of his assistants, was headed down the path to the left of the battery, and just as he emerged from the woods the enemy column closed off his exit route with a burst of fire that forced him to retreat. The general's coach, which was on its way to Jalapa, was

The American troops in blue charge up a steep incline and, using bayonets in close combat, capture the Mexican flag.

peppered with shot, the mules killed or captured, as was a wagon which carried sixteen thousand pesos received the day before to rescue the troops.... Cerro Gordo was lost!... Mexico was wide open to the iniquities of the invader's evildoing!...

General Santa Anna fleeing the battlefield. Both lithographs allude to the capture of Santa Anna's coach. Among the personal posses-sions seized was the general's cork peg leg. (He had lost his leg in the war against the French in 1839.) This sad trophy was soon exhibited to the public, and to this day is part of the collection of the Illinois National Guard and Militia Historical Society.

This may be the very first daguerreotype ever taken of a battlefield amputa-
tion. Two Mexican soldiers hold a third who has fainted. Pedro Vander Linden,
a surgeon of Belgian origin, holds the amputated leg in his left hand.

Vander Linden, who was an inspector general of the Mexican Military
Medical Corps, was captured at the Battle of Cerro Gordo, where this
daguerreotype was taken on April 18, 1847. A curious detail is that Mexican
and American soldiers can be seen together in this picture, the latter threaten-
ing the surgeon with bayonets. There was no neutrality for ambulances, and
the International Red Cross did not yet exist.

General anesthesia was discovered by the American doctors Morton and
Wells during the war on Mexico, and Mexican doctors Miguel Jiménez and José
Pablo Martínez del Río began using chloroform on Mexico's wounded in
September 1847.

Before anesthesia, narcotic brews made from opium or Spanish fly mixed
with liquor were used. Many amputees died after the operation because they
never recovered from the shock or fell prey to infection.

The American troops who advanced along the main road to Jalapa must have enjoyed this view. Scott stayed in Jalapa from April 19 until May 20, 1847.

IN THE HOSPITALS OF JALAPA

[José María Roa Bárcena, *Recuerdos de la invasión norteamericana*]

Those living near the hospitals were terrorized by the practically continuous screeching of the saw, the screams of the amputees who had not yet been treated with chloroform, and the sight of pieces of legs and arms taken out for cremation or burial. For a bit of emotional variety they had the spectacle of the funeral corteges, marching silently with heads bowed behind a simple pine coffin painted black, or, if the cortege was of soldiers, they could listen to a symphony of tin whistles, which is the saddest thing I have ever heard...

A NEW RULE IN ALGEBRA.
Five from Three and One remains !!
or
"The Three Mexican Prisoners, having but one leg between them all."

A morbid American cartoon about the most common medical treatment during the war: amputations. The caption says: "A New Rule in Algebra. Five from Three and One remains!! or 'The Three Mexican Prisoners having but one leg between them all.'"

*An American soldier meets a
street vendor.*

*A typical Mexican rooming house
from the book* Mexican War *published at the end of the war.*

Mexican Inn, between Jalapa and Puebla.

THE OTHER AMERICAN

Offering greater solace, no doubt, was the motley crew of volunteers [for the American side] who, attired in the most curious collection of clothing, many of them wearing local varieties of palm-leaf hats, entered or exited the city on horseback or by foot, or strolled its streets in groups, stretching out on benches whenever they felt tired, smoking pipes or chewing Virginia tobacco, eating bread with tallow instead of butter, and gnawing on pineapples and cactus pears with the peel still on.

They showed much more enthusiasm for cane liquor, the abuse of which could not be avoided despite the restrictions and heavy taxes put on its sale. A few sips of that liquid were enough to twist their senses into drunken fury or tearful sentimentality, and to predispose them to losing their weapons or their lives, since some members of the town's unscrupulous lower classes did not hesitate to take them one by one into the outlying suburbs or the countryside and kill them...

They abstained from bothering the local residents and behaved themselves in the churches. Besides the Irish, there were few Catholics among them. Many Protestant soldiers carried their Bibles with them. They were generous to beggars and made friends with the vendors of fruit and trinkets, and since the vendors wanted them to understand and they pretended to learn and speak the local language, a dialect was born whose vocabulary and idioms would make a very curious book for philologists if ever compiled and written down. What was most remarkable about these people was their respect for women, which is traditional in peoples of their race...

BROAD-BRUSH MERMAIDS

Desiring feminine company and able to visit only a very few private homes, they improvised parties attended by women of easy virtue who nevertheless were courted with the most exquisite politesse, which gave the boys of my days cause for great laughter. A few of those broad-brush mermaids caught a prey, and when the army retreated along they went to the United States, married more or less civilly...

GUERRILLA ACTION

Precarious and nomadic were the lives of state officials after the battle of Cerro Gordo... Ever since Santa Anna climbed up to Puebla with the troops that had met up in Orizaba, the resistance in nearly all of the east came to rely nearly exclusively on guerrillas. They were active in the states of Veracruz, Puebla and Mexico, just as they had been in Tamaulipas, where at the orders of generals Urrea, Romero and Canales they caused serious damage to the enemy in the days following the battle of La Angostura...

Guerrillas and counter-guerrillas played a key role during the American invasion. Resistance fighters were organized in the states of Puebla, Mexico, Veracruz and Tamaulipas under such outstanding leaders as Joaquín Rea, Juan Clímaco Rebolledo, José Urrea and Antonio Canales. Some of the fighters were local militia and others belonged to the army. Guerrilla attacks cost the Americans hundreds of men, as well as wagons, mules and supplies of food and clothing. This lithograph depicts a guerrilla skirmish with the Americans.

Panoramic view of Puebla.

PUEBLA DISCOURAGED

[Carlos María de Bustamante, *El nuevo Bernal Díaz del Castillo*]

Ever since the first fugitives from Cerro Gordo turned up in Puebla, this city has been in turmoil. Mothers and relatives of soldiers...headed out to the road to await their sons and learn the fate of those who had not yet arrived. And in any case the first to return home told so many lies that consternation soon turned into fear. The stories circulating heightened people's terror and led many families to flee.

The nuns who heard this exaggerated news in their cloisters were reduced to the bitterest anguish, praying continually for God to spare them from the coming calamity. The monks and friars, instead of preaching defense of the fatherland and inspiring people to fight, encouraged prayer and penance. And they paraded down the streets in solemn processions bearing crosses, medallions and scapularis, four or five thousand of them who would have done better had each carried a rifle. That was the state of the city of Puebla when the rest of our army arrived...

WIDESPREAD DISDAIN IS UNABLE TO PREVENT THE
YANKEES FROM ENTERING PUEBLA

[Ramón Alcaraz et al., *Apuntes para la historia de la guerra...*]

Once General Santa Anna arrived and was lodged in the governor's palace, he tried to take some measures. One of them was to violently commandeer horses in order to rebuild the cavalry, which was truly in a deplorable state. The circumstances of war justified this sort of measure, but those enforcing it did so in a manner that made it odious... Still, what contributed most to the utter absence of any defense was the apathy and fear that had taken hold of the inhabitants...

THE DISILLUSIONED HISTORIAN

[Carlos María de Bustamante, *El nuevo Bernal Díaz del Castillo*]

The neighborhood showed no sign of alteration. Besides the clothing stores, which were closed, the entire city looked as it always does, and no one would have known that it was awaiting the arrival of an enemy army. Curiosity to see the Yankees outweighed the very natural momentary alarm, and the rabble were out on all the street corners and nearly all the balconies were filled with the curious. Even I fell prey to curiosity, and breaking with my intention to stay inside I went out to meet our new lords.

What disillusion I felt, and everyone felt, when instead of the centaurs we expected, I saw coming toward me a hundred or so men decrepit in appearance, dressed in poorly made and ill-fitting uniforms. Many of them were in shirt-sleeves, armed with swords, carbines and common pistols, and their horses, though sturdy, were dull and ungainly like all of their breeding, poorly ridden and harnessed only with a packsaddle and a plain bridle without any sort of adornment. So as not to offend, I'll say only that for every ten men in good shape one could point to several who were skinny, rachitic and even crippled... None of this is exaggerated...

Following the defeat at Cerro Gordo, Santa Anna decided not to fight outside the Valley of Mexico. He regrouped his forces to defend the capital city. Above, Mexican troops pass through the town of Río Frío, located near the entrance to the Valley of Mexico.

MEXICO CITY PREPARES A FINAL STAND

[Ramón Alcaraz et al., *Apuntes para la historia de la guerra...*]

The advance of the Americans on the capital city, so many times declared to be underway and always disproved, finally occurred in the first days of August when they marched out of Puebla, leaving behind a small garrison. On August 7, 8, 9 and 10 in succession, the Twiggs, Quitman, Worth and Pillow divisions set out...

However, the defense of the capital faced obstacles difficult to overcome. Being a city open on all sides, new well-made fortifications ought to be built all around it to protect it from an enemy strike, and both a sizeable army and a large number of artillery pieces were essential...

The Main Fortifications

Among the fortifications were a few that were a credit to their creators. The best was the one at Peñón Viejo, built by the able engineer officer D. Manuel Robles, and since it was the first one the enemy would come upon on the direct road from Puebla to Mexico, it was the one believed most likely to be attacked. It defended the eastern front. In the south there were breastworks at Mexicalcingo, San Antonio, and the convent and bridge at Churubusco, a few of them still unfinished. In the southwest was Chapultepec Castle, whose artistic construction enhanced its natural defensive position, and whose artillery could reach both the road heading west to the fortified blockhouse at San Cosme and the one at Santo Tomás. In the north there were no advance fortifications: the entire defense was reduced to the blockhouses at Nonoalco, Vallejo and Peralvillo. In the villa of Guadalupe there was the Northern Army, which later marched to Texcoco to be able to fire on the Americans' flank from that excellent position...

This map drawn by the Americans shows Mexico City's main defenses. Two roads lead through the valley to the capital: the main one passed by fortified Peñón Hill, where Santa Anna lay in wait; the other ran through swamps alongside Chalco and Xochimilco lakes. On the former, the U.S. Army risked a confrontation not to their advantage; on the latter, artillery transport would be more difficult. Scott chose the latter. Two forts awaited him in the southern part of the city, at San Antonio hacienda and Churubusco convent. Nearby each was the Pedregal, broad fields of petrified lava.

DIFFERENT REACTIONS

[Abraham López, *La revolución de los polkos o la cruzada de México en el siglo XIX*]

The terrible blast from a 16-pound artillery piece at two in the afternoon on August 9, and the simultaneous general call to all army divisions in Mexico City, announced that the enemy with all its entourage of war had begun its march on this capital city. Every single man felt an urge to take to the battlefield. The middle class and the unfortunate class ran to the barracks to help defend their fatherland. The wealthy class and the aristocracy did no more than hide their riches and prepare to travel wherever their pusillanimity would lead them. Wagons piled high with furniture could be seen heading in all directions, for fear had finally taken hold of that class that had always wished for a foreign prince.

DICTATORSHIP AND CENSORSHIP, ALWAYS HAND IN HAND

General D. Antonio López de Santa Anna had become a dictator. Freedom of the press was abolished and the only law was his will, but it was said this was for the good of the fatherland.

THE NATIONAL GUARD

[Ramón Alcaraz et al., *Apuntes para la historia de la guerra...*]

The 10th [of August] is the day chosen for the march. General Anaya's regiment sets out for the battlefield; in the great plaza of Mexico City a multitude seethes, the balconies and rooftops of the palace crowned with anxious people... The National Guard is on parade, stirring up patriotic fervor among all. Its "Victory" battalion made up of the young merchants of Mexico, representing immense fortunes with their luxurious uniforms and their elegant pages; "Hidalgo" battalion made up of those exempted from regular service, including ardent youth, old folks enfeebled by sedentary living, heads of family bearing those social titles that always garner respect; "Independence" and "Braves" battalions, made up of hardworking artisans with their modest attire, their faces filled with pride...and whose weapons and dress betray a history of privation...

El Peñón: First Point Foreseen
for Defending the Capital

General León's regiment, composed mostly of National Guardsmen, was stationed at El Peñón beforehand...

On the 11th they paraded for review; "Victory" battalion was designated to hold the summit... On the morning of that day, with a splendid retinue and accompanied by numerous aides, General Santa Anna arrived at El Peñón. Honor guards and enthusiastic shouts of "Viva!" greeted him. At that moment a crowd appeared, rushing to put up stands, eateries, stalls, bars; improvising a portable city that sprung forth from the earth...

The military encampment at El Peñón where Santa Anna awaited the enemy in vain.

To God What Is God's

The celebration of mass on the summit of that hill on Sunday the 15th also took on the silent and magnificent pomp of such events in an encampment... The altar was raised and covered with gold cloth and ornaments. The National Guard performed the Eucharist; the vendors remained silent. The canopy of the altar was the diaphanous sky, the lamp lighting that vast temple was our glorious sun. Our weapons resounded... Raise up the sacred host, hear the fervent murmur of the soldier who believes, and to Holy God, the God of armies, offer the miserly implement of man's life... At that very moment the enemy came into view: the general alarm was sounded,

The pre-battle mass. This water-color shows a soldier laying down his weapon, paying homage to the benediction of the Holy Sacrament.

along with the call to march, and not a single voice, not a single movement interrupted the religious ceremony!...

A FOILED BATTLE EQUALS DEFEAT

The movements of the enemy on August 16 and 17 left no doubt that they intended to take another route...and that a large part of their forces had gone to the southwest. It would be ridiculously superstitious to believe it, but that movement on the enemy's part, which foiled the battle at the spot where confidence had taken root and which the mind viewed as unassailable, produced an extremely unfavorable effect. On the night of the 17th, the order was given for Señor Anaya's regiment to head out before dawn the following day. As soon as it was announced, the gathering began to disperse; General Santa Anna went off and there was a certain humiliation, a certain disappointment in returning to the city without having fought.

The regiment of Señor Anaya set up camp in Churubusco. The following day, that is the 19th, the "Victory" and "Hidalgo" battalions were ordered to advance to San Antonio, considered by the commander in chief to be the next place to come under threat...

PADIERNA:
SELFISH IN-FIGHTING LOSES THE BATTLE

[Near San Angel] the craggy rock-strewn terrain reveals itself stretch by stretch, amid puny shrubs and weedy brush, along paths that are more like cracks upon which the locals tend to stumble and slide more than walk. On that stony ground, beyond a gorge carved by the waters of the Magdalena... rises the hamlet of Padierna...

These are the places where on August 19 and 20 this year the Northern Army fought under the orders of General D. Gabriel de Valencia...

Before taking Padierna, the Americans split into two groups: one attacked the hamlet, and the other set up in the rocky terrain, harassing our left flank. The artillery fire was incessant... General Valencia ordered the cavalry regiment from Guanajuato down the road to hold them off... There was a short gun battle, part of the regiment was cut off; the enemy slipped through one by one and took refuge in the woods surrounding San Jerónimo... At that moment, General Pérez's regiment appeared on the Toro Hills that overlook the road... Now it was the Americans who were cut off; now everything was going our way... And yet the call for General Pérez to retreat was sounded three times, and General Santa Anna held back, as did General Pérez's regiment whose presence made the enemy hesitate and made General Scott fear for the battle's outcome... The opportune moment was lost...

All the while that Santa Anna's forces remained inexplicably immobile, the firing escalated in several directions...

After the evening prayers, and over the sound of the rain, several cannon blasts were heard from the hills of Olivar de los Carmelitas, where Santa Anna had retreated. What sounded like his relief was in fact his good-bye...

To avoid the strong points of the Mexican defense in the South at the San Antonio hacienda and the Churubusco convent, Scott and his troops tried to cross the Pedregal, an unfavorable spot for them where they were attacked by General Gabriel Valencia. This battle, not planned by either Scott or Santa Anna (even though Santa Anna had already transferred his troops from El Peñón to the southern approach to the city), became a bloody confrontation that lasted two full days. The first day forecast a Mexican victory over the Americans, who were trapped between the forces of Valencia and Santa Anna.

This playing card from the deck depicting the life of Santa Anna carries the following inscription: "Santa Anna abandons Valencia and retreats to Mexico City, 1847."

Santa-Anna abandona á Valencia en Padierna y se retira á México. 1847.

NIGHT ARRIVES AND WITH IT THE NEWS THAT DASHES ALL HOPE

Santa Anna ordered General Valencia to defend San Ángel, but Valencia believed it was wiser to contravene Santa Anna's express orders and advance to the hamlet of Padierna along the road to the town of Contreras. The Mexican position in Padierna had many disadvantages, cornered as it was in the southwest of the Valley of Mexico—their flanks were unprotected and their way forward was obstructed by scrub growth and rugged lava rocks in the part known as the Pedregal. That landscape provided perfect cover for the enemy. During the night, the Americans found in a gully the outlines of a road which led to Valencia's rearguard. Under a torrential downpour, they reinforced it and advanced to where the unsuspecting officer awaited, on the side he thought was inaccessible.

The soldiers had not eaten; after the exertion of combat they didn't even have a bit of bread or a piece of firewood with which to warm themselves, or even a place to lie down. They were soaked from the rain and yet no one complained, not a murmur, not a single sign of discontent.

General Valencia took refuge in a lean-to beside the artillery batteries. At nine o'clock Ramiro and del Río arrived, saying they had been sent by General Santa Anna. They began to relate his orders when Valencia interrupted, asking about the general's whereabouts. They told him, and it was then that Valencia learned of Santa Anna's retreat. Now faced with an impossible situation, he abandoned his usual circumspection and respectful demeanor, and in a livid voice, his eyes blazing, he erupted into a furious tirade against General Santa Anna...

At dawn the enemy forces advanced in three columns...

When dawn broke on the 20th, everyone anxiously turned their eyes toward San Ángel, and when they were convinced that no help was coming, several soldiers deserted and everyone's spirits collapsed... Defeat was practically assured!

Two escape routes remained: one by the inaccessible hills of San Jerónimo, the other by way of Anzaldo, both of them cut off by the Americans. Those who took the first route tumbled to their deaths, like a torrent from the heights, soldiers, mules, riderless horses; wounded men peopled the air with their cries, and howling women rolled hither and thither like furies. This entire shapeless mass of humanity was crushed under the enemy's horses and shot by the victorious barbarians... When those who took the Anzaldo road also broke ranks and fled in a frenzy, they met up with the column of Americans that had advanced, and the Americans opened fire and murdered our own...

Such was the memorable defeat of Padierna. When it was over, ambition and envy smiled with satisfaction, and the loss of our lovely capital city was seen to be near and all but inevitable...

The American forces took Zacatépetl hill, just to the east of Padierna, and General Scott directed operations from its summit, where he could observe the positions of the troops as if on a map laid out on a table,  *p. 279.*

Mexican army

American army

Scott and his aides

Padierna

The convent at Churubusco was the strongest fort on the southern approach to the city. This painting depicts Saint Paul's church and bell tower inside the convent.

BATTLE OF THE CONVENT OF CHURUBUSCO

The enemy followed within reach of our troops, giving chase as they retreated in a headlong rush, harassed by fire from the American columns that followed close by and to whom they offered no resistance. And in this condition they passed by the convent at Churubusco where they found Generals Rincón and Anaya...

Santa Anna corroborated the news that the enemy was approaching his rearguard, and after recommending that a vigorous defense be made in Churubusco he pulled out. The troops also continued their march...

All prepared for the attack, the defenders of Churubusco awaited, with guns in hand, the arrival of the enemy.

The Americans meanwhile advanced on the convent, which they believed they could take at very little cost, since the ease with which they had come so far led them to assume that our entire army had retreated all the way to the capital.

The fact that no one opened fire on them despite their being within range of the fortifications must have confirmed that belief, but it was the explicit order of Generals Rincón and Anaya not to fire until the enemy was very close, so as not to waste any powder.

That's what transpired, and the terrible decimation the blasts produced in the American ranks obliged them to hold off for a moment, intimidated and surprised. However, they soon continued to advance, sending one force toward the front of the parapet, and another larger one to the right flank...

Several lithographs produced in Mexico bear inscriptions in both Spanish and English. They were probably to be sold to American soldiers as "war souvenirs." The one below was done by Ignacio Cumplido, one of Mexico's most important lithographers. During the war, Cumplido fought as a captain in the "Victoria" regiment of the National Guard. Once the battles were over, he went back to his lithography business, selling souvenirs to the occupiers.

og. de Cumplido.

ATAQUE DE CHURUBUSCO.
por la division del general WORTH, el dia 20 de Agosto, de 1847.

ATTACH AT CHURUBUSCO.
by the division of general WORTH, on the 20th day of August, 1847.

GRAL. TWIGS.—"¿Dónde está el parque?"
GRAL. ʌNAYA.—"Si hubiera parque no estaria Vd. aqui."

*General Anaya surrenders his
sword to General Twiggs after the
Battle of Churubusco. The text
sums up the words exchanged
between the two generals: Twiggs
asked for the location of the
remaining munitions, to which the
defending general offered the
famous reply: "If we still had
munitions, you would not be here."*

MISTAKEN CALIBER OF SHELLS DISARMS THE ARMY

...The American division under General Twiggs, who launched the first attack, had just been driven back. The arrival of others, who hurriedly came to his rescue, not only afforded the means to renew the assault, but allowed them to attack the convent on several sides. The gallant men of Churubusco did not flinch... However, the plight of these courageous combatants was critical: their rearguard, the only point where they could save themselves in case of disaster, was under attack by General Worth's division...

Even worse, munitions were running low and they could foresee the moment when the utter lack of ordnance would prevent them from presenting an effective resistance. General Rincón had realized from the beginning this might occur, and he had sent his two aides...to request munitions from General Santa Anna.

Moved...by what they told him, Santa Anna sent as reinforcements several pickets from Tlapa and Lagos and the St. Patrick's battalion. He also sent along a munitions wagon which turned out to carry nineteen half-drachm shot while the rifles were of a different caliber, and thus desperation reached a climax...

The only ones whose weapons were the right caliber for that ammunition were the soldiers of the St. Patrick's battalion. Their conduct deserves the highest praise, since during the entire attack they maintained their fire with extraordinary bravery. Many of them succumbed in combat; those who survived were more unfortunate than their mates, and suffered a cruel death...

Three hours and a half the action lasted, with the repeated efforts of the Americans failing to achieve a decisive victory. The spirit of our troops did not slacken: facing their enemy, the soldiers were more intent on prolonging the combat with every passing moment. Unfortunately the ammunition was nearly gone... The shooting began to quiet down from our side, as ordnance became more and more scarce. It finally ran out and from that convent, which not long before had spit fire from all sides like a tower of fireworks, not a single shot emerged, as if none of its defenders remained standing... Our soldiers, meanwhile, filled with despair, rested on their useless weapons...

[The Mexican soldiers] in that courageous defense had put twenty-two bullets through the tattered American flag that Twiggs carried in his hands. A moment later it fluttered above the convent of Churubusco, presiding over the scene of death, desolation and tears which that religious monument, so placid and tranquil in other times, presented on August 20, 1847...

THE IRISH OF ST. PATRICK'S BATTALION ARE PUNISHED

[Letter from Guillermo Prieto]

What made such a deep impression on me were the pleas of the Irish prisoners, members of the St. Patrick's battalion... Those unfortunate souls had once served in the U.S. Army and it was mostly religion that seduced them to change sides, since they were all Catholics.

The members of St. Patrick's had won heartfelt sympathy for their irreproachable conduct and the bravery and enthusiasm with which they defended our cause. When the impending execution of the Irish was announced, alarm spread, all sorts of strings were pulled, money was forthcoming and all sorts of efforts were made [to save them]. Finally, the town's most distinguished and respectable ladies made a heart-wrenching appeal to Scott, pleading for the lives of his prisoners. Neither entreaties nor tears nor human considerations were able to soften that hyena's heart, and he ordered the terrible death sentence to be carried to its brutal and inescapable end.

Behind the plaza of San Jacinto, heavy timbers were raised in a row with thick beams set horizontally on the upper

The St. Patrick's Battalion was made up of Irishmen who deserted from the U.S. Army and joined the other side, drawn by their Catholic faith and the enticements the Mexicans offered during a public relations effort when the American troops were stationed in Matamoros, ☞ p.58. Many U.S. soldiers were recent immigrants and yearned above all to improve their lot. Once enlisted in the Mexican Army they fought loyally and fiercely. They entered history as either great heroes or traitors, depending on who is writing about them.

Of the eighty-five Irish who were captured and tried as traitors, about fifty were condemned to the gallows. The executions were carried out in three groups. Samuel Chamberlain offered the following description to accompany his portrait of the third group: "The execution of the last number was attended with unusual and unwarranted acts of cruelty. The day selected was the one on which the Fortress of Chapultepec was to be stormed, and the gallows was erected on a rising piece of ground just outside of the charming little village of Mixcoac, in full view of the attack on the Castle. Colonel [William S.] Harney, on account of the proficiency he had acquired as an executioner in hanging Seminoles in Florida, was selected to carry out the sentence. The man who 'had ravished young Indian girls at night, and then strung them up to the limb of a live oak in the morning' was certainly well fitted to carry out the barbarous order: 'To have the men placed under gallows with ropes around their necks, to remain until the American flag was displayed from the walls of Chapultepec, and then swing them off.'"

With his arm raised, sword clenched in his fist, Colonel Harney is about to give the order for the horses to pull the wagons out from under the condemned men; another moment and the execution will have occurred.

portion, from which vertical ropes were hung. The prisoners were put in horse-drawn wagons under the beams. Amid shouts and the cracking of whips, they tied nooses on the ends of the hanging ropes and put them over the necks of the prisoners...and with cries they set the horses galloping, leaving those defenders of the fatherland hanging in the air wracked with horrendous convulsions and visible pain...

THE ARMISTICE

[Ramón Alcaraz et al., *Apuntes para la historia de la guerra...*]

The fateful day of August 20 was drawing to a close with the cannonade still echoing in the ears of all Mexicans. The bloody battles of Padierna and Churubusco were over and the triumphant invading army was at the gates of the city...

In such distressing circumstances, General Santa Anna retired to his palace in a state of ghastly despair over the wretched course the war had taken. His ministers and other persons of distinction gathered there... Various opinions were expressed, but the one that utterly dominated favored negotiating a suspension of hostilities...

Our cabinet...named Generals Mora and Villamil and Quijano to work out the armistice with Major General Quitman and with Brigadier Generals Smith and Pierce...

Those leaders met on the 22nd in the town of Tacubaya... It was stipulated that the American army not impede the flow of food to city residents or to our army, and in Article 7 our civil and military authorities agreed, likewise, not to obstruct the flow of food from city or country to the American army. This final concession in Article 7 of the agreement, made perhaps with too little forethought as will be seen later on, brought with it disastrous consequences for both parties...

El Pueblo apedrea los Carros.

DEATH TO THE YANKEES, DEATH TO SANTA ANNA!

[On the morning of August 27...] more than a hundred wagons of the invading army, backed by Article 7 of the agreement, penetrated the city's main streets to collect money from a few foreign homes and to provide the troops with fresh supplies. Our people, in whose imaginations the bloody scenes of the past few days were still vivid, and who harbored a justifiable fury against the invaders, viewed that incursion with indignation and soon resolved to wreak vengeance. The avenues of the Plaza of the Constitution, where some of the wagons sat, filled up with people: a shower of stones fell on the wagons and their drivers, and everywhere was heard the cry "Death to the Yankees!"

The government, of course, ordered its officers to put down this revolt, and when the crowd saw our lancers defending the Americans it grew more incensed. Our soldiers were called "cowards" and there were those who called out "Death to Santa Anna," since they blamed him for what they viewed as a betrayal...

In addition, a woman from the lower classes angrily threw a stone at one of those men [the Americans] and knocked him down, gravely wounded. Caught *en flagrante* by police officers, she exclaimed with incalculable frenzy, "I wanted to kill him, and I'd kill them all. Because of them I've lost my poor son, and now instead of fighting back, we're supposed to let them come and take our food. This is so unfair..." In light of her sorrow, they set her free immediately...

The people acted on proper instinct; they were indignant. The people, after all, wanted vengeance... but despite all this, that article [of the armistice agreement] was still adhered to. It was agreed that the enemy should take under shadow of night whatever its agents would have acquired during the day. Having observed this, one night the people rioted again in the little plaza of San Juan de Letrán and along Ancha Street, looting the supplies which the Americans had stored there.

Unacceptable Proposal

On the afternoon of that very day, the 27th, commissioners from both sides met for the first time in the town of Azcapotzalco, and they exchanged their respective proposals...

[According to the peace treaty proposed by the North Americans] the Mexican Republic would lose, besides Texas, all of New Mexico, a large part of Tamaulipas, large parts of Coahuila and Chihuahua, also half of Sonora, both Californias, the lovely navigable rivers in those lands and control over the Bermejo Sea or Gulf of Californias...

In response, the Mexican government gave our commissioners a note, dated September 5, in which they were told definitively that the government did not agree to an extension of the armistice, much less to the ceding of New Mexico whose inhabitants had in so many ways manifested their desire to remain within the Mexican Republic...

From that moment preparations for war began anew...

At the peace negotiations held in the town of Azcapotzalco from August 27 to September 6, 1847, the United States sought not only to take an immense portion of Mexico's northern territory, it also demanded duty-free transit for its citizens across the Isthmus of Tehuantepec. When the Mexican government refused to accept these proposals, the Americans resumed hostilities the very next day.

After the battle of Churubusco, General Scott set up his headquarters in Tacubaya, from where he sent his troops to Molino del Rey and Chapultepec.

THE ATTACK ON MOLINO DEL REY AND CASA MATA

West of Chapultepec Hill there is a building known as Molino del Rey, which is divided in two sections separated by an aqueduct. One part of the building is a flour mill...and the other is the old gunpowder mill, which in the period we are speaking of was used as a foundry for cannons... Outside these buildings there is a threshing floor that is entirely open... To the northeast of the mills there is another building off by itself which was used as a gunpowder magazine, and it is called Casa Mata... These buildings were protected by the firepower of Chapultepec Castle, which was crowned with cannons...

When dawn broke on the 8th [of September], enemy batteries...opened fire on the mill, and the Chapultepec artillery responded in kind... Soldiers from General León's brigade were spread along the rooftops and the aqueduct. As soon as the Americans were within range, our forces blazed away at them with their rifles...

The battle spread. The roar of the cannon and musketry was like the eruption of a volcano, and smoke enveloped all the combatants...

The position of the mills finally fell into enemy hands and our lines were broken, but not without leaving that part of the battlefield strewn with the bodies of American soldiers, the cream of their officers having perished...

Once inside Molino del Rey, the Americans found a few munitions and cannon molds which they blew up, destroying part of the building in the process, as can be seen in this illustration.

Nicolás Bravo was commander-in-chief of the defense of Chapultepec Castle, leading eight hundred soldiers and fifty Military College cadets. He survived the battle and retired from politics, dying together with his wife in 1854, probably poisoned by his political enemies.

Only one road led to the summit of Chapultepec Hill, and General Quitman fought his way along it, ☞ p. 288. The ascent on the other sides had to be made by scaling the cliffs. General Pillow attacked on the much more dangerous western slope, ☞ p. 290. He was saved by Worth's soldiers coming from Molino del Rey.

CHAPULTEPEC

On the 12th, at dawn, enemy batteries located on the church grounds opened fire on the guardhouse at Niño Perdido, with no more purpose, as we have been able to deduce from the later writings of the American officers, than to draw our attention and allow them to calibrate the artillery that would blast Chapultepec...

In fact, in a few minutes these same batteries began to fire on Chapultepec. At first they caused no damage at all, but after their aim was rectified the walls of the building began to grow white from the fire coming from all directions, the roof also suffering great damage from shells tossed by a mortar...hidden in a courtyard amid the buildings of Molino del Rey...

On the 13th at dawn, enemy batteries opened fire once again on Chapultepec, more intensely than the previous day... General Bravo, observing enemy troop movements, sent an urgent call to General Santa Anna for ordnance and reinforcements... Unfortunately, General Santa Anna—who at every opportunity in this war failed to grasp the enemy's points of vulnerability, or his own, or when he ought to

CHAPULTEPEC
1847.

attack decisively—concluded that there would be no assault on Chapultepec and thus sent no reinforcements, focusing instead on defending the approaches on the Anzures and Condesa Causeways...

ASSAULT ON THE SACRED HILL

The enemy, seeing that their plan of attack was working, and that their feints were being vigorously resisted, directed the bulk of their columns to the assault on the hill entering by way of the Molino. Flanked and preceded by sharpshooters, they started up the hill, one column by the ramp, the other by the accessible part on the northeast, while a cloud of sharpshooters scrambled up on the northern and western slopes. Taking advantage of hillocks, thickets, blind spots and the poor layout of our fortifications, the sharpshooters either shut down our defenders or drew their attention away from the storming parties, who faced no more formal resistance on the ramp and at the foot of the hill than that posed by the gallant and intrepid Lieutenant Colonel D. Santiago Xicoténcatl and his San Blas battalion. But when Xicoténcatl's troops were outflanked and surrounded, and he and most of his officers and soldiers were killed, the enemy advanced along the second stretch of the causeway with their flag held high. Although the flag went down several times when the flag-bearers were killed and the columns had to retreat a few steps, others took it up and the advance continued to the embankment where our few defenders, dizzy from the bombardment, exhausted, sleepless and hungry, were stabbed with bayonets and thrown on the rocks or taken prisoner. A company from the New York regiment climbed to the highest part of the edifice, from where a few cadets continued shooting, but they were the final defenders of the Mexican flag, which soon came to be replaced by the American...

A depiction of the monument commemorating the Child Heroes, the six cadets who died defending Chapultepec Castle and who eventually became the subject of the war's greatest legend. It took time for the myth to emerge. The misfortunes of 1847 were not officially celebrated until 1871, during the government of Benito Juárez, when the young cadets of the Military College were first exalted as examples of loyalty and sacrifice. The names of Augustín Melgar, Vicente Suárez and Francisco Montes de Oca are well documented, but those of Juan de la Barrera, Juan Escutia and Francisco Márquez are not. On September 13, 1882, this monument was erected in their memory in Chapultepec Forest.

PSYCHOLOGICAL IMPACT OF THE FALL OF CHAPULTEPEC

The few people knowledgeable in the arts of war insisted that Chapultepec Castle was a very insignificant and poorly defended fortification. But people generally considered it to be an unassailable fortress... Thus when the Americans took the castle, it was as if the capital of Mexico had fallen, and the spirit of the city's inhabitants was overwhelmed by dread and discouragement. Yet the efforts of our troops did not slacken; they remained resolutely in their positions and the National Guard regiments remained nearly intact. And on this point it is painfully lamentable that an intelligent leader did not take advantage of all the elements still in our favor.

THE FINAL DEFENSE: THE BLOCKHOUSES

The enemy infantry advanced along Belén Causeway, and were repulsed by artillery situated below the arches and by infantry shooting from the blockhouse loopholes and from the building's flanks. Then General Quitman decided to hit the blockhouse with the heavy pieces that had caught up to him... General Santa Anna was convinced that this artillery fire would not turn into an assault, and thus he headed off to San Cosme, where he learned that General Rangel had abandoned Santo Tomás and was retreating toward the center of Mexico City without holding the blockhouse...

At the Belén blockhouse a final effort was underway... In the end, at five in the afternoon the two blockhouses were occupied by Generals Worth and Quitman...

On the night of the 13th, Quitman's division built a breastworks in the Belén blockhouse... Before dawn on the 14th, several messengers from the Citadel arrived carrying a white flag, inviting him to occupy it and saying that Santa Anna had abandoned the city...

Eight roads led to Mexico City, each of them protected by a blockhouse, a fortified gate with a paved square and a building where taxes on the goods entering the city were collected. Having decided to attack on the western approach, the U.S. Army had to take the two blockhouses at San Cosme and Belén. The moment captured below is just before they forced their way through the gate at Belén. American shelling of the civilian population and Mexican soldiers caused great damage.

Popular Resistance

In the days following the capture of Chapultepec Castle, groups of civilians resisted the invaders, not with lances, swords or guns, but with cobblestones that the municipal government had ordered pulled up and stockpiled on the rooftops when fighting began at Chapultepec.

The population of Mexico City, which over the previous days had showed more signs of indolence than of patriotism, could not stomach the sight of the invaders proudly taking possession of the city...

We have heard infinite versions of where the first shot was fired, and though it is hard to know which among so many is accurate, we will stick to the one most often repeated, which recounts that the shot was fired from López Alley. Colonel Carbajal of the National Guard, together with other officers, had drawn up a plan to strike at the enemy when they entered the city... A civilian named Esquivel pulled the trigger ahead of time and, believing that to be the signal, everyone opened fire... The shot was intended for General Worth, who was on horseback at the corner of López Alley, but it missed him and hit Colonel Garland, wounding him in the leg... At once, the Americans spread down the streets, blasting away, knocking down doors, looting homes and committing a thousand other atrocities...

The part of the population that fought did so mostly without weapons of war, except for a handful who were luckier than the rest and had a carbine or a rifle. The others relied on sticks and stones, and as a result suffered considerable punishment at the hands of the American forces. Some National Guardsmen, who the previous night had been forced to abandon their positions, came out of their homes carrying their rifles to take part in the fray. They occupied several tall buildings and churches from where they could cause more damage to the enemy...

Throughout the day, innumerable victims shed their blood on the streets and plazas of the city. It is painful to note that this generous struggle on the part of the poor was acrimoniously deplored by most of the privileged wealthy class, who viewed the humiliation of the fatherland with indifference as long as they could preserve their interests and comfort...

During the war, more soldiers died off the battlefield than on it. This litho-graph of the funeral of several Americans appeared in a Mexican calendar with the following commentary: "The multitude of Americans wounded in our skirmishes, the many who fell ill from shock when our attacks interrupt-ed their attempts to eat, made us believe that nature herself was helping us diminish the numbers of our enemy... The diseases they most commonly fell prey to were typhoid, consumption, mancenteritis and, in some cases, tuber-culosis... The casualties they suffered from the month of September to December of that year [1847], due to wounds or illness or assassination in the barrios...could have reached two thousand Americans, because quite often the number of funerals surpassed twenty per day... The most surprising and curious thing was the sort of funeral honors these men offered their brave companions fallen in an enemy country: They ground up their remains."

During the months the negotiations lasted, the situation remained tense and American soldiers continued dying.

While General Scott made his triumphal entry into Mexico City, guerrilla fighters attacked an American garrison stationed in Puebla, launching a siege of the barracks that lasted twenty-eight days. Though their capital and the entire northern part of their country was occupied by the enemy army, the Mexican people did not surrender. Guerrillas, with the support of the army, were active throughout the country. Santa Anna visited the guerrillas besieging American troops in Puebla in hope of recovering the city.

A View of the Occupied City

[Diary of Carlos María de Bustamante]

On this day [September 15] during which valiant Mexicans never entirely ceased shooting in any quarter, fearful of becoming a stupid victim if I showed myself on the street, I closed myself into my house with my family; yet in the end I decided to go for a walk nearby. Very soon, in the plaza of Santo Domingo, not far from the doorway of the Inquisition, I came upon five unburied bodies being devoured by dogs. Never had I seen such a horrendous sight and that image will be fixed in my memory as long as I live. No Mexican could venture into the street without becoming filled with horror, beginning with the terrible caricatures these new North American vandals seemed to be. Most of them were armed with rifles or pistols which, instead of concealing, they carried openly in order to strike fear into us. They entered homes and searched and looted at their pleasure, taking whatever they wished...

State of Siege

[Ramón Alcaraz et al., *Apuntes para la historia de la guerra...*]

The days following September 14, 15 and 16, 1847, the Americans posted troops all around the city and placed artillery pieces aimed at the causeways in each blockhouse; and during the night they took all appropriate precautions, both to be ready to resist a new uprising and to avoid being surprised in their barracks by any of the many groups of guerrilla fighters said to be roaming the towns of the Valley of Mexico. But by the time a month had passed, the Americans had regained a certain confidence...

The Americans set up several military bases to better control the occupied territory in which guerrillas were active. One of their principal barracks was located in San Ángel, a town near the capital.

During their stay in the capital, many American soldiers entertained themselves with prostitutes, whom they called "Margaritas." In this picture from a period calendar, an American soldier dances with one of them, mimicking a popular step, perhaps the "zapateado del jarabe" (the "syrup stomp").

FROM THE THEATER OF OPERATIONS TO THE THEATER OF ENTERTAINMENT

Proud of the conquest they had achieved, quite happy to find themselves in nearly complete control in the capital of the Republic and convinced that the risk of an uprising was very remote, the American officers set about organizing a system of entertainment...the owner of the National Theater had no great difficulty renting out the place, and the conquered city was soon showing off its attractions to the victors. Some mule drivers and soldiers put on comedies in German and in English in the New Mexico Theater... Those who weren't theater fans organized dance halls imitating the American style. One such dance hall was set up on Coliseo Street across from the Principal Theater, another on Belemitas Alley, and the most popular was in the Bella Unión Hotel. The rooms of that hotel were filled with officers...

On the lower floors of the Bella Unión, there were gaming rooms; higher up were saloons, billiard rooms and dance halls; on the top floors flourished what decency will not allow to be expressed. From nine in the evening until two or three in the morning these orgies lasted.

AMERICANIZATION OF THE CAPITAL

This continual influx of foreigners, most of whom spoke English, also wrought changes in commerce. Tailor shops that had previously called themselves Mexican became American tailors, and barbers, storekeepers, innkeepers and restaurateurs were influenced by the conquistadors' language and hurried to replace their signs and notices with ones in English. Commerce, which remains commerce no matter where, adjusted quickly to the new rulers, and all those inclined only to reckon their pecuniary profits started doing business and speculating...

How much does it cost?

DIFFERENT ATTITUDES TOWARD THE INVASION

The wealthy, ensconced in their homes or retired to their haciendas, viewed what was happening with indifference; avaricious merchants speculated; and those belonging to the middle class sometimes had to beg for alms. Selfish employees who had some other means of subsistence abandoned their government posts, believing that the conquest would last. The poor, heroic at first, persisted for a number of days wreaking vengeance, their knives making American soldiers disappear every day, but in the end they allowed themselves to be humiliated by the insolent conquistadors...

American soldiers make purchases in a street market.

This image from a Mexican calendar shows the punishment meted out to Mexicans involved in the resistance. Here one of them, tied to a lamppost, is being whipped by an American soldier.

Los azotes dados por los Americanos.

THE EXERCISE OF POWER

Although at first it seemed that the superficial harmony between the American authorities and the councilmen would not be broken, there was cause for daily antipathy. To punish slight infractions by our common people, the Americans would condemn Mexican prisoners to the shame of public whippings. The municipal government protested and the enemy responded that it was a right and custom established in their military laws. At night the city was insecure, doleful, given over to the mercy of counter-guerrilla thieves and traitors, and drunken American volunteers who roamed about armed, committing robberies and disturbances.

After Mexico City fell, General Santa Anna resigned from the presidency and retreated with his troops to Puebla to support the last pockets of resistance. Because of Mexico's defeat, Santa Anna was deposed from his position as commander-in-chief by Provisional President Manuel de la Peña y Peña. In October 1848, Santa Anna, having lost all respect and political support, chose to go into exile. This playing card from the deck that portrays his life shows him leaving Mexico.

Santa-Anna sale de la Republica. 1847

 *XI*   *The Price of Peace*

*F*ormal peace negotiations were begun anew once the Mexican government, led by provisional president Manuel de la Peña y Peña, was established in the city of Querétaro. The negotiations were held in a climate of great tension since much of the country was occupied by the invaders, who also maintained a blockade on the main ports and had seized the government's tax revenue.

At the same time, not all of Mexico's political groupings were in agreement with the suspension of hostilities. Some believed that military defense was still feasible, while others thought that annexation of the entire country to the United States was inevitable. What's more, the debate on whether to set up a monarchy came back to the fore.

As if this weren't enough, secession movements were active in several states, including Yucatan, and a number of state governments would not cooperate with federal authorities. In light of all this, the Mexican government chose to sue for peace in order to avoid greater suffering and loss.

Following arduous negotiations, Mexican commissioners Bernardo Couto, Miguel Atristáin and Luis G. Cuevas signed a treaty on February 2, 1848, in the town of Guadalupe-Hidalgo. It was ratified on May 19 by the Chamber of Deputies and on the 25th of that month by the Senate. The war was soon engraved on Mexico's collective memory as a deep trauma.

THE TERRITORY UNDER NEGOTIATION

*A*rticle five of the Treaty of Guadalupe-Hidalgo drew a new border between Mexico and the United States. Besides losing Texas, Mexico lost the territory between the Nueces River and the Rio Grande, as well as all of New Mexico and Upper California, though it held on to Baja California, which remained linked by land via Sonora. The dividing line was placed along the Rio Grande and Gila rivers. In all, Mexico lost about two and a half million square kilometers. The Americans agreed to pay fifteen million pesos in compensation.

This map shows the territory Mexico lost in yellow, what Mexico managed to retain in green, and in red the territory sold to the United States in 1854 by the treaty of La Mesilla.

LOSS OF TERRITORY, BUT NOT INDEPENDENCE

[Testimony to the Supreme Government by the Comissioners who signed the Peace Treaty with the United States]

The Peace Treaty we have signed no doubt represents the great disgrace suffered by our weapons in the war, but we believe we can guarantee that it does not contain any of the stipulations of perpetual burden or ignominy to which nearly all nations in circumstances perhaps less unfavorable than ours have had to submit. We will suffer a loss of territory but, regarding what we conserve, our independence will be full and absolute, without limitation or restriction of any sort. Upon accepting this treaty, we will be unbridled and free to seek our own interests and to maintain policies that are exclusively Mexican, as much as we were at the moment when we won our independence. The loss we have conceded in order to secure peace was necessary and inevitable. This sort of treaty is really composed during the campaign, according to the battles won or lost; all the negotiators do is translate into written form the final result of the war. There [on the battlefield], not in the treaty, is where the territory now in the hands of the enemy was lost.

This map compares the territories of the United States and Mexico after the war, *p. 12.*

A TREATY OF RECUPERATION

What the treaty has achieved is not only to keep that loss from growing, via a continuation of the war, but also to recover most of what fell to the victorious arms of the United States: the accord is more aptly one of recuperation than one of relinquishment... Even should our luck in the near future be less adverse than to date, and even should we win a few advantages in the interior of the country, who would posit with any probability that these would procure for us all that this treaty achieves? Who would bet that by force of arms we could return our flag, never mind to San Francisco in California or the banks of the Sabina, but even the parapets of Ulúa [Veracruz]?

LEGITIMACY AND JUSTIFICATION OF THE NEGOTIATIONS

Although the northern territories were thinly populated, there were still thousands of Mexicans who suddenly changed countries without moving. What fate awaited them? The peace treaty guaranteed freedom for Catholics to practice their religion and exercise their civil rights; similarly, it protected the property and other assets of the inhabitants of the territories ceded to the United States. Nevertheless, as might be expected, there was a large discrepancy between what the law said and what occurred. An interesting case was that of five hundred residents of Laredo, Texas, who crossed the Rio Grande to found the town of Nuevo Laredo in Coahuila.

Some have wished to dispute the competence of the supreme authorities in political society to make territorial concessions: a vain contention, more suited to the idleness of a schoolboy than to the serious concerns and positive approach of a man of state. If one were to ask whether a person in a good state of health has the right on a whim to cut off a limb needlessly, the question would perhaps be taken as a sign of senility in whoever asked it; but the instinct of self-preservation declares to the entire world that when a part can no longer live with the rest of the body without risk of causing death, it is necessary to save life by separating that part, no matter how painful the operation may be. In this case, to question the competence of the Mexican government to reach an agreement such as the one which we have signed is in substance to dispute its right to lessen the sorrows of a nation. In other words, it is to place in doubt the nation's right to remake itself by the only route open, conserving the most important part of what had been lost...

Peace treaties are in essence transactions; in them the causes which motivated the combatants are set aside, and the facts are taken as they exist. And without making any judgments regarding previous rights, a friendly adjustment of differences is achieved, and rights are created for the future.

It is the obligation of each government to seek from that adjustment the most favorable conditions possible for its people, given the circumstances. And that duty has been categorically fulfilled by the government...

 AFTERMATH OF A SHIPWRECK

One of the less visible repercussions of the end of the war was the political defeat of what were called the "savage tribes:" Comanches, Cheyennes, Papagos, Pimas, Apaches, Pueblos and Cherokees, among many others. The Mexican government assumed no legal responsibility for them; on the contrary, the treaty called on the U.S. government to patrol the border to keep them from moving to the "Mexican side."

The task entrusted to us by the Supreme Government was in essence to pick up the pieces after a shipwreck... Our territory has been considerably reduced and some of our brothers will perhaps be left outside our political society; such losses are among the most painful a people can endure. However, considering the size, features and advantageous position of the territory we retain—remember for example that Baja California alone is equal in size to England, and Sonora equal to half of France—considering that the rich mineral deposits of the cordillera and the fruits of two climatic zones remain on our soil, that on both seas we still possess a lengthy coastline, and that we can therefore still maintain a profitable trade with Europe, America and Asia, we are convinced that if Mexico does not become some day a contented nation or a great one, its misfortune will not be the result of lack of territory...

Pray to the All-powerful that the hard lesson we just learned will serve to make us take heed of good advice, and will cure us of old vices. Without that, our downfall is assured...

LEGISLATIVE APPROVAL OF THE PEACE TREATY

[Ramón Alcaraz et al., *Apuntes para la historia de la guerra...*]

The debate [on the Peace Treaty] in the House was animated, civilized, decent, instructive. Both sides went through all of their strongest reasons, their most powerful arguments for and against the issue at hand... Taken to a vote, it was approved by fifty-one votes to thirty-five... The Senate then took up the matter... The vote was thirty-three to four... On May 30 treaty ratifications were exchanged in Querétaro, thus definitively concluding one of the most historically significant acts in the annals of our history.

THE HISTORIAN'S UNTENABLE IMPARTIALITY

On such an important matter, scrutinized down to its smallest details in public gatherings and the press, we could say much. We will abstain, however, from doing so for three reasons: First, we remain firm in the purpose that has guided us throughout this work, and do not wish to violate it now or substitute the commentaries of the critic for the simple narration of the facts. Second, as we are still painfully affected by an event that destroyed our dearest illusions and reduced us to a dismal state of depression, misfortune, discredit, we feel incapable of speaking with the impartiality appropriate to a historian. Third and last, because among the very authors of these notes there has existed and still exists a great diversity of opinion on this point, with some being tenacious advocates of war and others staunch defenders of peace...

The Consequences of the War

The U.S. military withdrawal from Mexican territory began in the middle of May 1848. On May 30 the two countries exchanged their respective ratifications of the Treaty of Guadalupe-Hidalgo. U.S. President James K. Polk chose July 4, anniversary of U.S. independence, to declare the war with Mexico over.

During Polk's term (1845–1849) of office in the United States, the presidency of Mexico faced incessant change. In the less than two years that the fighting lasted, eight men served as president, with eleven changes of office, evidence of the extreme instability that plagued Mexico's domestic politics.

The war against the American invasion was a traumatic event. Mexico had to cede more than half its territory after sacrificing many lives and spending enormous resources trying to defend it.

The dramatic end of the war underscored the failure of the country's first experience as a republic and obliged intellectuals and political leaders to search for a new way forward following the bitter defeat.

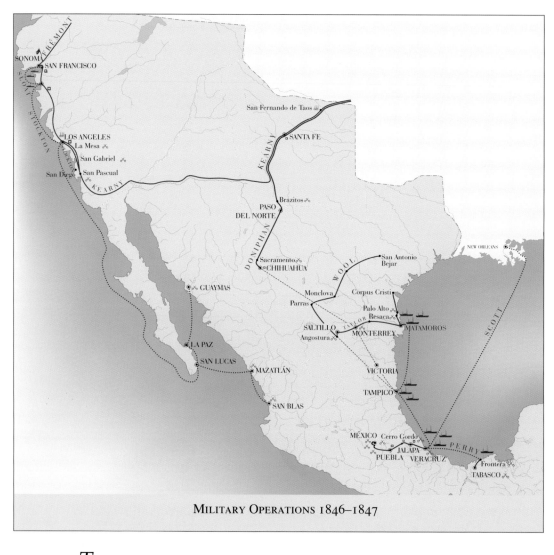

FRÉMONT

SONOMA

SAN FRANCISCO

STOCKTON

LOS ANGELES
La Mesa
San Gabriel
San Diego   San Pascual

KEARNY

San Fernando de Taos

SANTA FE

KEARNY

Brazitos

PASO
DEL NORTE

DONIPHAN

Sacramento
CHIHUAHUA

GUAYMAS

WOOL

San Antonio
Bejar

Monclova   Corpus Cristi
Parras

Palo Alto
Resaca

TAYLOR

SALTILLO   MATAMOROS
Angostura   MONTERREY

NEW ORLEANS

SCOTT

LA PAZ

SAN LUCAS

MAZATLÁN

SAN BLAS

VICTORIA

TAMPICO

MÉXICO   Cerro Gordo
         JALAPA   PERRY
PUEBLA   VERACRUZ
                     Frontera
                   TABASCO

MILITARY OPERATIONS 1846–1847

*T*hroughout this book the various military campaigns have been shown sepa-
rately. To give a sense of the full dimensions of the invasion, this map shows
the entire deployment of forces and territory occupied by the Americans during the war. The red lines indicate the campaigns of

- *Taylor*
- *Wool*
- *Kearny*
- *Doniphan*

- *Stockton*
- *Perry*
- *Scott*

POOR POLITICAL CALCULATIONS

["Frutos de la guerra," *El Monitor Republicano*, July 7, 1848]

War befell our Republic, in our view, without the least justification that could exonerate the nation which waged it on
us and from whom it was least expected given our identical
systems of government, our joint interest in blocking the
establishment of a monarchy on this continent, the close
proximity of the two nations, the similarities between our
struggles for independence and other considerations, all of
which would seem to call on the two to forge close links, be
perpetually joined, and make common cause on whatever
matters to either of them. But all such political calculations
disappeared in light of calculations based on selfish interests, and as we said before a war befell us that our nation
should never have suffered...

THE BLINDNESS OF PRIDE

No thinking person at all familiar with the character,
customs and morality of our neighbors failed to perceive
how far our conflicts with the United States would lead,
unless war was avoided by ceding or selling Texas. It was
even acknowledged that managing this issue with skill and
ceding that part of our territory could have been most bene-
ficial instead of damaging, whether by setting up a friendly
sister republic there rather than a rebellious daughter, or by
saving the great expense involved in keeping her subdued
and continually quelling her endeavors to win separation, or
by taking advantage of the millions we could have received
from recognizing her independence, secession or sale, or
lastly, by having Texas serve as a buffer between us and the
United States...

For our part, we sinned, and if the United States sinned
out of ambition, we did so out of pride. Led by the lofty
conception we had of ourselves, as well as by the very low

*The text reproduced here is the
political rationale offered by the
Mexican government negotiators
for the signing of the treaty.
Given the military superiority of the
enemy, they presumed that reason
should prevail over sterile confrontation; to continue fighting would only
prolong the occupation, perhaps
permanently, bringing more
disastrous losses of territory.*

one we had of the Americans, we scorned everything that common sense counseled, listened only to the advice of vanity, and put everything at risk.

FINAL LESSONS

We have lost much in the war; but allow us to say that we have also won much. Some will be scandalized by this proposition. To dispel any qualms, note that the war has placed the nation in a position where it is able to undertake reforms that would never have been possible had it remained as it was, much less so if our fate on the battlefield had been to achieve victory. Paradoxical though it certainly seems, if we look beyond shocking appearances to the substance of things, it could be that defeat was much more useful for the Republic than victory.

As a result of the war, reform of the army has become necessary, and not only necessary but with the great advantage that no one disagrees. A few years ago reform of the army was already crucial; without it the Republic was headed rapidly for ruin. But before the war the problem was nearly impossible to correct and indeed grew steadily worse and threatened to destroy the nation. The war placed us in a very advantageous position to pursue that reform without opposition, because what officer would have the nerve to protest?...

Enarbolan el Pabellon Mexicane.

On June 12 the U.S. Army pulled out of Mexico City. At six in the morning the American flag flying on the National Palace was lowered, and the Mexican tricolor was raised. Both armies solemnly witnessed this ceremony.

The American troops retreated from the city at 9 a.m. on the same day. The last U.S. soldiers left Veracruz on July 30, 1848.

American Voices

Mexico in the Eyes of the U.S. Minister Plenipotentiary

When the English established their first colony on the American continent in 1607, the Viceroyalty of New Spain was already an economic and cultural power with Mexico City as its hub. Over the course of the seventeenth century, the British attempted to conquer a number of Spain's colonial possessions.

Besides being great political and economic rivals, the Spanish and British empires were divided by religion: the Puritans, who spearheaded the colonization of New England, considered Catholics to be anti-Christs and moral degenerates. In addition, the fact that miscegenation was taboo in the English colonies led its inhabitants to view race-mixing in New Spain as another indication of that society's moral decay. After the United States achieved independence, its citizens by and large held fast to the prejudices of their colonial past.

On December 12, 1822, soon after Mexico's independence from Spain, the government of the United States recognized the country as a sovereign nation. A year later, President James Monroe announced that U.S. policy toward the newly independent nations of Latin America would seek to impede any new European expansion on the American continent and to promote representative democracy as the most appropriate political system for the Western Hemisphere. This stance became known as the Monroe Doctrine.

With this cultural baggage in tow, special envoy Joel Robert Poinsett arrived in Mexico in 1825.

This view of the main plaza of Mexico City was painted by German artist Carl Nebel, who visited Mexico from 1829 to 1834. The result of his trip was Viaje pintoresco y arqueológico sobre la parte más interesante de la República Mexicana (*Picturesque and Archeological Travels in the Most Interesting Part of the Mexican Republic*), a collection published first in Paris and later in Spain.

Nebel used this very same perspective when he sketched the capital city's main plaza on the day it was occupied by U.S. troops. The striped awning over the balcony above the wine store is the same one a woman is raising in the lithograph he made twenty years later, p.292.

The Price of Spanish Domination

[Joel R. Poinsett, Minister of the United States in Mexico to Martin van Buren, Secretary of State, Mexico]

Joel Robert Poinsett (1779–1851) first served as U.S. special envoy to Argentina and Chile, and was expelled from the latter for interfering in the country's internal affairs. From August 1822 to January 1823, he was in Mexico on a special mission, and was named minister plenipotentiary of the United States in Mexico two years later. His term of office was fraught with difficulties, leading the Mexican government to request his departure in 1830.

March 1, 1829

The character of this people cannot be understood nor the causes of their present condition be fully developed without recurring to the oppression under which they formerly labored. It would lead you into error to compare them with the free and civilized nations of America and Europe in the nineteenth century. They started from a period nearer to the age of Charles the V, and it is even a matter of some doubt whether this nation had advanced one step in knowledge and civilization, from the time of the conquest to the moment of declaring themselves independent. No portion of the Spanish dominions in America was watched over by the mother country with such jealous care as Mexico. Its comparatively dense population, its extensive and fertile territory, its rich and varied productions, and especially its mineral wealth rendered it a source of great profit to Spain: while the history of the ancient splendor of Mexico, and the glory of its conquest could not fail to enhance the value of its possession in the eyes of that chivalrous people. In order to preserve that possession every precaution was taken that human prudence could devise to prevent the access of strangers to Mexico and to keep the people in profound ignorance of their relative position with regard to other nations. Until the publication of the voyage of Baron Humboldt, the nations of Europe and even their immediate neighbors were ignorant of the very names of the fertile districts and populous cities which the first described…

Creole Nobility and Church Hierarchy

The nobility and gentry then as now, inhabited spacious hotels, built after the fashion of those of their mother country, solid and substantial; but still more destitute of all comfort or convenience. Their style of living was not generous or hospitable although they sometimes gave costly and ostentatious entertainments… There never did exist that social intercourse among the higher orders, which in every other country forms the chief charm of life. Here every man of distinction considered it beneath his dignity to visit his friends or neighbors and remained in his own house, where in a large gloomy apartment dimly lighted and miserably furnished he received a few visitors of inferior rank who formed his tertulia of every night. It is not to be wondered at, therefore, that the sons of these men equally uneducated than themselves, fled from the gloomy mansion of their fathers to the theater, the coffeehouses or the gambling tables; and this circumstance united to the absence of all excitement to industry, from the preference given by the Council of the Indies to Europeans for all appointments rendered the aristocracy of Mexico an ignorant and immoral race.

Carl Nebel's collection,
Viaje pintoresco y arqueológico...,
depicts scenes of daily life in the
cities he visited. Among them is
this lithograph of a religious
procession in Mexico City's Santo
Domingo Square.

The same state of society existed among the higher orders of the clergy and marked their character in the same unfavorable manner. The regular clergy formed from the very dregs of people, was then and is now disgustingly debauched and ignorant…

LACK OF A FREE PEASANTRY

But what more particularly distinguishes the condition of people in the Spanish colonies is the character of the laboring classes. That portion of America conquered by Spain was inhabited by a people in a high state of civilization for the age in which they lived. The higher classes fell a sacrifice to the cruelty and rapacity of their conquerors, and the common

Because American society was made up of immigrants from among England's poor and persecuted, it was economically less hierarchical than those of the Spanish colonies and boasted a great diversity of religious denominations. What's more, the English colonists refused to intermarry with the Indians and did not consider them part of their society. In New Spain, on the contrary, miscegenation was common. This painting depicts the eight castes of Mexico's complex racial society, each defined by various mixes among whites, Indians and blacks. In Mexico, there was only one official religion: Catholicism. Placing the Virgin of Guadalupe at the top of the painting symbolizes the protection she provides to all Mexicans.

people were reduced to a state of the most abject slaving. The existence of this degraded race had a singular effect upon the character of the Spanish settler. The poorest white man scorned to be placed on a level with the unfortunate Indian. His color ennobled him, and Spaniards and their descendants would have perished rather than degrade their "casta" in America working in the field, or by following any other laborious occupation in which the Indians are habitually employed. Here therefore is wanting that portion of a community which forms the strength of every nation, but especially of a republic, a free and virtuous peasantry. The Indians cannot as yet be regarded in that light. They are emerging slowly from the wretched state to which they had been reduced; but they must be educated and released from the gross superstition under which they now labor before they can be expected to feel an interest in public affairs…

Lack of Interest in Educating the People

Less attention has been paid by this government to the establishment of primary schools than in any other part of Spanish America. This has been a lamentable oversight, for not only does the great mass of the population require to be educated in order that the real principles of a representative government may be carried fully into operation; but to inspire them with a decent pride and to induce them to more constant labor and to employ their earnings in rendering this habitation comfortable and in purchasing clothing for themselves and families.

Poverty a Result of Ignorance

At present, seven-eighths of the population live in wretched hovels destitute of the most ordinary conveniences. Their only furniture, a few coarse mats to sit and sleep on, their food Indian corn, pepper and pulse, and their clothing miserably coarse and scanty. It is not that the low price of labor prevents them from earning a more comfortable subsistence in spite of the numerous festivals in each year, but they either gamble away their money, or employ it in pageants of the Catholic Church, in which pagan and Christian rites are strangely mingled, and these evils if not cured entirely would be greatly mitigated by education…

The "Scotsmen" Side with England

It is proper here to mention, that the party in opposition to President…were organized and connected together in a society under the rules and regulations of the Scotch Masons, and were therefore called "escoceses." At this period the affairs of Mexico wore the most favorable aspect. Loans had been affected in London to a sufficient amount to enable the government to augment the number of their troops which they did without necessity, to arm and clothe them, and to purchase ships of war. The large sums of money introduced into the country by the English mining companies contributed in no small degree to the prosperity of the people. Their trade increased to a surprising degree, and the whole country wore the appearance of abundance. The Treasury was overflowing, pensions and salaries were paid with punctuality, and both the government and people appeared to think that the millions they had borrowed formed part of their annual income. The "escoceses" considered this state of things as the effect of their political combinations and without thinking of the future called upon the people to admire their work. But the party in opposition looked upon these proceedings with gloomy foreboreings [forebodings]…

Mistrust between the United States and Mexico, and the Delicate Question of the Border

Such was the state of this country when we entered in the spring of 1825. We soon perceived that we were objects of distrust, dislike to the ruling party composed as it was of the aristocracy, the high clergy, the monarchical faction and the Spaniards; it was natural they should look coldly upon the representative of a republic. They did more, they displayed a hostile feeling towards us, and actually talked of receiving us in a style different from that in which the English chargé d'affaires had been received…

In the decade of the 1820s, only a few Mexicans participated actively in politics, and political parties were a new phenomenon, circumstances that opened the door to meddling by foreign powers. Outside interference in Mexico's politics took place via the Masonic lodges that came to define the country's main ideological currents. The lodge that followed the rites of the Scotch Masons, set up by Spanish officials during the War of Independence, constituted a strong, centralized force and came under the influence of British interests.

In 1819 Spain and the United States negotiated the Adams-Onís Treaty (also known as the Transcontinental Treaty, and referred to by Poinsett as the Treaty of Washington) which established the border between New Spain and the United States. When Mexico won its independence in 1821, the new government asked the United States to confirm that agreement. The United States refused, hoping to get Mexico to cede a piece of territory so that Texas would reach to the Rio Grande (or Bravo).

This 1792 map indicates clearly that the Nueces River was the border between the colonial provinces of Texas and Tamaulipas, not the Rio Grande as the United States insisted.

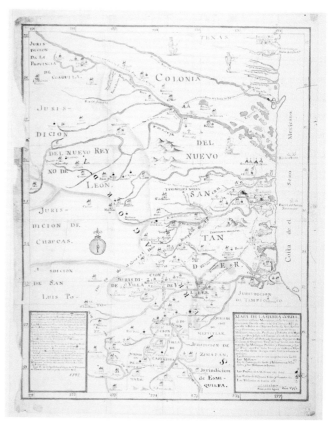

In combination with the Secretary of Foreign Relations D. Lucas Alaman, he had firmed a plan to negotiate a new treaty of boundaries by which we were to be reduced to the margin of the Mississippi, for they believed that by the treaty of Washington, we had unjustly deprived Spain of a large portion of her territory. They were exceedingly surprised therefore when no objection was made by this legation to renew the negotiations on that subject altogether with a declaration that in that event, the United States would assume the line of the Río Bravo del Norte, as the boundary…

The Congress more wisely compelled the executive subsequently to confirm that treaty. The party in power availed itself of this question and publicly accused us of ambitious views and of jealousy of the rising greatness of Mexico.

Natural Empathy between
Liberals and North Americans

In proportion to the repugnance with which the aristocratic faction regarded us were the cordial advances of the democratic party, and if our principles had not induced us to seek our associates among the latter, we should have been driven to do so by the conduct of the former.

Implementing the Monroe Doctrine

Under these circumstances it became my duty to consider the policy the United States would pursue regarding these countries and especially regarding Mexico. For various reasons one was most interesting to us: It was an undeniable fact that G. Britain had used great exertions to acquire an ascendancy in them all, and had to a certain degree succeeded in doing so… and the question to be resolved by me was whether I should permit a European nation the most unfriendly to our prosperity to acquire unbounded influence in a neighboring republic or whether I ought to oppose views so hostile to the interest of America.

The great powers of Europe have established their separate influence over the inferior nations of that continent after a long struggle with each other; and it must be manifest, that the contest for power will be renewed by them in America. Are we to take no part in this contest? Are we to sit tamely by and see G. Britain and France contending for sway in the Americas, nor to concern ourselves in a question which may hereafter so essentially affect our interests? Is the policy of the United States in relation to Europe and to these countries the same?

I think not, if we do not exercise a direct and salutary influence over the councils of the American states we ought not to permit any European nation to do so. It is not obvious that if Great Britain should establish such a dominion over

This colored daguerreotype from 1847 shows the symbolic attire worn by an American Mason.

During the nineteenth century, the United States feared England's economic and political clout on the American continent. As soon as he arrived in Mexico in 1825, Poinsett sought to counteract British influence by encouraging liberal and radical politicians to join together in the York Masonic lodge. This interference in domestic politics, plus the territorial demands he made generated widespread condemnation and led Mexico to request his departure in 1830.

this country as she exercises over Portugal that this state of things might prove highly detrimental to our interests. That this ambitious nation has attempted, and will continue to exact a vast means to effect this object cannot be doubted. In my opinion the United States ought not to permit it, and with this view, of the subject I have acted. I found the British united with the aristocratic and monarchical party who governed the country and I felt gratified that this party should act towards us in a manner which not only justified, but to a certain degree compelled us to seek our friends altogether among the Creoles and democrats…

POINSETT DECIDES TO INTERVENE AND SETS UP THE YORK MASONS

At the earnest desire of some of the most distinguished men in the country, and with the full approbation of the government, I sent for charters for the five lodges already existing in the country and installed the Grand Lodge of Ancient York Masons in Mexico. Their opponents had long been organized under the Scotch rite and had used this institution altogether for political purposes. They supposed, what proved to be the fact, that the York Masons would follow their example and, being more numerous, would be able with an equal organization to carry all their measures; with this perversion of a purely philanthropic institution to the purpose of political intrigue, I took no part, but on the contrary withdrew myself from their meetings so soon as the intentions of the party became manifest.

The First American Settlers in Texas

In August 1821, barely a month after Mexico won its independence, Moses Austin moved from Louisiana to Texas with the first three hundred American families. To escape the difficult economic situation in the United States, these settlers took advantage of a provision in the 1819 Transcontinental Treaty between Spain and the United States which gave the inhabitants of Louisiana the right to move to Texas.

The Louisiana Territory, a former French colony under Spanish rule since 1763, had been returned to France in 1800, only to be sold three years later to the United States. The economic crises which engulfed the United States between 1800 and 1820 left many Americans penniless. When Mexico opened its borders, offering considerable incentives, settlers migrated en masse to Texas in search of an opportunity to regain their lost fortunes.

*P*ortrait of Stephen Austin, son of Moses Austin, the first American settler in Texas. Although this portrait was painted in Mexico City, where Austin had traveled in 1833 to settle Texas's affairs, he is posing with his rifle before a backdrop that is supposed to show the Brazos River in Texas.

THE LIFE AND MIRACLES OF MOSES AUSTIN
AS PENNED BY HIS SON

[Stephen Austin, "Apuntes relativos a la Colonia de Texas," June 1828]

Moses Austin, a native of the northern State of Connecticut, was remarkable for his enterprising and active spirit; owner of a lead mine in the State of Virginia, he was the first to introduce skilled miners and craftsmen from Europe into his operation, and the first in the United States of the North to manufacture small munitions, lead shot, clothing irons and metal buttons, for which he brought over master craftsmen from England. In the year 1798, having received word of the rich mines in the upper Louisiana, then belonging to Spain and now part of the State of Missouri, he made a trip to explore that territory under the protection of passports from the Spanish Minister with whom he maintained a friendship. The result of his voyage was a determination to emigrate to the upper Louisiana, and from the Spanish Gov[ernment] he won a concession for the principal lead mines. He moved there with his family in the year 1799, acquiring a considerable fortune from the mines and the vast improvements he introduced; but in the year 1818 he suffered great losses due to the bankruptcy of the Bank of Saint Louis and other misfortunes. Having heard talk of Texas from some travelers, he got the idea to set up a new colony in its empty tracts and to that end, in the fifty-sixth year of his life, he set off from Misuri [sic] to Bexar, capital of Texas some six hundred leagues distant, and on January 17, 1821, he received from the Commanding General of the Eastern Internal Provinces, Gen. Joaquín Arredondo, and from the Most Excellent Deputation of the Provinces in Monterrey, authorization to establish three hundred foreign families in Texas. He returned to Misuri [sic] and in May of the same year died from a chest illness contracted during the rigors of the winter on his return trip between Bexar and Nachitoches, leaving his son Stephen F. Austin in charge of carrying forward the colonization enterprise...

Moses Austin, his son Stephen and the rest of the Americans who colonized Texas were typical of those who settled the United States. Their ancestors had come to America in search of a better life and, above all, property. Without a place to call home, they were prepared to go anywhere they might find opportunity. They viewed moving as an expression of enterprising spirit and progress.

This text was originally written in Spanish by Stephen Austin, and contained a number of spelling mistakes.

The American settlers in Texas were known as "pioneers," and they were rugged individualists. Land speculation was the primary focus of their efforts to accumulate wealth, and they rarely hesitated to obtain land illegally. As the historian Avery Craven notes, "They were emphatically provincial and self-centered. Immediate material gain... not national interest, prompted them. They had not hesitated to expatriate themselves when personal benefit lay in that direction. When necessary, they had claimed as natural rights everything, material and spiritual, which they considered conducive to individual happiness... They were a restless race and they were always resentful of restraints and impatient under failure to make rapid progress... Their methods were direct; their faith in themselves unbounded."

THE INHOSPITABLE LAND OF TEXAS

In those days all of Texas, with the sole exception of the two small districts of Bexar and La Bahia, was nothing but unpopulated land infested with barbarian Indians at war with the Mexicans and decidedly hostile to any new settlement of civilized people... The government in that epoch was in turmoil and all of Mexico was in revolution. In this state of affairs there was little on which to base hope, and the idea of colonizing Texas was ridiculed by the friends of Austin's son, who sought to persuade him to abandon the effort; nevertheless, having inherited some of his father's enterprising nature and respectful of his last wishes in this regard, he pressed forward, and in the month of December 1821 traveled on the Brazos River from Louisiana with the first families and founded the new colony.

THE FIRST YEAR IN THE COLONY

These first settlers went with their families to the middle of the desert, surrounded by enemy Indians, with no resources but those provided by nature in an unpopulated country, and with no hope of protection other than that provided by their own fortitude. Austin sent schooners from [New] Orleans loaded with foodstuffs, tools, seeds, etc., but they never arrived. One was lost on the unfamiliar coastline and another was shipwrecked and the cargo stolen by Indians, leaving the settlers a choice between abandoning the effort and returning to Louisiana or maintaining themselves by hunting.

The enterprising spirit which had brought them to the desert sustained them in their hardships, and their guns offered security from the Indians and provided them with food from the bisons, bears, deer and other wild animals in the countryside....

PAPERWORK THAT TOOK
AN ENTIRE YEAR

....in March of the year 1822, Stephen Austin visited Bexar to settle matters regarding the colony with the government, and the Governor of Texas D. Antonio Martínez told him that he had to travel to Mexico City to obtain from the newly installed national congress a confirmation of the concession made by the Spanish authorities to his father Moses Austin. This news discouraged him greatly... The roads in those days were infested with thieves, and after all there was little order or discipline in any branch of the police... To protect himself from thieves, Austin disguised himself as a beggar; he had a compatriot with him who had been an officer under Gen. Mina, and that helped out with the ruse; they said they had lost everything in Mina's expedition, and were going to Mexico City to seek recompense from the government for their services to the fatherland.

When he arrived in Mexico City, Austin found himself in a rather embarrassing situation, a foreigner without any knowledge of the Castilian language, without acquaintances or friends, with the government in turmoil and public opinion unpredictable regarding the political system to be adopted. Shortly after his arrival, Iturbide was proclaimed Emperor and the resulting events, plus the incidents of the month of August with the jailing of the Deputies, and those of the end of October with the dissolution of Congress, occupied the attention of the government to such an extent that Austin did not manage to get his business attended to until February 18, 1823, the day on which he received from the Emperor full authority to establish his new colony in Texas. However, he did not leave Mexico, for it was evident that big changes were on the political horizon; in effect, that occurred and Iturbide was dethroned in the month of March and Congress was re-established with all its rights and freedoms. To further solidify the legality of his enterprise, Austin presented to Congress

The sheer distance between Texas and Mexico City, the lack of proper communications, and even the concessions the Mexican government offered the American settlers in Texas, encouraged them to remain aloof from the rest of Mexican society. Culturally and economically, they remained linked to their country of origin.

In its edition of October 15, 1823, the Missouri Advocate *of St. Louis described the generous concessions which the Mexican government offered the settlers of Texas in these terms: "The difference is too great not to produce its effects between a republic which gives first-rate land grants, and a republic which will not sell inferior land for what it is worth... Mexico does not think of getting rich by land speculation...but by increasing the number and wealth of her citizens."*

the order he had received from the Emperor on February 18, which was approved by Congress on the 11th day of April and by the Supreme Executive Power on April 14 that same year 1823.

With the great and momentous business that motivated his visit to Mexico concluded, Austin departed at the end of April, one year after his arrival/return [sic] to Texas, having in this time learned Spanish.

THE SETTLERS' INABILITY TO ADAPT

A wagon train of settlers meets a herd of wild horses, thousands of which lived on the Great Plains.

The settlers did not understand a word of the Castilian language, and there were no translations, not even a single copy of the laws of the country, nor were they aware of the customary procedures in trials and civil processes, or even the talents and character of the people and government of the nation that they had adopted. Austin had general instructions for administering justice, preserving order and, in sum, governing the colony as best he could until it could be organized in another fashion, and by virtue of this authority he set down some provisional regulations for administration in all areas...

PROBLEMS WITH THE ABORIGINAL INHABITANTS OF TEXAS

In the early years the Indians harassed the colony, notably by stealing many horses and killing a considerable number of settlers, among them an entire family, including the mother and three children. Austin sought to contain the Indians at first with gifts and entreaties until he acquired sufficient force to fight them, and then he took the offensive and made several expeditions against the Indians... Dealing with the Indians and undertaking several expeditions against them

The indigenous population of Texas was made up of a variety of tribes with different ways of life. The Caddos lived in eastern Texas on the banks of the Sabina River, while the Pueblos lived north of the Rio Grande (near Santa Fe, New Mexico). These two groups were sedentary and lived peacefully with the inhabitants of European origin.

In the central and western parts of Texas, the Comanches and Apaches, nomads who never became assimilated, attacked the settlers incessantly and made incursions as far south as the states of Zacatecas and San Luis Potosí. The situation was further complicated in 1839 when the U.S. government relocated the Cherokees and other groups to the northern reaches of Texas, in Comanche territory.

The year 1820 marked the rise of King Cotton in the United States. Thanks to Eli Whitney's invention of the cotton gin, cotton became the country's most important export. This reinforced the economic basis of slavery. By 1830, Texas had become part of the "Kingdom of Cotton."

On December 20, 1826, Benjamin Edwards and a group of settlers living near the town of Nacogdoches, supported by the Cerote Indians, tried to declare an independent country. The alliance with the Indians was not well received by the rest of the American settlers, and Stephen Austin himself opposed the idea. The rebellion was put down and Edwards fled to the United States in January of 1827.

was very costly to Austin... It ought to be noted that at that time there were not fifty national soldiers in all of Texas because the garrisons of Bahia and Bexar had utterly fallen apart due to lack of funds, and the inhabitants of those two places suffered so many miseries they barely survived...

PROSPEROUS LIFE IN THE COLONY

The colonies [sic] of Austin today is flowering in the areas under the control of its inhabitants: agriculture and animal husbandry have advanced, water mills have been set up for sawing boards and grinding grain, there are cotton gins and other machines, schools have been set up, the nearby Indians subjected. In sum, nature's crude and savage appearance in the desert has been exchanged for the graceful and pleasing countenance of civilization.

The inhabitants are farmers, enterprising, industrious, peaceful and easy to govern; proof of this last quality is that from the beginning Austin has governed without the support of a single soldier, without any need of force, and even without a jail or prison of which there are none in the jurisdiction to this day, and never has there been a capital crime committed by a settler and only a single case of simple robbery.

SOLIDARITY WITH MEXICO

They have given unequivocal proof of patriotism and honor, and of loyalty to their adopted government—they have freely spilled their blood fighting against the savage enemies of the Mexicans, and in last year's events at Nacogdoches, through their firm and quick support for the Mexican flag, they quelled a nascent revolution in its infancy, saving the country from a brutal war against the barbarian Indians and adventurers...

The Constitution of 1824 prohibited trading and owning slaves, and declared all who entered Mexican territory to be free. However, the settlers of Texas were granted an exception. Five years later, federal legislation outlawed slavery throughout the country and emancipated all slaves. Stephen Austin managed to convince President Vicente Guerrero to exempt Texas once more.

The threat that slavery might eventually be abolished in Texas was one motivation behind the separatist movement.

The two paintings on the left depict scenes from the lives of slaves in Virginia. The image below shows a slave market: Among the people shackled are a mother with her children; the whites carry whips, and in the background one of the black workers is being flogged. On the horizon, the Capitol Building flying the U.S. flag seems to offer its blessing to the scene.

UNITED STATES SLAVE TRADE.
1830.

Advantages for Mexico
of the Colonization of Texas

This establishment has not cost the government a cent, not for setting it up, not for governing it, not even for defending it; on the contrary, besides the services noted, it has supplied the soldiers and inhabitants of Bejar [Bexar] and Bahia with food at much more reasonable prices than had been known since the year 1811. To get a proper idea of the important advantages for the nation of this colony, one only has to ask: What was the situation of Texas in the year 1821 and what is its situation today? And how much would it have cost the nation to set up an equal number of Mexican or European families in these deserts under similar circumstances? Now all the difficulties of settling Texas have been eased: it is no longer a desert, there is food everywhere and in abundance, there is the physical force of militias to put down the Indians, and there will be no problem setting up other settlements under the protection of those already established... Austin laid out the path and now it can be easily followed...

...Progress and advancement of a large part of the states of Chihuahua, Cuahuila and Texas, Neuva León and Tamaulipas and the territory of New Mexico depend on the progress of the new colonies of Texas, because if these fall behind and the country becomes depopulated of civilized people it will soon be occupied by the barbarian Indians of the north, who are emigrating in large numbers every year, and by the vagabond adventurers and fugitives from both neighboring nations, and these plus the native Indians of the country would utterly destroy the estates and towns of the Rio Grande, and Texas instead of being of benefit would go back to being a dead weight and even a threat to the Mexican nation...

III   *Texas Secedes*

The population of American settlers in Texas, about 2,500 in 1821, reached 40,000 by 1836. Some of them were legal residents, and others, a large proportion, were there without proper documentation. Mexican government policy toward the settlers between 1821 and 1835 was enormously generous. Besides giving out land—at first for free, later at extremely low prices— the government exempted the settlers from customs duties and allowed them to maintain their own judicial institutions.

Even though the settlers had promised to convert to Catholicism, they retained their Protestant churches, as well as their language and business connections with the neighboring populations of the United States, especially in the port of New Orleans. Throughout, they held firm to the idea of turning Texas into a free and sovereign state.

The separatist movement of Anglo-American Texans gained strength at the beginning of the 1830s when Mexico refused to recognize Texas as a state separate from Coahuila, eliminated the customs duties exemption, and insisted that the slaves be set free.

Then when Mexico moved from a federal constitutional system to a centralized one in 1835, Texans saw an opportunity to rebel—and rebel they did. When the Mexican Army attacked the forts at Goliad and the Alamo to put down the rebellion, the Texans declared independence from Mexico.

TEXAS IN 1840,

OR THE

EMIGRANT'S GUIDE

TO THE

NEW REPUBLIC;

BEING

THE RESULT OF OBSERVATION, ENQUIRY AND TRAVEL
IN THAT BEAUTIFUL COUNTRY.

BY AN EMIGRANT,

LATE OF THE UNITED STATES.

Land of the prairies, hail!
Of birds and music, of flowers and beauty,
Of loveliness and hope,—Peace be thy lot,
Joy thine inheritance, and Holiness thy praise!

WITH AN INTRODUCTION BY THE
REV. A. B. LAWRENCE,
OF NEW ORLEANS.

NEW YORK:
PUBLISHED BY WILLIAM W. ALLEN,
AND SOLD BY ROBINSON, PRATT & CO., 73 WALL STREET,
COLLINS, KEESE & CO., 254 PEARL STREET,
AND BY THE BOOKSELLERS GENERALLY.
1840.

This book is an example of the promotional material used to encourage emigration to the new country of Texas. Published in New York by "an emigrant, late of the United States," it praises Texas from the very first page as a country of meadows, beauty, peace and hope. The frontispiece is a view of "The City of Austin, the new capital of Texas in January 1, 1840."

THE CONTRIBUTIONS MADE BY TEXANS, AND THE HARASSMENT THEY FACE

[Message of Samuel Houston]

Washington [-on-the-Brazos]

December 12, 1835

Your situation is peculiarly calculated to call forth all your manly energies. Under the Republican constitution of Mexico, you were invited to Texas, then a wilderness. You have reclaimed and rendered it a cultivated country. You solemnly swore to support the Constitution and its laws. Your oaths are yet inviolate. In accordance with them, you have fought with the liberals against those who sought to overthrow the Constitution in 1832 when the present usurper was the champion of liberal principles in Mexico. Your obedience has manifested your integrity. You have witnessed with pain the convulsions of the interior and a succession of usurpations. You have experienced in silent grief the expulsion of your members from the State Congress. You have realized the horrors of anarchy and the dictation of military rule. The promises made to you have not been fulfilled. Your memorials for the redress of grievances have been disregarded and the agents you have sent to Mexico have been imprisoned for years without enjoying the right of trial agreeable to law.

CHANGEOVER TO A CENTRALIST SYSTEM

The federation has been dissolved, the Constitution declared at an end, and centralism has been established...

The usurper dispatched a military force to invade the colonies and exact the arms of the inhabitants. The citizens refused the demand, and the invading force was increased.

During the War of 1812, Samuel Houston fought under the command of Andrew Jackson, with whom he formed a close friendship. Accused of fraud in 1832, he was exonerated with the assistance of his friend Jackson, who at that point was president of the United States. After the trial Houston was commissioned to negotiate with the Indian tribes along the Texas border. That was when he decided to remain in Texas and immediately he became involved in local politics. Before long, he was a leader of the separatist movement.

In 1832, several leaders in Texas demanded the territory be split off from the state of Coahuila. They held a state constitutional convention and wrote up a draft constitution. Stephen Austin was sent to Mexico City to present the request to the Mexican government. After two years of petitioning, Austin returned with the government's refusal.

The question then was shall we resist the oppression and live free, or violate our oaths and bear a despot's stripes? The citizens of Texas rallied to the defense of their constitutional rights...

RECRUITING OF VOLUNTEERS

The Texas rebellion against the change in government structure soon became a secessionist movement. Since the settlers had no military experience, Houston recruited American volunteer soldiers with the promise of land.

The army of the people is now before Bexar... Though called together at a moment, the citizens of Texas, unprovided as they were in the necessary munitions of war and supplies for an army, have maintained a siege of months...

Since our army has been in the field, a consultation of the people, by their representatives, has met and established a provisional government... A regular army has been created and liberal encouragement has been given by the government. To all who will enlist for two years or during the war, a bounty of twenty-four dollars and eight hundred acres of land will be given. Provision has also been made for raising an auxiliary volunteer corps to constitute part of the army of Texas which will be placed under the command and subject to the orders of the Commander-in-Chief. The field for promotion will be open. The terms of service will be various: to those who choose to tender their services for or during the war will be given a bounty of six hundred and forty acres of land; an equal bounty will be given to those who volunteer their service for two years; if for one year, a bounty of three hundred and twenty acres... The rights of citizenship are extended to all who will unite with us in defending the republican principles of the Constitution of 1824...

The services of five thousand volunteers will be accepted. By the first of March next, we must meet the enemy with an army worthy of cause and which will reflect honor upon freemen... Liberal Mexicans will unite with us.

BATTLE OF THE ALAMO

On March 5 and 6 of 1836, respectively, the Mexican Army attacked the forts at Goliad and the Alamo, held by Texas rebels and American volunteers. The Mexican government had warned on December 30, 1835, that "foreigners who enter the Republic with hostile intentions will be punished as pirates..." And captured volunteers were in fact executed. Those executions led the federalist movement of Texas to become openly separatist.

The unequivocal defeat of the Mexicans on April 21, 1836, on the banks of the San Jacinto River, and the capture of Santa Anna the following day, decided the fate of Texas. The Mexican troops pulled back to the other side of the Rio Grande. Although Mexico did not recognize Texas's secession, from then on it was a fact.

The Declaration of Independence of Texas was based on the one proclaimed in 1776 by the Continental Congress of the English Colonies of North America. Texas claimed the Rio Grande as its southern border. The declaration was made in the Texas town of Washington; after the Civil War, the name of the town was changed to Washington-on-the-Brazos, for the river running through it.

DECLARATION OF INDEPENDENCE OF TEXAS

[Declaration of Independence, made by the Delegates of the People of Texas in General Convention]

March 2, 1836

Nations, as well as individuals, are amenable for their acts to the public opinion of mankind. A statement of a part of our grievances is therefore submitted to an impartial world in justification of the hazardous but unavoidable step now taken of severing our political connection with the Mexican people, and assuming an independent attitude among the nations of the earth.

The Mexican government, by its colonization laws, invited and induced the Anglo-American population of Texas to colonize its wilderness under the pledged faith of a written constitution, that they should continue to enjoy that constitutional liberty and republican government to which they had been habituated in the land of their birth, the United States of America.

In this expectation they have been cruelly disappointed, inasmuch as the Mexican nation has acquiesced in the late changes made in the government by General Antonio López Santa Anna, who having overturned the constitution of his country… These and other grievances were patiently borne by the people of Texas, until they reached that point at which forbearance ceases to be a virtue.

WE DECLARE OURSELVES FREE

We, therefore, the delegates, with plenary powers, of the people of Texas, in solemn convention assembled, appealing to a candid world for the necessities of our condition, do hereby resolve and declare, that our political connection with the Mexican nation has forever ended, and that the people of Texas do now constitute a free, sovereign and independent republic...

IV *Annexation*

E*ver since the Transcontinental Treaty of 1819, the United States had claimed the territory of Texas as part of Louisiana. For that reason, the American people generally supported the Texas emancipation movement and provided both material support and volunteers to fight against the Mexican Army. However, the stance of the U.S. government during the war was more cautious. President Jackson remained steadfastly neutral; he received Texas's request for annexation politely, but gave no indication of support. The farthest he went was to formally recognize an independent Texas on March 2, 1837.*

Nevertheless, the U.S. government soon showed renewed interest in the goal of annexing Texas. On April 12, 1844, the United States signed a treaty with Texas taking responsibility for the new country's public debts. In return, Texas ceded to the federal government all its publicly owned land. That treaty, however, did not win the two-thirds majority in the Senate required for ratification. President John Tyler then proposed that Texas be annexed by means of a Joint Congressional Resolution—a procedure which, unlike the treaty, involved both houses of Congress and required only a simple majority. The Joint Resolution was approved on March 1, 1845.

*T*he Texas question drew the attention of the world's great powers. France recognized the independence of Texas in 1839, and a year later Holland, Belgium and Great Britain followed suit. Britain gained great influence as the principal buyer of Texan cotton, and soon provided the new and highly indebted republic with loans. The growing ties between Texas and Great Britain were the most compelling reason for the United States to revive its plan to annex the territory.

This campaign banner is from the 1844 U.S. elections: James K. Polk and George Mifflin Dallas were the Democratic candidates for president and vice-president. Polk appears surrounded by twenty-six stars symbolizing the states that then made up the United States—thirteen of them slave states, thirteen free states. The blue star off by itself represents the lone star of the Texas flag. The design of this campaign pennant alludes to Polk's promise to annex Texas to the United States.

MATTY MEETING THE TEXAS QUESTION.

John C. Calhoun, ☞ p. 304, the principal spokesman for Southern slave-holders, was named Secretary of State in 1843. In May of 1836, right after Texas declared independence, he explained why it should become part of the Union: "...the Southern States, owning a slave population, were deeply interested in preventing that country from having the power to annoy them."

PREVIOUS ATTEMPTS TO ANNEX TEXAS

[Instructions of John C. Calhoun, Secretary of State, to William Shannon, Minister of the United States in Mexico]

Washington D.C., September 10, 1844
No measure of policy has been more steadily or longer pursued and that by both of the parties into which the union is divided. Many believed that Texas was embraced in the cession of Louisiana and was improperly, if not unconstitutionally surrendered by the treaty of Florida in 1819. Under that impression and the general conviction of its importance to the safety and welfare of the Union, its annexation has been an object of constant pursuit ever since. It was twice attempted to acquire it during the administration of Mr. Adams; once in 1825, shortly after he came into power; and again in 1827. It was twice attempted under the administration of his successor, General Jackson; first in 1829, immediately after he came into power; again in 1833, and finally in 1835, just before Texas declared her independence. Texas herself made a proposition for annexation in 1837 at the commencement of Mr. Van Buren's administration, which he declined; not however on the grounds of opposition to the policy of the measure.

In this cartoon, two senators are carrying the new country on their shoulders; Calhoun is the one on the right. Texas is represented as an angry witch bearing handcuffs and a whip, the symbols of slavery. In the right-hand corner Polk tells Dallas, "She's not the handsomest Lady I ever saw, but that $25,000 a year—Eh! It's worth a little stretching of Conscience!" The figure alludes to the salary of the president of the United States.

Texas's nine years of independent life were plagued with domestic problems. It achieved sovereignty at the cost of a sizeable public debt incurred on account of the war against Mexico. The debt grew larger because Texas needed a standing army to defend itself against attacks by Indians and Mexicans seeking to recover their lands.

The United States had previously acknowledged her independence and the example has since been followed by France and Great Britain. The latter, soon after her recognition, began to adopt a line of policy in reference to Texas which has given greatly increased importance to the measure of annexation, by making it still more essential to the safety and welfare both of her and the United States.

WE WILL NOT LOSE
THIS GOLDEN OPPORTUNITY!

In pursuance of this long cherished and established policy, and under the conviction of the necessity of acting promptly in order to prevent the defeat of the measure, the present administration invited Texas to renew the proposition for annexation, which had been declined by its predecessor. It was accepted and, as has been stated, is now pending. The question recurs, shall we stand by quietly, and permit Mexico to defeat it, without making an effort to oppose her? Shall we, after this long and continued effort to annex Texas, now, when the measure is about to be consummated, allow Mexico to put it aside, perhaps forever? Shall the golden opportunity be lost, never again to return? Shall we permit Texas, for having accepted an invitation tendered her at a critical moment, to join us and consummate a measure, essential to theirs and our permanent peace, welfare and safety, to be desolated, her inhabitants to be butchered or driven out…

…The president would be compelled to regard the invasion of Texas by Mexico while the question of annexation is pending as highly offensive to the United States. He entertains no doubt that we had the right to invite her to renew the proposition for annexation, and she, as an independent state, had a right to accept it, without consulting Mexico, or asking her leave. He regards Texas, in every respect, as independent as Mexico, and as competent to transfer the whole or part of Texas as she would be pleased…

The Texas question sparked deep divisions within the United States. The free industrial states of the North saw that annexation would strengthen the agrarian slave states of the South, thus upsetting the balance in Congress, where this division took on a partisan cast: the Democrats favored annexation, while the Whigs (later to become the Republicans) opposed it. This cartoon depicts the Congressional battle and predicts a Democratic victory. On the right is Polk waving the U.S. flag to welcome Texas, depicted as a boat on which Austin and Houston bear the flag of Texas, easily recognizable by its lone star. Below the bridge the abolitionists, who sought to block annexation, fall to defeat, among them Henry Clay, ☞ p. 301, then Whig candidate for the presidency.

War is the Only Option Left

Nor will our honor, any more than our welfare and safety, permit her to attack Texas, while the question of annexation is pending. If Mexico has thought proper to take offense, it is us who invited a renewal of the proposition and not she who accepted it, who ought to be held responsible and we, as the responsible party, cannot, without implicating our honor, permit another to suffer in our place…

Annexation at Last

[Joint Resolution of Congress annexing Texas to the United States]

March 1, 1845

Resolved by the Senate and House of Representatives of the United States in Congress assembled, That Congress doth consent the territory properly included within, and rightfully belonging to the Republic of Texas, may be erected into a new State, to be called the State of Texas…

And be further resolved, That the foregoing consent of Congress is given upon the following conditions, and with the following guarantees, to wit:

First, Said State to be formed, subject to the adjustment by this government of all questions of boundary that may arise with other governments, and the constitution therof [sic], with the proper evidence of its adoption by the people of said Republic of Texas, shall be transmitted to the President of the United States, to be laid before Congress for its final action, on or before the first day of January, one thousand eight hundred and forty-six.

The "Manifest Destiny" of American Expansionism

*F*rom the debate on the annexation of Texas, a current of thought emerged called "Manifest Destiny," a term coined by John Louis O'Sullivan. It provided a moral justification for the territorial ambitions of American society, as articulated by its politicians during the decade of the 1840s.

Manifest Destiny, which proclaimed the superiority of representative democracy and "progress," had a dark side: all non-Anglo-Saxon peoples, be they Indians, Mexicans or Africans, were considered to be inferior and therefore could be rightfully dispossessed of their property and their freedom. The doctrine posited the expansion of the United States as the extension of the realm of freedom. In fact, it was precisely the opposite: in Texas, slavery was legalized following its annexation by the United States.

"*A*merican Progress," painted in 1872 by John Gast, is perhaps the best allegory of Manifest Destiny. It portrays a gigantic woman adorned with a star, chasing away shadows and darkness as she flies by. In one hand she carries a book, in the other telegraph wires. Following her are hardworking settlers and railroads. Before her flee Indians and herds of buffalo and wild horses. The woman is headed from right to left, which on the map is east to west; on the extreme left of the painting lies the Pacific coast.

MANIFEST DESTINY

[John L. O'Sullivan, "The Great Nation of Futurity," *The Democratic Review*]

From their earliest Puritan beginnings, the American people considered themselves to be exceptional, graced with a divine mandate to extend the territorial reach of their institutions for the good of humanity.

November 1839

The American people having derived their origin from many other nations, and the Declaration of National Independence being entirely based on the great principle of human equality, these facts demonstrate at once our disconnected position as regards any other nation; that we have, in reality, but little connection with the past history of any of them, and still less with all antiquity, its glories, or its crimes. On the contrary, our national birth was the beginning of a new history, the formation and progress of an untried political system, which separates us from the past and connects us with the future only; and so far as regards the entire development of the natural rights of man, in moral, political, and national life, we may confidently assume that our country is destined to be the great nation of futurity.

THE GREAT NATION OF THE FUTURE

America is destined for better deeds. It is our unparalleled glory that we have no reminiscences of battle fields, but in defence of humanity, of the oppressed of all nations, of the rights of conscience, the rights of personal enfranchisement. Our annals describe no scenes of horrid carnage, where men were led on by hundreds of thousands to slay one another, dupes and victims to emperors, kings, nobles, demons in the human form called heroes. We have had patriots to defend our homes, our liberties, but no aspirants to crowns or thrones…

We have no interest in the scenes of antiquity, only as lessons of avoidance of nearly all their examples. The expansive future is our arena, and for our history...

We are the nation of human progress, and who will, what can, set limits to our onward march? Providence is with us, and no earthly power can. We point to the everlasting truth

In the decade of the 1840s, U.S. society and government were different from others in the world. The country's population was composed of immigrants who had come from a variety of countries with different historic, cultural, religious and linguistic backgrounds, in hope of finding a better life. The only link that tied them together was their belief that the country's political and economic system would provide them with a better future. Thus, what united Americans was not their past, but their future.

More than a few European intellectuals looked favorably on the U.S. invasion of Mexico. Among them were Karl Marx and Friedrich Engels, the fathers of scientific socialism. Engels wrote on January 23, 1848: "[W]e have witnessed the conquest of Mexico and have rejoiced at it. It is also an advance when a country which has hitherto been exclusively wrapped up in its own affairs, perpetually rent with civil wars, and completely hindered in its development, a country whose best prospect had been to become industrially subject to Britain —when such a country is forcibly drawn into the historical process. It is to the interest of its own development that Mexico will in future be placed under the tutelage of the United States."

on the first page of our national declaration, and we proclaim to the millions of other lands, that "the gates of hell"—the powers of aristocracy and monarchy—"shall not prevail against it."

The far-reaching, the boundless future will be the era of American greatness. In its magnificent domain of space and time, the nation of many nations is destined to manifest to mankind the excellence of divine principles; to establish on earth the noblest temple ever dedicated to the worship of the Most High—the Sacred and the True. Its floor shall be a hemisphere—its roof the firmament of the star-studded heavens, and its congregation an Union of many Republics, comprising hundreds of happy millions, calling, owning no man master, but governed by God's natural and moral law of equality, the law of brotherhood—of "peace and good will amongst men."

THE ANNEXATION OF TEXAS, PART OF OUR MANIFEST DESTINY

[John L. O'Sullivan, "Annexation," *United States Magazine and Democratic Review*]

July 1845

It is time for opposition to the annexation of Texas to cease, all further agitation of the water of bitterness and strife, at least in connection with this question… But, in regard to Texas, enough has now been given to party…

Texas is now ours. Her star and her stripe may already be said to have taken their place in the glorious blazon of our common nationality…

The next session of Congress will see the representatives of the new young state in their places in both our halls of national legislation, side by side with those of the old Thirteen. Let their reception into "the family" be frank, kindly, and cheerful, as befits such an occasion…

HUNTING INDIANS IN FLORIDA WITH BLOOD HOUNDS.

In the brilliant future foreseen by Manifest Destiny, there was no place for the people who had inhabited the American continent for thousands of years. The rhetoric of progress presumed the huge question of exterminating these people, many of whom lived in nomadic tribes. Several wars were waged against the Indians, some as brutal as the one fought against the Seminoles (1835–1842) in which trained attack dogs were used in battle, as depicted in this painting. The general wearing a Panama hat and riding a white horse is none other than Zachary Taylor, who would later become commander-in-chief in the war against Mexico and, at its end, President of the United States.

The Americans' territorial ambitions did not stop at Texas; they wanted the western portion of England's dominion (Oregon) as well as Mexico's California. They took California in a manner similar to the way they conquered Texas, via the migration of American settlers who by 1845 had already spread to both New Mexico and California. Some of them, such as the traders in New Mexico, arrived legally, while others, such as the Mormons in what was then part of California, did not.

AFTER TEXAS, CALIFORNIA

California will, probably, next fall away from the loose adhesion which, in such a country as Mexico, holds a remote province in a slight equivocal kind of dependence on the metropolis. Imbecile and distracted, Mexico never can exert any real government authority over such a country. The impotence of the one and the distance of the other, must make the relation one of virtual independence; unless, by stunting the province of all natural growth, and forbidding that immigration which can alone develop its capabilities and fulfill the purposes of its creation, tyranny may retain a military dominion, which is no government in the legitimate sense of the term.

In the case of California this is now impossible. The Anglo-Saxon foot is already on its borders. Already the advance guard of the irresistible army of Anglo-Saxon emigration has begun to pour down upon it, armed with the plough and the rifle, and marking its trail with schools and colleges, courts and representative halls, mills and meetinghouses. A population will soon be in actual occupation of California, over which it will be idle for Mexico to dream of dominion...

And they [los emigrantes] will have a right to independence—to self-government—to the possession of the homes conquered from the wilderness by their own labors and dangers, sufferings and sacrifices—a better and a truer right than the artificial title of sovereignty in Mexico, a thousand miles distant, inheriting from Spain a title good only against those who have none better. Their right to independence will be the natural right of self-government belonging to any community strong enough to maintain it distinct in position, origin and character, and free from any mutual obligations of membership of a common political body, binding it to others by the duty of loyalty and compact of public faith. This will be their title to independence; and by this title, there can be no doubt that the population now fast

Mass migration to California and Oregon began during the first half of the nineteenth century and was considered to be evidence of Manifest Destiny. In covered wagons, thousands of families crossed the immense wilderness that today forms part of the United States.

This study for a mural in the U.S. Capitol is an allegory of the arrival of the pioneers on the Pacific coast. Wagon trains emerge from the darkness and head toward the glimmering sun and sea. Skeletons and destroyed wagons give testimony to the hardships and dangers the settlers faced in the crossing. Those who made it climb the Rocky Mountains in triumph.

The scene is framed by vignettes featuring the mythological or historical heroes whose feats inspired the American pioneers. There is Moses, Hercules, the Vikings and Christopher Columbus. Below are portraits of the explorers Daniel Boone and William Clark, as well as one of San Francisco Bay. The parchment on which an eagle is perched bears the title of the painting: "Westward the Course of Empire Takes its Way."

streaming down upon California will both assert and maintain that independence.

Whether they will then attach themselves to our Union or not, is not to be predicted with any certainty. Unless the projected railroad across the continent to the Pacific be carried into effect, perhaps they may not; though even in that case, the day is not distant when the empires of the Atlantic and Pacific would again flow together into one, as soon as their inland border should approach each other. But that great work, colossal as appears the plan on its first suggestion, cannot remain long unbuilt.

RAILROADS AND TELEGRAPH WIRES: INSTRUMENTS OF MANIFEST DESTINY

Its necessity for this very purpose of binding and holding together in its iron clasp our fast-settling Pacific region with that of the Mississippi Valley—the natural facility of the route—the ease with which any amount of labor for the construction can be drawn in from the overcrowded populations of Europe, to be paid in the lands made valuable by the progress of the work itself—and its immense utility to the commerce of the world with the whole eastern coast of Asia, alone almost sufficient for the support of such a road—these considerations give assurance that the day cannot be distant which shall witness the conveyance of the representatives from Oregon and California to Washington within less time than a few years ago was devoted to a similar journey by those from Ohio; while the magnetic telegraph will enable the editors of the *San Francisco Union*, the *Astoria Evening Post*, or the *Nootka Morning News*, to set up in type the first half of the President's inaugural before the echoes of the latter half shall have died away beneath the lofty porch of the Capitol, as spoken from his lips.

 Declaration of War

On May 11, 1846, U.S. President James Knox Polk asked Congress for a declaration of war against Mexico; two days later Congress obliged him.

There were both internal and external causes of the war. As of 1844, confrontation between the protectionist free states of the North and the free-trade slave states of the South was out in the open. One way of maintaining the Union was to offer both regions an opportunity for expansion.

Even though neither territory had been part of the United States, President James Knox Polk promised "the re-annexation of Texas" and "the reoccupation of Oregon"—the former to satisfy the demands of the South, the latter those of the North. The treaty he negotiated with Great Britain regarding Oregon in 1846 offered the northern states little comfort since it did not provide them with a port on the Pacific coast. Polk did not wish to add a conflict with England to the one already brewing with Mexico. So he acceded to the deal with Great Britain and resolved to force Congress to declare war on Mexico, so that the territories of New Mexico and California could be conquered along with Texas.

Batralion of Artillery. — 8th Infantry. — 2nd Dragoons. — 7th Inf. — 5th Inf. — Light Artillery. — 3rd Inf. — 4th Infantry. — Town
1st Brigade.   2nd Brigade.   3rd Brigade.
GENL WORTH.   COL TWIGGS LT COL McINTOSH   COL WHISTLER.

Birds-eye view of the

CAMP OF THE ARMY OF OCCUPATION,

COMMANDED BY GENL TAYLOR.

Near Corpus Christi, Texas, (from the North) Oct. 1845.

O*nce Polk decided in favor of annexing Texas, he sent the army to reinforce the Texas militias in case they came to blows with Mexico. General Zachary Taylor was named commander-in-chief of what was known as the Army of Occupation.*

In July 1845, nearly a year before war was declared, an encampment was set up at Corpus Christi on the banks of the Nueces River—inside the territory claimed by both the Texas Republic and Mexico. At the end of that year, the camp held four thousand soldiers, fully outfitted for war. While awaiting battle, many of them died of dysentery due to the pitiful sanitary conditions in the camp. Worst of all for the troops were the rattlesnakes that invaded their tents, and the abrupt changes in weather, which took a heavy toll.

In this illustration, we have a bird's-eye view of the U.S. encampment at Corpus Christi.

U.S. PRESIDENT JAMES KNOX POLK EXPLAINS
WHY WAR WITH MEXICO IS INEVITABLE

[James Knox Polk, Message to Congress on War with Mexico]

Daguerreotype of President James K. Polk, taken circa 1847.

May 11, 1846

The existing state of the relations between the United States and Mexico renders it proper that I should bring the subject to the consideration of Congress...

The strong desire to establish peace with Mexico on liberal and honorable terms, and the readiness of this Government to regulate and adjust our boundary and other causes of difference with that power on such fair and equitable principles as would lead to permanent relations of the most friendly nature, induced me in September last to seek the reopening of diplomatic relations between the two countries... An envoy of the United States repaired to Mexico with full powers to adjust every existing difference... His mission has been unavailing...

THE FAILED MISSION OF MR. JOHN SLIDELL

It now becomes my duty to state more in detail the origin, progress, and failure of that mission... On the 10th of November, 1845, Mr. John Slidell, of Louisiana, was commissioned by me as envoy extraordinary and minister plenipotentiary of the United States to Mexico, and was intrusted with full powers to adjust both the questions of the Texas boundary and of indemnification to our citizens. The redress of the wrongs of our citizens naturally and inseparably blended itself with the question of boundary...

Mr. Slidell arrived at Vera Cruz on the 30th of November, and was courteously received by the authorities of that city. But the Government of General Herrera was then tottering to its fall. The revolutionary party had seized upon the Texas question to effect or hasten its overthrow. Its determination to restore friendly relations with the United States, and to receive our minister to negotiate for the settlement of this

Mexico considered the annexation of Texas to be a violation of the border treaty by which the United States recognized Texas as part of Mexico's territory. Mexico broke off diplomatic relations and declared the annexation to be a causus belli, an "act of war" rather than a "declaration of war." Mexico wished to avoid war and thus received an "envoy" (John Slidell)—several ranks below a minister plenipotentiary—sent to negotiate "the Texas problem." However, Mexico refused to address other controversial topics, such as compensation for damages to U.S. citizens, which as far as Mexico was concerned had been resolved in 1843. For his part, Slidell had instructions to demand the sale of California and New Mexico.

An Irish soldier in the U.S. Army.

Nearly half of General Taylor's army was made up of recently arrived immigrants of whom 24 percent were Irish. Some of them had enlisted before acquiring U.S. citizenship. Many Irish went over to the other side, motivated primarily by their identification with the Mexicans as Catholics and attracted by Mexico's offer of land, which was communicated via leaflets, p. 135–136.

Training of recruits.

question, was violently assailed, and was made the great theme of denunciation against it. The Government of General Herrera, there is good reason to believe, was sincerely desirous to receive our minister; but it yielded to the storm raised by its enemies, and on the 21st of December refused to accredit Mr. Slidell upon the most frivolous pretexts… Five days after the date of Mr. Slidell's note General Herrera yielded the Government to General Paredes without a struggle, and on the 30th of December resigned the Presidency. This revolution was accomplished solely by the army, the people having taken little part in the contest; and thus the supreme power in Mexico passed into the hands of a military leader. Determined to leave no effort untried to effect an amicable adjustment with Mexico, I directed Mr. Slidell to present his credentials to the Government of General Paredes and ask to be officially received by him…

Mr. Slidell, in obedience to my direction, addressed a note to the Mexican minister of foreign relations, under date of the 1st of March last, asking to be received by that Government in the diplomatic character to which he had been appointed. This minister in his reply, under date of the 12th of March, reiterated the arguments of his predecessor, and in terms that may be considered as giving just grounds of offense to the Government and people of the United States denied the application of Mr. Slidell. Nothing therefore remained for our envoy but to demand his passports and return to his own country…

PREPARING FOR WAR

In my message at the commencement of the present session I informed you that upon the earnest appeal both of the Congress and convention of Texas I had ordered an efficient military force to take a position "between the Nueces and the Del Norte." This had become necessary to meet a threatened invasion of Texas by the Mexican forces, for

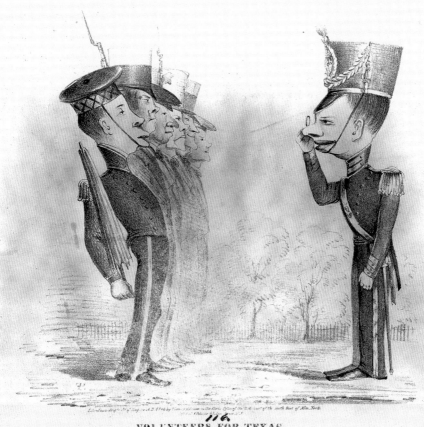

VOLUNTEERS FOR TEXAS

Deposited in the Clerks Office for the So. Dist. of NewYork May 13. 1846.

This cartoon satirizes the widespread enlistment of volunteers for defending Texas. The regular U.S. Army was relatively weak, since low pay and a harsh life fighting Indians made a military career fairly unattractive.

In this drawing, the artist contrasts the gallant figure of an officer with that of the volunteers he is training, by underlining their incorrect posture, home-sewn uniforms (note the variety of hats) and shoddy weaponry. The first in line carries an umbrella in place of a rifle.

During the entire war there were disagreements and fights between regular soldiers and the volunteers, who lacked discipline and military experience.

Even U.S. politicians questioned Polk's claim that the Texas border was the Rio Grande. The congressional resolution by which Texas was annexed to the United States does not mention that border. On this map, the territories of the Mexican states of Tamaulipas and Coahuila clearly extend beyond the Rio Grande, here called the Rio del Norte.

which extensive military preparations had been made. The invasion was threatened solely because Texas had determined, in accordance with a solemn resolution of the Congress of the United States, to annex herself to our Union, and under these circumstances it was plainly our duty to extend our protection over her citizens and soil.

This force was concentrated at Corpus Christi, and remained there until after I had received such information from Mexico as rendered it probable, if not certain, that the Mexican Government would refuse to receive our envoy.

Meantime Texas, by the final action of our Congress, had become an integral part of our Union. The Congress of Texas, by its act of December 19, 1836, had declared the Rio del Norte to be the boundary of that Republic...

Our own Congress had, moreover, with great unanimity, by the act approved December 31, 1845, recognized the country beyond the Nueces as a part of our territory...

It became, therefore, of urgent necessity to provide for the defense of that portion of our country. Accordingly, on the 13th of January last instructions were issued to the general in command of these troops to occupy the left bank of the Del Norte. This river, which is the southwestern boundary of the State of Texas, is an exposed frontier. From this quarter invasion was threatened...

The Army moved from Corpus Christi on the 11th of March, and on the 28th of that month arrived on the left bank of the Del Norte opposite to Matamoras [sic], where it encamped on a commanding position, which has since been strengthened by the erection of fieldworks.

A depot has also been established at Point Isabel... 30 miles in the rear of the encampment...

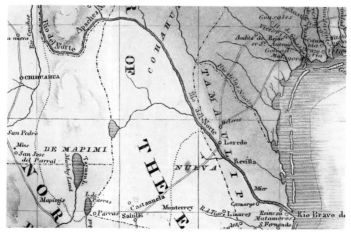

Although it has been said that the war of 1846–1848 was the first war to be photographed, this claim ought to be taken with a certain grain of salt. Due to the long exposures required for daguerreotypes, it was absolutely impossible to photograph the fighting.

This daguerreotype, the only one known to exist of the departure of the U.S. Army, shows volunteers in Exeter, New Hampshire, ready to depart for the war. Dressed in their uniforms and tall hats, these men have thousands of kilometers of marching ahead of them. An invisible detail, perhaps the most surprising, lies in their footgear: both boots were made from the same mold. Only as of 1850 were soldiers' boots made for left and right feet.

Drums lead the way. In so many of the lithographs that illustrate this book, dead soldiers are depicted in the foreground, decorating the battlefield with their drums.

It was the 25th, not the 24th of April 1846 when the first encounter between the armies of Mexico and the United States took place, in the hamlet of Carricitos, Tamaulipas—not in Texas and nowhere near the United States. Even before this skirmish, Polk was preparing to ask Congress for a declaration of war against Mexico. Originally, the text of his speech referred only to Slidell's mission, but on May 8, having received Taylor's report on the skirmish at Carricitos, he added the argument that Mexico had invaded U.S. territory. On May 11, Polk sent Congress his request and two days later Congress declared war on Mexico.

HOSTILITIES BEGIN

The Mexican forces at Matamoras [sic] assumed a belligerent attitude, and on the 12th of April General Ampudia, then in command, notified General Taylor to break up his camp within twenty-four hours and to retire beyond the Nueces River, and in the event of his failure to comply with these demands announced that arms, and arms alone, must decide the question. But no open act of hostility was committed until the 24th of April. On that day General Arista, who had succeeded to the command of Mexican forces, communicated to General Taylor that "he considered hostilities commenced and should prosecute them." A party of dragoons of 63 men and officers were on the same day dispatched from the American camp up the Río del Norte [or Bravo], on its left bank, to ascertain whether the Mexican troops had crossed or were preparing to cross the river, "became engaged with a large body of these troops, and after a short affair, in which some 16 killed and wounded, appear to have been surrounded and compelled to surrender."

Mexico has passed the boundary of the United States, has invaded our territory and shed American blood upon the American soil. She has proclaimed that hostilities have commenced, and that the two nations are now at war.

In this illustration, General Taylor is writing to the War Department the message Washington so anxiously awaited: the fighting had begun.

General Taylor writing to the War Department.

VII   Taylor's Campaign

In June 1845, certain that Texas would embrace annexation to the United States, President Polk ordered General Zachary Taylor to move his troops to the southern banks of the Nueces River, occupying territory claimed by Texas even though it had never been part of that province. Once annexation was ratified in July, he ordered Taylor to advance to the Rio Grande. In December of 1845, after Texas was accepted as a state in the Union, Polk sent Taylor new orders to cross the Rio Grande and occupy the river town of Matamoros and Mier, both in the state of Tamaulipas.

General Taylor reached the Rio Grande at Matamoros on March 28, 1846, and began building Fort Texas, later called Fort Brown. A month later, on April 25, the first confrontation between American and Mexican forces took place in Carricitos. This skirmish was followed by battles at Palo Alto and Resaca de Guerrero. While Taylor advanced toward Monterrey, General Wool occupied the state of Chihuahua and the western part of Coahuila. By January of 1847 the army under Wool's command met up with Taylor's in Saltillo.

General Zachary Taylor was sixty-one years old when President Polk named him commander-in-chief of the Army of Occupation. He had acquired his military experience in the wars against the Indians along the southern frontier, ⚙ p.203. Never had he led an army as large as the one he commanded now. His campaign turned into a chain of unbroken victories that carried him to the White House. His audacity and modesty won the admiration and affection of his soldiers, who called him "Rough and Ready." His popularity can be deduced from the large number of portraits made of him—he was without question the general most often painted in this war.

In this painting we see him with his aides-de-camp in the woods of Santo Domingo, a place near Monterrey the Americans called Walnut Spring. Old Whitey, his famous white stallion, appears in this picture.

THE BATTLES OF PALO ALTO AND RESACA

[Letter of Lieutenant Edmund Kirby Smith to Frances K. Smith]

Matamoros, May 20, 1846

You may now banish all concern for our safety. The war is pretty much over, two thousand men were it our policy could with ease march to the City of Mexico—never were a people so completely cut up—so panic-struck, as the Mexicans now are—all their energies, all their resources have been expended in one grand effort—for more than a year they have been preparing for this occasion. They have staked their all upon the turn of a die, and at one fell swoop they have been laid perfectly helpless. In the battle of the 8th which lasted from 1/2 past two P.M. till dark, the Mexicans acknowledge the loss of 500 killed besides the desertion of a large body of Cavalry and two pieces of Artillery. Our loss was between 40 and 50 killed and wounded. This great disparity in loss is owing to the destructive effect with which our Artillery was served, the schrapnel shells sometimes bursting in the very midst of their columns.

General Taylor realized that the battle had been won by mobile cannon, known as flying artillery. The author of this innovation, Major Ringgold, died from his wounds two days after the battle, and became the first American hero of the war.

On the 9th we attacked them in their entrenchments… We stormed their works, captured all their Artillery, and entirely routed a force of 7,180 regular troops—500 with their priest were drowned in crossing the Río Grande. Our men expected no quarter, and fought with perfect desperation—it was hand to hand conflict—a trial of personal strength—in many instances, where the bayonet failed, the fist even was used—but in moral courage as well as personal strength—we were far their superiors, and have given them a lesson, which ages cannot remove…

THE BASIS OF OUR VICTORY

[Report of Lieutenant Jeremiah Mason Scarritt to Colonel Joseph G. Tottem]

May 12, 1846

There was a great deal of personal gallantry shown and the most enthusiastic and determined spirit both in officers and men. But the light artillery was the back bone of our success. I will not dwell on this fight for it demonstrates only the efficiency of our artillery and the daring of our officers and men.

In this war the Americans used bronze cannons for the first time, which were lighter than the iron ones used by the Mexicans. Mounted on two wheels, these cannons could be moved more quickly, but still required the strength of six horses or oxen to accomplish the task. The effectiveness of the Mexicans' heavy iron cannons depended on the precise calculation of the trajectory of the ball, something military engineers had to determine before the battle began, since changing position during the fighting was a complicated affair. For this reason, Mexico's shells caused few casualties among enemy ranks, while the American artillery was devastating.

The war of 1846–1848 was the first to be covered by correspondents. Outstanding among them was George Wilkins Kendall, whose dispatches arrived quickly and were rarely lost since he sent copies of each story with several different messengers. If one got caught in a skirmish with the enemy, there was always the chance that another would get through. Kendall was present at several battles. After the war he published a book called The War Between the United States and Mexico Illustrated, *which included twelve lithographs of the battles of Taylor and Scott's campaign, all based on illustrations by Carl Nebel. Kendall carefully chose the most dramatic moments to illustrate his book, and these lithographs became perhaps the most well-known images of the war.*

Road to Fort Texas
blocked by Mexican artillery

Dry grass on fire

Mexican cavalry

Mexican army

Flying artillery

American army

Gen. Taylor

Road to
Fort Isabel

The "Battle of Palo Alto" is the first in the series of illustrations by Carl Nebel for the book The War Between the United States and Mexico Illustrated.

The Mexicans chose this battlefield under the mistaken impression that it would favor a cavalry assault, but the ground turned out to be too swampy. The combat soon became an artillery duel, giving the Americans an enormous advantage since they had the more advanced cannons, introduced by Major Ringgold, ✒ p. 217. The oxen that pulled the artillery pieces to the battlefield can be seen at the center.

The plains of Palo Alto were covered with thorny cactuses and weeds so high they reached the shoulders of the troops. The day of the battle was hot and the dry grass seems to have caught fire from the heavy artillery shelling; a number of soldiers died in the fire.

Nebel portrays the moment when the grass between the two armies is burning fiercely. The Americans are taking advantage of the dense smoke to collect the wounded and repair damage.

We can see the American light artillery in the mid-distance and the Mexican cavalry, useless under these circumstances, on the far right. In the right foreground, surrounded by his aides, is General Taylor on his white stallion, Old Whitey.

In this drawing, Nebel was so faithful to detail that some soldiers are seen wearing Panama hats, which they used instead of shakos due to the heat.

The war was a great boon to the press, since people were anxious for news, and it coincided with the invention of the lithograph, which allowed for images to be reproduced easily. Many battlefield pictures based on eyewitness sketches were published immediately in special editions.

Occupation of "Matamoras"

[Letter of Lieutenant Jenks Beaman to C. R. Mallory]

Matamoras, May 29, 1846

After the Battle of the 9th of May we remained on the field so gloriously won until 2 o'clock p.m. of the 12th burying the dead, taking care of the wounded (both of our men and Mexicans) and sending our prisoners & captured property to Point Isabel. We then marched to our old ground opposite Matamoras [sic] for which we had been fighting so hard. Arrived there, we encamped. On the morning of the 17th Genl. Taylor ordered us to be ready to march, at 2 o'clock, up the River to cross, for the purpose of taking Matamoras [sic]. There we thought the enemy would give us a hard fight as the town is strongly fortified, and we had a larger river to cross in flat & small boats to reach it, but about 11 o'clock (before we got under way), a "parley" was sounded from the Mexican side, to which we replied, and a boat with three of Genl. Arista's officers came over. They acknowledged in their Genl.'s name that they had been badly whipped, and had been sent by him to ask for an Armistice—which Genrl Taylor most peremtoraly [sic] declined them… They then asked the Genl. upon what terms he would except [sic] the City if it was surrendered to him. He replied, "That they must leave all their arms & munitions of war, and all public property of all kinds, belonging to their government, excepting provisions enough to take them to Monterey". They promised him an answer at 3 o'clock, till which time he waited and the answer not arriving, we commenced our march up the river and marched three miles [and] halted, and as soon as it was dark commenced crossing our army. At day light on the morning of the 18th, we had several pieces of Artillery & 600 men over —and were crossing the rest. About 8 o'clock the Alcalda, Prefect &c [Civil authorities] came and asked to see Genl. Taylor—and then reported that Genl. Arista and Army had the night previous evacuated the city…

Occupied on May 17, 1846, Matamoros remained under U.S. control until the end of the war and was used as a rearguard and disembarkation point for new troops.

March to Camargo

[John R. Kenly, "The Maryland Volunteer"]

Taylor's army remained in Camargo from July to September 1846. The sanitary conditions in the town were horrendous, and nearly fifteen hundred men died of dysentery and dehydration, almost as many as the total combat casualties during the entire war. Finally, on September 9, Taylor began the march to Monterrey.

August 15, 1846

Left Matamoras [sic], to march with the brigade to Camargo… by what was called the mountain road.

Our march was over desert rather than a mountainous country; from the time we left the Río Grande at Matamoras [sic] until we struck the San Juan River on the 23d of August, not a stream, rivulet, brook, or spring, did we see or hear of, the only water to be had being found in ponds or tanks as they were called, in which rain-water had been collected for the use of the cattle.

We suffered very much, and our march was more that of a routed army of stragglers than the advance of a well-organized brigade.

We marched in the middle of the day, with a burning sun overhead, and burning sand beneath our feet; not a drop of rain had fallen in this section of the country for months, and the dust raised by the tramp of so many men hung over our heads with smothering denseness from which there was no escape… At noon of the third day… I fell in the road utterly broken down, and I saw men toward night frantically digging with their bayonets in the dry bed of a water-course in the vain hope of finding water beneath the surface, but all was as dry as the arid country around.

This drawing shows American tents and cannon in the main plaza of Camargo.

Grand Plaza, Camargo.

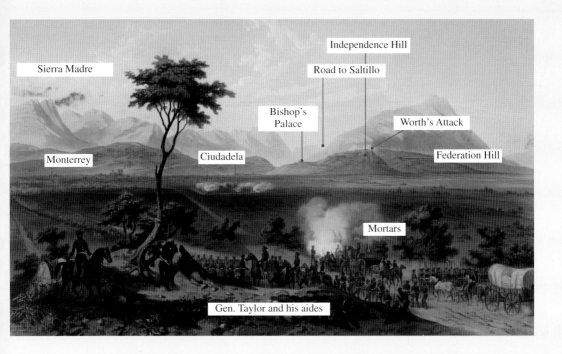

On September 19, General Taylor and his army reached the outskirts of Monterrey and began to implement his strategy for conquering the city. The battle lasted three days. Taylor's troops attacked Monterrey from the east and the west.

This drawing by C. Nebel 🔫 p. 168, sums up the events in a panoramic view:

- At a fork in the road northeast of the city, Taylor can be seen on horseback, surrounded by his aides, directing the assault on the city from the east.
- At the center of the drawing is the Ciudadela, a well-built fort defending the city's northern flank. The Americans decided not to attack it, since it was the best fortified point in Monterrey.
- In the distance, to the right of the Ciudadela, can be seen Independence and Federation Hills, each of them fortified. On the lower flanks is the Bishop's Palace. Plumes of smoke indicate an attack on Worth's troops who lie hidden in the valleys.
- Behind the Bishop's Palace is a pass through the Sierra Madre, where the road to Saltillo and Rinconada runs, now cut off by Worth.

The "Capture of Monterrey"
by Carl Nebel for the book
The War Between the United
States and Mexico Illustrated,
p 219.

THE MOVEMENT OF WORTH'S FORCES
TO THE WEST OF MONTERREY

[Letter of Lieutenant Edmund Bradford to Caroline Bradford]

Taylor split up his forces and ordered the troops under Worth's command to attack Monterrey from the west. The lithograph on the opposite page shows American soldiers advancing along the road to Saltillo. It is the morning of September 21. The skirmish has just finished. In the background, the last horsemen ride off through the trees; on the road lie the dead, abandoned. A similar scene must have been contemplated by Lieutenant Bradford, one of Worth's soldiers and author of the letter published here. On the left side of the drawing is Independence Hill, on the right Federation Hill. The fighting that Bradford mentions took place on both hills.

Monterrey, September 27, 1846

Now that I am somewhat settled I will try and give you some description of the battles. On the 19th the whole Army arrived in sight of Monterrey and encamped about 2 1/2 miles from the town. Several reconnoitering parties were sent out in different directions to ascertain the position of the enemy... The next morning the 1st Division... were ordered to take with them two days provisions and one blanket for each man. The Division was under the command of Genl. Worth. ...in our advance we could see there was a battery of the enemy planted on the top of a very high hill which commanded the road on which we were marching. Below the battery and on the same hill there was a large fortified building called the Bishop's palace. Beyond this was another hill about the same height with a battery on the top, and a stone fort lower down, both of which commanded the road... Just as the sun was setting a heavy shower of rain came up which drenched us to the skin and in this condition we were obliged to remain all night...

The next morning, the 21st, we rose before day light, and commenced our march. We now knew we were to storm the two heights and take the guns of the enemy, thereby cutting off their retreat by the Saltillo road... About 7 o'clock A.M. we heard a firing of musketry in our advance between the Mexicans and our skirmishers.... I could distinctly see the enemy running in every direction. In the charge we passed over the dead bodies of several men and horses. Lances, pistols, holsters &c were lying in every direction. The force of the enemy was estimated at 300 cavalry supported by a column of Infantry. As they retired, our batteries opened on them with shells, making great havoc. I have since ascertained one single shell killed and wounded thirty Mexicans...

CAPTURE OF FEDERATION HILL

Three companies of the Arty Batn and two companies of Texans were ordered to join Capt. Smith for the purpose of storming the 2nd hill. The command started about 12 1/2 o'clock P.M... About 1/4 2 o'clock we saw the firing commencing by our troops and the Mexicans running up the hill. We then raised such a shout as I have hardly ever heard. In a few minutes Capt. Smith was on the top. He had followed them so fast that they had not had time to carry off one of their guns. This gun was immediately captured and turned on them. The very first shot made with it struck the other gun (which they had placed in the fort) directly on the muzzle breaking it off. Just at the [sic, that] time the 2nd Brigade charged the Fort and drove the enemy from it. The guns were now turned on the castle on the opposite hill and an incessant firing kept up between the two forts...

CAPTURE OF INDEPENDENCE HILL

Worth took two points that were essential for Monterrey's defense: Independence and Federation hills. Below Independence Hill lay another smaller rise with a fortified building called the Bishop's Palace, where gory fighting took place, as depicted in this lithograph.

On the morning of the 22nd Capt. Scott's, Lieut. Ayers and my company of the Arty. Batn., three companies of the 8th Infy and the Texans received orders to storm the 1st hill and castle. We started at 3 o'clock in the morning and reached the foot of the hill just as the day began to appear. I suppose we were discovered from the castle as four rockets were thrown up at different times. As we commenced ascending the hill, a heavy fog enveloped the top of it, which prevented the enemy from discovering our exact position. When we came within fifty yards of the summit, the enemy commenced their fire; our men did not return it until we were almost on the top; we then opened our fire and charged at the same time. The enemy retreated very rapidly and we pursued them half way to the castle and the[n] came back to our position on the summit. We planted the American flag amid a shower of bullets from the castle and gave it three cheers…

Capture of the Bishop's Palace

After the firing had been continued an hour, we heard the sound of the trumpets of their cavalry who were coming up the hill to charge us… I could see a body of lancers coming up. We immediately fired on them and made them retreat; the company on my left charged down the hill towards the castle followed by mine. In running down, I could see the top of the castle lined with men. Lieut. Ayers of the 3rd Arty was 1st officer in the castle, and I was the second. Lieut. Ayers, handed down the colors. The men lined the castle in an instant, and commenced firing at the retreating Mexicans… In a very short time they had all disappeared… The American flag was hoisted on the earth immediately…

The day after the capture of the Bishop's Palace, Captain Whiting made a sketch of the building as viewed from Independence Hill. On the far left of the drawing, in the distance to the north of the city, smoke can be seen rising from the Ciudadela, the last bastion defending Monterrey.

MARCHING INTO TOWN

The next day, the 23d we marched into the town; we advanced very cautiously expecting every moment to be fired on from the houses. My company with two others formed the reserve—as we went along we broke the doors of every house we passed so as to be able to get into them, in case we should be obliged to retreat.

When we had penetrated the city about a mile, the enemy opened on us with grape and musketry. The men were immediately put in the houses, and then the work of cutting from house to house commenced. We seized on all the crowbars and pickaxes we could find. The stone of which the houses are built is so soft that we could cut through a wall two feet thick in 20 minutes. By dark our troops had advanced to within one square of the main plaza, where the cathedral is…

View of the plaza of Monterrey from a rooftop, drawn by Captain Whiting. This drawing shows the important defensive features of such rooftops, with their walls and rainspout openings which could be used as gunports. Some of the stones carried up to throw at the invaders can be seen still there. On the left of the plaza are the Mexican cannons captured by the enemy, p. 74.

TRUCE

The next morning the 24th the firing commenced as usual. About 8 A.M. a flag of truce was sent in by Genl. Ampudia to Genl. Taylor asking to capitulate. During the whole day Genl. Taylor and Genl. Ampudia were agreeing on the terms… At 3 o'clock P.M. Genl. Taylor made his last offer and gave Ampudia one hour to consider it. The Genl. agreed that the Mexicans should march with their muskets, sabres and six pieces of field artillery. At the end of the hour we all thought we should be obliged to commence fighting again, but when the flag returned we were told that Ampudia had agreed to the terms. That night at 10 o'clock the stipulations were signed. By them, all hostilities are to cease for eight weeks or until the two Genls. were able to hear from their respective countries. Neither Army is to advance beyond a certain line half way between this and Saltillo.

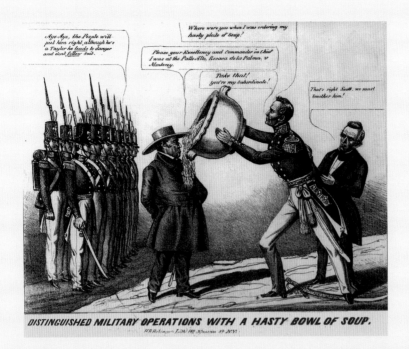

DISTINGUISHED MILITARY OPERATIONS WITH A HASTY BOWL OF SOUP.

According to the cease-fire, ☛ p. 75, agreed between Generals Taylor and Ampudia, hostilities were suspended for two months. Polk, impatient to end the war quickly and also to put an end to Taylor's growing popularity, decided to remove Taylor and bestow command on General Scott, whom he ordered to pursue a new line of attack from Veracruz toward Mexico City.

This satirical cartoon refers to events at the beginning of the war, when Polk passed over Scott, then head of the army, and named Taylor to lead the U.S. forces against Mexico. In response to Polk's letter informing him of the decision, Scott answered beginning with the phrase, "[Your] letter... received at about 6 p.m., as I sat down to take a hasty plate of soup..." The soup anecdote became a constant theme of the ridicule directed against Scott. In this illustration he can be seen emptying an enormous bowl of soup on Taylor, while asking, "Where were you when I was ordering my hasty plate of soup?" Taylor responds, "Please your Excellency and Commander in Chief, I was at the Palo Alto, Resaca de la Palma and Monterey." Behind Scott, Polk is egging him on, "That's right Scott, we must smother him!"

The story of a young Mexican woman who died while helping the wounded of both armies inspired several American writers to compose poems, songs and plays about "The Maid of Monterrey."

A MEXICAN WOMAN
WHOSE GENEROSITY KNEW NO ENEMIES

["Touching Incidents," *Louisville Journal*]

September 19, 1846

Hungry and cold I crept to one corner of the fort to get in the sunshine and at the same time to shelter myself from the bombs that were flying thick around me. I looked out, and, some two or three hundred yards from the fort, I saw a Mexican female carrying water and food to the wounded men of both armies. I saw her lift the head of one poor fellow, give him water, and then take her handkerchief from her own head and bind up his wounds; attending one or two others in the same way, she went back for more food and water. As she was returning I heard the crack of one or two guns, and she, poor good creature, fell; after a few struggles all was still—she was dead! I turned my eyes to heaven and thought, "Oh God, and this is war!" I cannot believe but that the shot was an accidental one. The next day, passing into another fort, I passed her dead body. It was lying on its back, with the bread and broken gourd containing a few drops of water. We buried her amid showers of grape and round shot, occasionally dodging a shell or twelve pounder, and expecting every moment to have another grave to dig for one of ourselves.

Once the cease-fire was lifted on November 16, 1846, Taylor occupied Saltillo. The troops under the command of General Ampudia had abandoned the city to join the forces Santa Anna was concentrating in San Luis Potosí. Saltillo became the operational headquarters for the Northern Army, since it allowed the Americans to control the only road which could handle artillery. Nevertheless, the American force was seriously weakened by the transfer of its best troops to Veracruz.

However, Taylor was unexpectedly reinforced by four hundred volunteers who arrived under General Wool's command. They can be seen posing for this daguerreotype on Calle Real in Saltillo.

Near Saltillo lies a mountain pass called La Angostura, and it was there that General Taylor decided to confront Santa Anna, who was marching in from San Luis Potosí with a force nearly three times as large as the American one. Closed off by steep mountainsides, the rough terrain offered the Americans strategic advantages: the deep gorges would make it impossible for the fearsome Mexican cavalry to attack and would also slow the advance of the Mexican infantry. The final battle in the northwest was known as the Battle of La Angostura or Buena Vista, in reference to the nearby hacienda San Juan de la Buena Vista, where the American troops bivouacked.

FROM A SKETCH TAKEN ON THE SPOT BY MAJOR EATON, AID DE CAMP TO GEN'. TAYLOR.

BATTL

LITH. PUB.& PRINTED IN COLORS BY H.R. ROBINSON, 142 NASSAU S.T.

OF BUENA VISTA.

The Battle of Buena Vista or La Angostura lasted two days. At the very moment when the American Army was on the verge of defeat, Santa Anna ordered a retreat. In the United States, Taylor was acclaimed as the "Hero of Buena Vista."

A dead soldier's body is looted.

THE BATTLE OF BUENA VISTA (LA ANGOSTURA)

[Letter of General Brigadier John E. Wool to Major W. W. S. Bliss]

Agua Nueva, Coahuila, March 4, 1847
About 9 o'clock, our picket stationed at the Encantada, three and a half miles distant, discovered the enemy advancing. Word was immediately despatched to the commanding general at Saltillo, and I ordered the troops at Buena Vista forthwith to be brought forward. Captain Washington's battery was posted across the road, protected on its left by a commanding eminence, and on its right by deep gullies…

The enemy was now seen pushing his infantry on his right towards the heights, showing evidently an intention to turn to our left in order to get possession of the key to our position—the eminence immediately on the left of Washington's artillery—and thus open a free passage to Saltillo…

At 2 o'clock, as the enemy's light infantry were moving up the side of the mountain and in the ravines, they opened a fire on our riflemen from a large howitzer posted in the road; and between 3 and 4 o'clock, Col. Marshall engaged the Mexican infantry on the side of the mountain, and the firing continued on both sides at intervals until dark…

The troops remained under arms during the night in the position they occupied at the close of the day… The enemy had succeeded during the night, and early in the morning, in gaining the very top of the mountain, and in passing to our left and rear…

At 8 o'clock, a large body of the enemy, composed of infantry, lancers, and three pieces of artillery, moved down the high road upon our center…

The rapidity and precision of the fire of the artillery scattered and dispersed this force in a few minutes with considerable loss on their side and little or none on our own.

This astonishingly detailed lithograph is made from a sketch done by Major Joseph Horace Eaton, aide-de-camp of General Taylor during the Battle of Buena Vista. It offers a good picture of the strategic topographic features of the battleground: in the background the mountains blocked any possibility of military action from that side, while to the left sudden deep gorges kept the Mexican cavalry from attacking.

The illustration portrays the field situation on the afternoon of February 23:

• Captain Washington's battery controls the Saltillo–San Luis Potosí road.

• Along the base of the mountains we can see the Mexican infantry and cavalry moving to outflank their enemy on the left.

• In the center of the picture, on the first plateau surrounded by gorges, stand six horsemen. The third from the left, mounted on a white horse, is General Taylor, protected by the infantry regiment under the command of Henry Clay, Jr. Beyond them lies O'Brien's battery, and on the other side Bragg's.

This moment is shortly before the fighting turned brutal. Santa Anna is gathering his troops at the bottom of the gorge; Taylor will send his regiment there; Captain Henry Clay, Jr. will die in the assault, p. 240.

Henry Clay, Jr., son of the Kentucky senator, died in the battle of Buena Vista, ☞ p.301. In Eaton's lithograph he is still on horseback leading the Second Volunteer Regiment of the Kentucky Infantry. The illustration above captures the moment of his death and carries the following description: "When shot down a second time, he drew a brace of pistols from his belt, handed them to Capt. Cutter, and requested him to deliver them to his Father, with this message: 'Say to him he gave them to me, and that I have done all that I can with them and now return them to him.'"

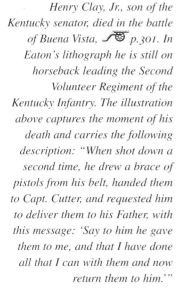

THE LOSS OF THE CANYON

In connexion with this movement, a heavy column of the enemy's infantry and cavalry and [the] battery of the side of the mountain moved against our left, which was held by… 2d Indiana regiment, and Lieutenant O'Brien's section of artillery, by whom the enemy's fire was warmly returned… The infantry, however, instead of advancing, retired in disorder; and, in spite of the utmost efforts of their general and his officers, left the artillery unsupported, and fled the field of battle… Lieutenant O'Brien, being unsupported by any infantry, and not being able to make head against the heavy column bearing down upon him with a destructive fire, fell back on the center, leaving one of his pieces, at which all the cannoneers and horses were either killed or disabled, in the hands of the enemy…

Daguerreotype of the grave of Henry Clay, Jr.

Mexican infantry

O'Brien's cannons

Bragg to the rescue

Gen. Taylor and his aides

THE TURNING POINT OF THE BATTLE

The Mexican column was now in rapid retreat, pursued by our artillery, infantry, and cavalry, and notwithstanding the effect of our fire they succeeded, for the greater part, favored by the configuration of the ground, in crossing the bed of the torrent and regaining the plateau from which they had previously descended. While this was taking place on the left and rear of our line, our center, under the immediate eye of the commanding general, although it suffered much in killed and wounded, stood firm and repelled every attempt made upon it.

The Mexican forces being now concentrated on the left, made a bold move to carry our centre by advancing with his whole strength from the left and front. At this moment Lieutenant O'Brien was ordered to advance his battery and check this movement. He did so in a bold and gallant manner, and maintained his position until his supporting force was

Kendall asked Carl Nebel to sketch the final and most dramatic fighting of the Battle of Buena Vista. In the foreground General Taylor can be seen on his white horse, together with his aides-de-camp; across from them Captain O'Brien's batteries seek to hold off an enormous contingent of Mexican infantrymen. O'Brien has already lost one battery. From the right, Captain Bragg gallops headlong into the heart of the battle to rescue O'Brien. From the left, infantry regiments advance to save both the commander-in-chief and the battle.

Carl Nebel's "The Battle of Buena Vista."

completely routed by an immensely superior force. His men and horses being nearly [all] killed and wounded, he found himself under the necessity of abandoning his pieces and they fell into the hands of the enemy… This was the hottest as well as the most critical part of the action; and at the moment when our troops were about giving way before the greatly superior force with which they were contending, the batteries of Captains Sherman and Bragg coming up most opportunely from the rear, and under the immediate direction of the commanding general, by a well directed fire checked and drove back with great loss the enemy who had come close upon the muzzles of their pieces… This was the last great effort of General Santa Anna; the firing, however, between the enemy's artillery and our own continued until night.

During the long months of their stay in the north of Mexico, the Americans established many relationships with Mexicans, especially with those women who followed the army. This illustration by a grateful soldier, Samuel Chamberlain, testifies to their importance—here, they can be seen collecting the wounded after a battle. Several of them carry the wounded on their shoulders, others bear stretchers, still others help the wounded on to mules.

When the war ended, some of them went to the United States with the troops. A harrowing fate awaited those who did not: they were executed as traitors to the fatherland.

Between November 1846 and February 1847, U.S. forces encamped on the outskirts of Saltillo. Conflicts between the soldiers and the civilian population led to great tragedies. On February 10, near Agua Nueva, the cruelest killings occurred: the Arkansas Frontier Mountain Voluntaries, known as the "Racksackers," found dozens of civilians hiding in a cave. They set about killing them by scalping, hacking off their hair with the skin attached. Many bleeding heads can be seen in this drawing. In the center, a soldier hoists a scalp. The custom of scalping was probably copied from the Indians of the northeast.

Samuel Chamberlain, who went to the cave with another group of soldiers to put an end to this macabre episode, left us this drawing and the following description:

"A fire was burning on the rocky floor, and threw a faint flickering light on the horrors around, nearly thirty Mexicans lay butchered on the floor,

most of them scalped. Pools of blood filled the crevices and congealed in clots. A sickening smell filled the place."

The Conquest of New Mexico

On May 13, 1846, after having signed the law which declared war on Mexico, President Polk met with his cabinet to discuss the formal declaration and the letter that would be sent to U.S. diplomatic missions abroad. For the latter, Secretary of State James Buchanan prepared a draft which explicitly stated that the United States had no territorial ambitions beyond the Rio Grande. When Polk read it, he affirmed that capturing Mexican territory was the only way to obtain payment of the debts still pending from claims acknowledged in the Convention of 1843. And he said he was prepared "to meet the war...which some or all the Powers of Christiandom might wage, and that I would stand and fight until the last man among us fell in the conflict...sooner than give the pledge...that we would not if we could...acquire...any other part of the Mexican Territory which we desired." Polk's words left no doubt that the Americans' purpose in this war was not to defend their claims to the territory between the Nueces River and the Rio Grande, but to conquer as much of Mexico as they wished. In fact, just their assertion that Texas should reach the Rio Grande implied taking over nearly half of the territory of New Mexico.

That very day, Secretary of War Marcy ordered Colonel Stephen W. Kearny, commander of the regiment based at Fort Leavenworth in Missouri, to march to Santa Fe, New Mexico, "to protect our traders."

SANTA FE.

*I*n this drawing, Santa Fe may appear insignificant, but located as it was on the route that linked St. Louis, Missouri, with Los Angeles on the Pacific coast, and Chihuahua in what is now the north of Mexico, the city acquired enormous economic importance after 1821 when Mexico opened up to trade with the United States. At the beginning of the war, President Polk ordered Stephen W. Kearny to occupy it as soon as possible. After a forced march of eight hundred miles (about twelve hundred kilometers), Kearny took Santa Fe without firing a shot.

The lithograph shows Mexicans returning to an occupied city, as evidenced by the Stars and Stripes flying in the center and on the hill overlooking the town.

TOWARD SANTA FE

[Letter of Andrew T. MacClure to his wife]

Río Viguita, August 22, 1846
You will see by the date of this letter that we have at length arrived at the long sought for place—Santa Fee [sic]. On the 18th, Genl. Kearney [sic] took formal possession of the capital of the province without having fired a single gun…

Our march…was the same unvaried monotony until [sic] within five days travel of Santa Fee [sic]—when the whole army was thrown into a state of excitement by the arrival of a flag and letter from Gov. Armijo. In the letter the Gov. informed Genl. K. "that he had advanced as far into the Mexican territory as he could with safety—and that he called upon him to retire immediately—but if he did not that he would meet him at the Vigas a stream about 20 miles off and give him battle." To this Genl. K. made a characteristic reply, that he would meet Gov. A. at the Vigas. You can well immagine [sic] the excitement created in camp by the interchange of civilities. Every one expected a fight [for] certain. And sure enough the next day the enemy advanced to within three miles of our encampment determined to oppose our passage through a narrow gap in the mountains.

On the next morning after this disposition of the enemies forces, Genl. K. marched out of his camp, in battle order, both himself and every man in the army, from the nature of the ground and reported strength of the enemy (about 2,000 strong) anticipating a bloody battle… We each of us stripped off our coats, shouldered our Rifles, and marched off—at double quick time to enter upon our career as soldiers.

As I said before, the enemy were posted at a gap in the mountains about three miles from our camp on the direct road to Santa Fee [sic]. This gap is formed by two mountains of the same range approaching to within 150 feet of each other suddenly terminating in [a] steep precipice—leaving a gorge through which the road passed… Genl. determined

General Kearny

When he was given the task of conquering Santa Fe, Stephen W. Kearny was fifty-one years old and had spent thirty of those years in Indian territory on the Great Plains. His march from Fort Leavenworth is tinged with heroism: He led 1,458 people and an enormous contingent of animals (459 horses, 3,658 mules, 14,904 oxen) across a wilderness that was a semi-desert—and all of them had to eat and drink. Later, he left Santa Fe and marched on to California. Given the distance he traveled,  p. 160, we might well think he was made of steel, but like so many other American officers he fell prey to dysentery and died in 1848.

that the infantry should scale the mountain on the right, pass in rear of the enemy, and cut off their retreat. So as the order was given we commenced the ascent of an allmost [sic] perpendicular mountain side, covered with rocks, about 400 feet high, and after hard puffing and scratching gained the summit. We immediately commenced our descent on the other side and in a few minutes were in the valley below, formed the company, marched up to the pass—and to our chagrin and surprise found it occupied by the dragoons—the enemy having suddenly recollected—

> that he that runs away
> will live to fight another day...

Thus ended the first great battle of this campaign.

SANTA FE IS CAPTURED WITHOUT RESISTANCE

To reach Santa Fe, Kearny made his men march thirty-two miles (about fifty kilometers) per day. Not all could withstand the pace; both men and beasts fell by the wayside. Lucky for them, they did not have to fight along the way, since the territory was thinly populated and the few Mexican troops present always retreated.

...we learned that Gov. Armijo with a force of 3,000 men occupied the narrow Pass between that point and Santa Fee [sic] and the only gap in the mountains through which it was possible for our army to pass—the pass being about twenty miles from Santa Fee [sic]...on the 17th encamped with 4 miles of the pass. Here again we expected to have had a battle, but on the evening of the 17th there arose a contest in the camp of the enimy [sic] as to the supreme command, the result of which was that the enimy [sic] dispersed without attempting to oppose our passage.

On the 18th we struck tents and marched off not knowing certainly w[h]ether we should have a fight or not... As we advanced, the mountains seemed to be gradually approaching each other until at length they seemed to have placed themselves in front of us, an impassable barrier, hundreds of feet in height and almost perpendicular. Here by turning the point of a mountain you are suddenly thrown into a pass through which the road was just wide enough for a waggon [sic] to pass or four men abreast...each side of the pass having walls of rock, perpendicular

Rout of the Mexicans.

hundreds of feet high—and entirely impossible for us to ascend. It was at this pass the enemy had made preparations to resist our passage, and it seems to me if they had availed themselves of the natural advantages of the place, thrown up a barricade, and upon it planted a battery—with one sixth of their force they could have effectually resisted every effort of ours to pass—but instead of doing so, although they doubled us in numbers, and were possessed of five excellent pieces of artillery under the effe[c]ts of fear and discord...

That evening as I have said in the first part of my epistle we took peaceble [sic] possession of Santa Fee [sic].

THE TAOS REBELLION

[Dispatch of Colonel Sterling Price to General Roger Jones]

Taos, February 15, 1847

I have the honor to submit to you a short account of the recent revolution in this territory, and a detailed report of the operations of the forces under my command consequent upon the rebellion.

About the 15th of December last I received information of an attempt to excite the people of this territory against the American government. This rebellion was headed by Thomas Ortiz and Diego Archuleta. An officer, formerly in the Mexican service, was seized, and on his person was found a list of all the disbanded Mexican soldiers in the vicinity of Santa Fe. Many other persons, supposed to be implicated, were arrested, and a full investigation proved that many of the most influential persons in the northern part of this territory were engaged in the rebellion. All attempts to arrest Ortiz and Archulet proved unsuccessful, and these rebels have, without doubt, escaped in the direction of Chihuahua. After the arrest above mentioned, and flight of Ortiz and Archuleta, the rebellion appeared to be suppressed; but this appearance was deceptive.

After declaring New Mexico to be part of the American Union—as a territory not a state—Kearny named as governor Charles Bent, a trader who had married a wealthy Mexican landowner. Everything seemed to indicate that the conquest of New Mexico had come off without a hitch, and Kearny marched confidently off to California. However, in the middle of December 1846, rumblings of discontent among the people of New Mexico rose to the surface. In Santa Fe, a group conspired to challenge American rule, but word leaked out and the conspiracy was stifled.

Guerrilla fighters of the Mexican North.

In January 1847, New Mexicans in the town of Taos rose up with the support of the Pueblo Indians. The rebels executed officials of the imposed American regime, among them governor-designate Brent. The American military leader, Sterling Price, crushed the insurrection. In a letter, fragments of which are published here, Price sums up the events of which he was the protagonist. By February 1847, the conquest of New Mexico by the United States had been consummated.

On the 14th of January, Governor Bent left this city for Taos. On the 19th of the same month, this valuable officer, together with five other persons, were seized at Don [sic San] Fernando de Taos by the Pueblos and Mexicans, and were murdered in the most inhuman manner the savages could devise. On the same day, seven Americans were murdered at the Arroya Honda, and two others on the Río Colorado. It appeared to be the object of the insurrectionists to put to death every American and every Mexican who had accepted office under the American government.

News of these events reached me on the 20th of January; and letters from the rebels calling upon the inhabitants of the Río Abajo for aid, were intercepted. It was now ascertained that the enemy was approaching this city, and that their force was continually being increased by the inhabitants of the towns along their line of march [sic]. In order to prevent the enemy from receiving any further reinforcements in that manner, I determined to meet them as soon as possible.

On the 1st of February, we reached the summit of the Taos mountain, which was covered with snow to the depth of two feet; and on the 2d, quartered at a small village called Río Chicito [sic, Chiquito] in the entrance of the valley of Taos. The marches of the 1st and 2d were through deep snow. Many of the men were frostbitten…

On the 3d, I marched through Don [sic] Fernando de Taos, and finding that the enemy had fortified themselves in the Pueblo de Taos, proceeded to that place. I found it a place of great strength, being surrounded by adobe walls and strong picked. Within the enclosure and near the northern and southern walls, arose two large buildings of irregular pyramidal form to the height of seven or eight stories. Each of these buildings was capable of sheltering five or six hundred men...the large church of the town was situated in the north-western angle... After having reconnoitered the town, I selected the western flank of the church as the point of attack; and about 2 o'clock, P.M., Lieutenant Dyer was ordered to open his battery at the distance of about 250 yards. A fire was kept up by the 6-pounder and the howitzers for about two hours and a half, when, as the ammunition wagon had not yet come up, and the troops were suffering from cold and fatigue, I returned to Don [sic] Fernando.

Early on the morning of the 4th, I again advanced upon Pueblo... The batteries opened upon the town at nine o'clock, A.M. At 11 o'clock, finding it impossible to breach the walls of the church with the 6-pounder and howitzers, I determined to storm that building... Small holes had been cut into the western wall, and shells were thrown in by hand, doing good execution... The enemy during all this time kept up a destructive fire upon our troops. About half-past three o'clock the 6-pounder was run up within sixty yards of the church, and after ten rounds, one of the holes which had been cut with the axes, was widened into a practicable breach. The gun was now run up within ten yards of the wall—a shell was thrown in—three rounds of grape were poured in the breach. The storming party...entered and took possession of the church without oppposition. The interior was filled with dense smoke... A few of the enemy were seen in the gallery where an open door admitted the air, but they retired without firing a gun...

It was now night, and our troops were quietly quartered in the houses which the enemy had abandoned. On the next morning the enemy sued for peace, and thinking the severe loss they had sustained would prove a salutary lesson, I granted their supplication, on the condition that they should deliver up to me Tomas [Baca]—one of their principal men, who had instigated and been actively engaged in the murder of Governor Bent and others...

The ruins of Casas Grandes in Chihuahua. The high walls give an idea of the sort of constructions built by the Pueblo Indians.

Once the rebellion was crushed, its leaders were tried. The Taos parish priest, Antonio José Martínez, considered the trial unfair because "neither the prosecutor nor the attorney for the defense spoke English yet the prisoners were informed of their [death] sentence in that language... Not to mention the quality of the jury—ignorant men corrupted by passion." Of the fifteen accused of "treason," six were found guilty and hanged.

After Santa Fe was conquered, part of Stephen W. Kearny's army, led by Alexander W. Doniphan, marched to Chihuahua. Their objective was to reinforce the division led by General John Ellis Wool, which however had not yet reached the city. Doniphan left with over 900 soldiers, all volunteers with no military experience (Doniphan himself was a lawyer) and 300 wagons. Doniphan's troops walked over 3,000 kilometers through semi-desert, suffering from the harsh climate, the scarcity of food and their own exhaustion. Even so, they won two important battles at Brazitos and Sacramento.

After occupying Chihuahua, they made another long march to Buena Vista, where they arrived after a bloody battle had ended. From there, the soldiers were sent to Matamoros. In all, after leaving Fort Leavenworth, they had marched about 8,800 kilometers. It should surprise no one that none of these soldiers re-enlisted.

This lithograph of the battle that took place on the banks of the Sacramento River is made from a sketch by soldier Elihu Baldwin Thomas, who took part in the fighting there. Doniphan's troops found good fortifications built by General José A. Heredia. Thomas chose the moment when the American artillery opened fire on the Mexican cavalry.

The Conquest of California

*T*he United States' desire to acquire California was as longstanding as its yearning for Texas. For many years Americans had been fishing and especially whaling off the California coast. During the recession of 1837, the flow of migrants to the Pacific increased. The U.S. minister plenipotentiary in Mexico, Joel R. Poinsett, was the first to suggest buying the territory, and later on his successor Anthony Butler openly proposed a deal. On that occasion, the U.S. government linked the sale of California to claims for damages suffered by U.S. citizens.

In 1842, during negotiations over the northern border with Great Britain, U.S. Secretary of State Daniel Webster told his British counterpart that the United States would accept the 49th parallel as the border if Britain would lean on Mexico to sell them California. By coincidence, that same year Commodore Jones, believing that war had been declared on Mexico, occupied the port of Monterey in California. Although the U.S. government later apologized, Jones's action brought U.S. intentions into the open.

When President Polk declared war on Mexico, taking California was one of his objectives.

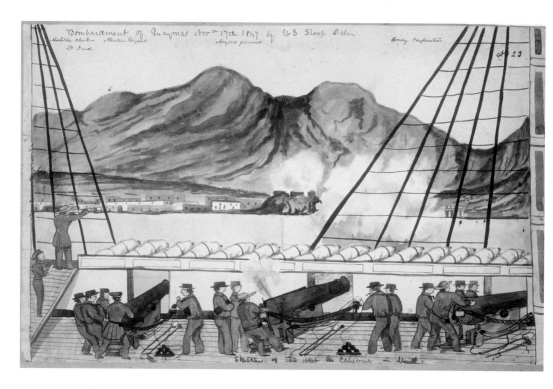

In July 1846, the U.S. Navy bombarded the California coast. American settlers, incited by the recently arrived John Charles Fremont, rebelled and proclaimed the Republic of California. Californians, however, rose up to fight against this takeover. Lacking soldiers, Commodore Robert F. Stockton decided to send his sailors ashore to quell the rebellion and support Kearny's troops, who were due in soon from Santa Fe.

Thanks to one of those sailors, artillery officer William H. Meyers, there are drawings of the main battles in California: San Gabriel, San Pascual and La Mesa.

The illustration above shows the attack of the warship Dale, *on which Meyers served. In addition to the artillery maneuvers, the drawing portrays a soldier writing or sketching—perhaps a self-portrait of Meyers himself.*

OCCUPATION OF THE CALIFORNIA COAST

[Letter of Lieutenant Archibald McRae to John McRae]

San Francisco, October 25, 1846

The Naval Forces under Commodore Sloat landed in the face of a hot sun and took possession of Monterey and San Francisco, meeting with no other loss than that of two men who took the first opportunity of getting drunk, and quietly stowing themselves away in a pig sty, while the military force galloped up and down the country on horse back proclaiming every where that they were looking for Genl. Castro and his Army; this was done so that Castro might have no idea of their movements and therefore would not guard against a surprise.

The war having progressed so far the aged hero Commodore Sloat thinking that he had gained laurels enough gave up command of the squadron to Commodore Stockton and proceeded to the U.S…. After Commodore Stockton took command he dispatched the vessels down the coast and took possession of all the towns on the sea coast of upper California; besides which he arrested the French Consul at Monterey in consequence of his writing some very insolent letters protesting against our taking possession of the country…

CONQUEST UNOPPOSED

No blood has been spilled on this side, nor have the hostile forces ever been near each other except in two instances, the first on the occasion spoken of on the preceding page, and the last at the town of Angeles (Pueblo de Los Angeles). It was known from some very bombastic proclamations of Genl. Castro that he was at that place with nearly all his force—some five hundred men—in consequence of which the Congress proceeded to San Pedro (a small port 30 miles from the Pueblo) landed about 400 men and marched up. But unfortunately the General left a few hours before the Commodore arrived, and so no one had an opportunity of

In May 1845, Minister of War George Bancroft instructed Commodore John D. Sloat that "in case of war" he should occupy San Francisco. This order was confirmed by Commodore Robert F. Stockton in October of that year. Once war was declared, the first step the Americans took was to occupy California's ports. The Americans needed access to the Pacific for two reasons: whaling was a profitable business and the fleet was expanding, and the United States had been trading with China since 1844 and planned to increase its Asian trade.

distinguishing himself, and what is still worse, it is said that Castro's five hundred cavalry made so much dust in their retreat that it was impossible to distinguish any one else....

WHY WINNING WAS SO EASY

As in the case of New Mexico, the U.S. occupation of California was achieved handily. In July and August 1846, the territory was declared to be part of the United States. However, on September 29 Governor Pío Pico led the Mexican population of Los Angeles in a rebellion that reclaimed the city from its occupiers.

At present all Upper California…is in our possession, and the Mexican Coast is blockaded at all of its principal ports...

It may appear singular to you that with so little force as we have employed out here the country could be taken possession of so quietly. But it is not at all so. The country is very thinly populated and the few Californians in it are divided in their political relations into three or four factions, so that any small number of resolute men—and such are those who are with Capt. Frémont [sic]—can do what they please. Besides this the number of Americans now in the territory is not much inferior to the number of Californians and the Americans are a hardy, brave set of men, used to handling fire arms from their infancy. As for the towns on the coast, all put together would not be a match for one good frigate…

THE BATTLE OF SAN PASCUAL

[Letter of John M. Stanley to *St. Louis Reveille*]

Stephen W. Kearny reached California in the midst of the uprising led by Pío Pico. On December 6, 1846, Kearny's and Pico's forces met at San Pascual. In the battle Kearny himself was wounded and had to retreat to San Diego.

San Diego, January 19, 1847
On the morning of the 4th of December we resumed our march, Genl. Kearny having previously sent an express to San Diego to inform Commodore Stockton of his arrival in the country, and on the 5th we met Capt. Gillespie and Lieut. Beall [sic], U.S.N., with an escort of thirty-five men. After making a late camp, General Kearny heard that an armed body of Californians were encamped about nine miles from us…

At 2 o'clock on the morning of the 6th the reveille sounded, and at 3 our force was formed in the order of battle and the march resumed. We arrived about daylight at the valley… The Californians were waiting in their saddles for our approach.

From a misapprehension of an order, the charge was not made by our whole force, or with as much precision as was desirable; but the Californians retreated, on firing a single volley to an open plain about half a mile distant... The retreat of the enemy was followed with spirit by our troops, skirmishing the distance of half a mile. When they reached the plains, our force was somewhat scattered in the pursuit. The Californians, taking advantage of this disorganization, fought with desperation, making great havoc with their lances. It was a real hand-to-hand fight, and lasted half an hour. They were, however, driven from the field; with what loss we could not learn.

We camped on the field and collected the dead. At first Gen. K[earny] thought to move on the same day. The dead were lashed on mules, and remained two hours or more in that posture. It was a sad and melancholy picture. We soon found, however, that our wounded were unable to travel. The mules were released of their packs, and the men engaged in fortifying the place for the night. During the day the enemy were in sight, curvetting [sic] their horses, keeping our camp in constant excitement. Three of Capt. Gillespie's volunteers started with dispatches to Com. Stockton. The dead were buried at night, and ambulances made for the wounded; and the next morning we started, in the face of the enemy's spies, being then about 38 miles from San Diego...

In the Battle of San Pascual, several soldiers were trampled to death by horses, as portrayed in this drawing by William H. Meyers. The rising sun can also be seen, indicating that the fighting began at dawn.

Naval Sketches of the War in California Meyers

CROSSING THE SAN GABRIEL RIVER

[Major William H. Emory, *Notes of a Military Reconnaissance from Fort Leavenworth, in Missouri, to San Diego, in California*]

Kearny and Stockton's forces regrouped in San Diego and marched toward Los Angeles. On January 8, 1847, as they crossed the San Gabriel River, they were attacked by the Mexicans. In this illustration, Stockton's sailors can be seen crossing the river, while a group of soldiers, already on the other bank, hauls forward an artillery piece. Above a cloud of smoke on the right flies the Mexican flag. The Californians are on horseback. Stockton used the classic infantry defense against a cavalry charge—deploying troops in the form of a hollow square.

The text presented here was written by William H. Emory, an engineer assigned to Kearny's troops to investigate possible routes for a railroad to California.

January 8.—We passed over a country destitute of wood and water, undulating and gently dipping towards the ocean, which was in view. About two o'clock we came in sight of the San Gabriel River. Small squads of horsemen began to show themselves on either flank, and it became quite apparent the enemy intended to dispute the passage of the river. The river was about 100 yards wide, knee-deep, and flowing over quicksand. Either side was fringed with a thick undergrowth. The approach on our side was level; that on the enemy's was favorable to him...

As we neared the thicket, we received the scattering fire of the enemy's sharp-shooters. As the same moment, we saw him place four pieces of artillery on the hill, so as to command the passage...

The 2d battalion was ordered to deploy as skirmishers, and cross the river. As the line was about the middle of the river, the enemy opened his battery, and made the water fly with grape and round shot. Our artillery was now ordered to cross—it was unlimbered, pulled over by the men, and placed in counter battery on the enemy's side of the river. Our people, very brisk in firing, made the fire of the enemy wild and uncertain. Under this cover, the wagons and cattle were forced with great labor across the river the bottom of which was quick sand. Whilst this was going on, our rear was attacked by a very bold charge and repulsed.

On the right bank of the river there was a natural banquette, breast high. Under this the line was deployed. To this accident of the ground is to be attributed the little loss we sustained from the enemy's artillery, which showered grape and round shot over our heads. In an hour and twenty minutes our baggage train had all crossed, the artillery of the enemy was silenced, and a charge made on the hill. Half-way between the hill and river, the enemy made a furious charge on our left flank... The 1st battalion, which formed the right, was directed to rush for the hill supposing that would be the contested point, but great was our surprise to find it abandoned. We have no means of pursuit, and scarcely the power of locomotion; such was the wretched condition of our wagon train. The latter it was still deemed necessary to drag along for the purpose of feeding the garrison intended to be left in the Ciudad de Los Angeles, the report being that the enemy intended, if we reached that town, to burn and destroy every article of food.

The Americans spent the night on the battlefield. This sketch by Meyers shows cannon, stacks of muskets and a double circle of guards. Witnesses say Kearny slept like any other soldier in a tent pitched on the ground, but Stockton traveled in a carriage complete with bed and night table.

During the Battle of La Mesa, Kearny's soldiers used the same strategy as during the fighting at San Gabriel: they formed a hollow square of riflemen to protect themselves from the Mexican cavalry. The dense rifle and artillery fire demolished the horsemen, as can be seen in this drawing by William H. Meyers.

THE BATTLE OF LA MESA

January 9.—The grass was very short and young, and our cattle were not much recruited by the night's rest; we commenced our march leisurely, at 9 o'clock, over the "Mesa", a wide plain between the Río San Gabriel and the Río San Fernando...

After marching five or six miles, we saw the enemy's line on our right, above the crest made by a deep indentation in the plain. Here Flores addressed his men, and called on them to make one more charge; expressed his confidence in their ability to break our line; said that "yesterday he had been deceived in supposing that he was fighting soldiers."...

As we advanced, Flores deployed his force, making a horse shoe in our front, and opened his nine-pounders on our right flank, and two smaller pieces on our front. The shot from the nine-pounders on our flank was so annoying that we halted to silence them. In about fifteen minutes this was done, and the order "forward" again given when the enemy came down on our left flank in a scattering sort of charge...

A round of grape was then fired upon them, and scattered... We all considered this as the beginning of the fight but it was the end of it. The Californians, the most expert horsemen in the world, stripped the dead horses on the field, without dismounting, and carried off most of their sad-dles, bridles, and all their dead and wounded on horseback to the hills…

The Battle of La Mesa secured the road to Los Angeles. Although California was already lost to Mexico, skirmishes continued even after a peace treaty was signed.

THE CITY OF LOS ANGELES SURRENDERS

It was now about three o'clock, and the town, known to contain great quantities of wine and aguardiente, was four miles distant. From previous experience of the difficulty of controlling men when entering towns, it was determined to cross the river San Fernando, halt there for the night, and enter the town in the morning with the whole day before us…

January 10.—Just as we had raised our camp, a flag of truce borne by Mr. Celis, a Castilian, Mr. Workman, an English-man, and Alvardo, the owner of the rancheria at the Alisos, was brought into camp. They proposed, on behalf of the Californians, to surrender their dear City of the Angels, provided we would respect property and persons. This was agreed to... We moved into the town in the same order we should have done if expecting an attack. It was a wise precaution, for the streets were full of desperate and drunken fellows who brandished their arms and saluted us with every term of reproach...

We were now in possession of the town; great silence and mystery was observed by the Californians in regard to Flores; but we were given to understand that he had gone to fight the force from the north, drive them back, and then starve us out of the town. Towards the close of the day we learned very certainly that Flores, with 150 men, chiefly Sonorians and desperadoes of the country had fled to Sonora, taking with him four or five hundred of the best horses and mules in the country, the property of his own friends. The silence of the Californians was now changed into deep and bitter curses upon Flores.

The Launch of the U.S. Sloop of War Dale Surprising the Mexican Camp at Bacochivampo Nov

Sketches of the war in California — Meyers

One of the many U.S. naval assaults on the California coast documented by artillery officer William H. Meyers.

The conquest of California was fought out in several pitched battles and numerous skirmishes waged by small groups. Throughout the war, the Americans continued increasing their troop strength in California, and did not stop at the conquest of Upper California. The U.S. Navy under Commodore W. Brandford Shubrick went on to occupy and control Baja California's ports. On March 29, he occupied San José and San Lucas; on April 13, La Paz; in October, Guaymas and Mazatlán. By the end of the war, he had taken control of the Pacific coast as far south as Acapulco.

X Scott's Campaign

*B*y January 1847, only seven months after declaring war, the United States had achieved its principal territorial ambitions. The war was apparently a great military success. Politically, however, the outlook was not nearly so favorable. Despite its losses, Mexico was not prepared to negotiate and the war went on much longer than President Polk and his cabinet had foreseen.

Given the need to legitimate the ground gained as soon as possible, the Americans opted for a change in strategy. On November 18, 1846, General Winfield Scott was ordered to advance from Veracruz to Mexico City to increase the pressure on the Mexican government.

Scott's campaign began on March 9, 1847, with a siege of the port of Veracruz. It culminated six months later with his triumphal entry into Mexico City on September 14 of that same year.

*E*ven though Winfield Scott had been at the head of the U.S. Armed Forces since 1841, President Polk did not make use of him in the first phase of the war. Only after the success of General Taylor's campaign, and out of fear that Taylor's popularity could turn him into a rival presidential candidate, did Polk tap Scott for the assault on Mexico City, p. 292.

Scott was known by the nickname "Fuss and Feather," due to his strict adherence to regulations and his penchant for dress uniforms. His personality contrasted sharply with that of Taylor, old "Rough and Ready."

General Scott launched his campaign with a spectacular amphibious assault on the port of Veracruz.

On March 9, 1847, U.S. forces began disembarking on the beach at Callao, not far from the city. Astoundingly, the most vulnerable operation of the entire campaign—landing soldiers with heavy artillery, wagons, horses and oxen—was accomplished without attack from the Mexicans. The U.S. forces did not lose a single soldier, and facing no resistance of any sort they set about preparing the siege of the city.

This drawing of the disembarkment—based on a sketch by Charles Crillon Barton, who took part in the operation—is quite detailed.

In the siege of Veracruz, the U.S. Navy used steam-powered ships for the first time. They were supplemented by the Mosquito Fleet, made up of lighter and quicker dreadnoughts. This illustration gives some indication of the effectiveness of the American armada in its assault on Veracruz. However, according to General Scott's plan, the main assault was to be by land.

SIEGE OF VERACRUZ AND THE CITY'S SURRENDER

[Letter of Lieutenant Colonel Ethan A. Hitchcock to Elizabeth Nicholls]

Veracruz, March 27, 1847

I am in…some 2 1/2 miles from Vera Cruz, and we moment[ari]ly expect the return of our Commissioners…with the Articles duly signed by the Mexicans, surrendering both the city of Vera Cruz and the celebrated Castle of St. Juan de Ulloa… On the 24th, a heavy battery of guns landed… [and] opened… The 25th—another heavy battery of [guns] commenced fire and more mortars being placed in position the firing during the night of the 25th was very destructive—perfectly terrific—nothing can exceed its horrors. The enemy commenced firing the day after we landed and continued to fire every day, but with very little effect. They ceased firing usually at night and on the night of the 25th they scarcely fired at all. Our mortars on the contrary… poured in a perfect stream of shells into all parts of the City, the very thought of

which makes me now shudder. The shells were filled with several pounds of pow[d]er and at night might be seen by their burning fuzes [sic] making their passage from the mortars… through an immense [sic] arc, rising very high and then descending into the denoted City & probably falling… into some house through the roof would there burst with an awful explosion, destroying whole families of women & children. It is horrible to think of.

The lithograph offers a view of the artillery assault by land. Six heavy pieces were disembarked and dragged some five kilometers through drifting sands and brush to a hill overlooking the city. This operation required two hundred soldiers. Using sandbags, they built a parapet with openings for the cannon. Each section was also protected by a lateral parapet in order to diminish the impact of the explosions.

The Mexican Army surrendered their flags and weapons; some four hundred muskets, sixteen British cannons and more became part of the enemy's arsenal.

OCCUPATION OF VERACRUZ

(Letter of Lieutenant Peter V. Hagner to Mary M. Hagner)

Veracruz, March 30, 1847
On the 29th the garrisons of the different forts & the Castle marched out to a plain near the city selected by the Genl. and there between two of the Divisions of the Army stacked their arms, gave their parole—not to fight during the War—& then march off—southwards…

Genl. Worth, as Gov. is bringing everything into order as fast as possible in a dirty Spanish town now nearly one third destroyed—full of rubbish—streets piled up with barricades or cut up by our shot & shells—houses shattered terribly in every street—few lazy half-clothed, dirty inhabitants, the most [of them] having left the city or hid themselves, as soon as our lines were opened to them…

Today I have been completing the visitation in the City and also at the famous castle of San Juan. It is a fine old fort —indeed old, very old, but in good military preservation— and it has been infinitely assisted in its protection by skilful Engineers. Barricades, piles of sand bags—at every corner… We get plenty of trophies, you see many of these fine old brass peices [sic] from Spain—and peices [sic] of ordnance —old Bombards by name—which must have been made as early as 1620. We get too, many fine peices [sic] of our own muskets—made at West Point Foundry for several years past with thousands of shot, shells & & & & [sic] English guns equally well supplied & of the latest patterns…

The city has few or no gardens and as our lines were around them for three weeks they had consumed the most of their fresh provisions…

We shall soon move towards the interior. I learn there we will have a more agreeable country & more pleasant time, I hope.

Once he had secured Veracruz, Scott ordered his troops to advance inland. On April 18, 1847, they met up with the Mexican Army at a place called Cerro Gordo, near Jalapa. There, Santa Anna had dug in on two hills, Telégrafo and Atalaya, which overlook the town.

To portray the battle of Cerro Gordo in his book, The War Between Mexico and the United States Illustrated, *the journalist George Wilkins Kendall,* ☞ *p. 219, chose the vantage point from which he himself had observed it: the rearguard. A company from Worth's division can be seen blockading the road to Jalapa to prevent any reinforcements from arriving. American troops are scaling Telégrafo on the right and left, like two swarms of bluish ants. The Mexican fortifications vanish behind the smoke enveloping the summit. The Americans advancing on opposite sides are obliged to reduce their fire so as not to kill each other. Atalaya can be seen on the left in the background,* ☞ *p. 115. In their assault on Telégrafo, the Americans are making use of the Mexican batteries they captured the previous night when they took Atalaya Hill.*

An assault during the battle of Cerro Gordo. On the right the fortifications on the summit of Telégrafo Hill can be seen.

Battle of Cerro Gordo

[Anonymous letter]

Jalapa, June 7, 1847

In the evening we succeeded after a great deal of labor, in getting our 24 pounder and two howitzers, and two other pieces of cannon on this hill… This was the night of the 17th. It was a shocking sight to behold the poor wounded riflemen and some artillery and infantry, about 100 in number, lying on the ground, with legs shot off, arms gone, and cut in every part, some with both legs and arm gone, some shot through the breast and other parts of the body, some just alive, all waiting for the surgeons who were busily engaged in dressing the wounds. We were obliged to encamp or rather lie down here, and notwithstanding the groans of the wounded and dying, and the rain which was falling fast, we slept soundly, such was our fatigue.

In the morning we were awakened early, and ascended the hill to our battery, and assisted in planting our guns. It was a very exposed position, in full range of the enemy's battery, and just concealed by a small growth of chappparel [sic]...

THE CAPTURE OF TELÉGRAFO HILL

We descended the hill on which was our battery under a heavy fire of grape, canister [sic] and musketry from the enemy, about five times our number. You have seen a hail-storm, and witnessed the falling of the hail-stones; accompanied by rain—then you have an idea of our situation. The shots fell around us, cutting down the low bushes, and passing through the clothes of some, and cutting down others of the brave fellows that were on to the charge. You can imagine my feelings—I thought of home and friends—and then such was the excitement of the moment, that all fear was done away. I looked—expecting to see some one of our brave little band fall—but they marched on after their brave officer until we reached the foot of Cerro Gordo [sic, El Telégrafo], where we rested but a moment to breathe, and then charged up the almost impassable height. The officers were obliged to use their swords for canes to help them up the hill, as did the soldiers their muskets. They fired briskly upon us, cutting down one after another, but still we pushed on, excited and maddened to a complete frenzy—that madness insensible to fatigue or even fear. We met them at the point of the bayonet, and drove them out of their fortifications, and then turned their own guns, these already loaded for us, upon them, making great destruction... After we had secured the position of the hill, and planted the flag of our country on the walls...

General Shield, who took Santa Anna's troops and carriage by surprise—and obliged the Mexican general to make a hasty retreat 🔫 *p. 117,—was severely wounded in that skirmish. Here he is in bed being visited by General Scott.*

SCOTT VISITING GENERAL SHIELDS—WOUNDED.

The U.S. Army
on Santa Anna's Hacienda

The battle of Cerro Gordo took place close to Hacienda Encero, a property belonging to Santa Anna. Because it was healthier than Veracruz, the Americans used it as a military base for the duration of the war. In the foreground of this picture a soldier is sketching the encampment. From this perspective, Santa Anna's house and the chapel connected to it dominate the long rows of military tents.

We pressed on until we came to Encerro [sic, Lencero], about eight miles from Cerro Gordo, where we encamped for the night. A great number of prisoners were taken and brought into camp that night, but all the soldiers were set at liberty again. In the morning we started for Jalapa, and after marching 10 miles through a most beautiful country, we reached Jalapa about 12 A.M.

CASTLE de PEROTE, MEXICO.

SURRENDERED APRIL 22ᴺᴰ 1847, TO THE U S ARMY COMMANDED BY GENL. WINFIELD SCOTT.

COL.F.M WINKOOP 1ˢᵗ REGT PENNA VOL. CIVIL & MILITARY GOVERNOR.

GARRISONED BY

Very close to Jalapa stands Perote Castle, a seventeenth-century building used as a prison before the war. The Americans turned it into a garrison, and from here they sought to defeat the guerrillas who would not leave them in peace,  p. 121.

THE AMERICAN ARMY IN PUEBLA

[H. Judge Moore, *Scott's Campaign in Mexico*, 1849]

At that time, Puebla was the second largest city in Mexico. In the middle of this picture stand the towers of the cathedral at the city center. Scott's troops bivouacked here from May to August 1847. Scott's lengthy stay was due to two factors: before advancing on Mexico City, he needed to increase his troop strength and the U.S. Congress seemed unwilling to make new appropriations or recruit more men; and U.S. negotiator Nicholas P. Trist had arrived to seek a peace agreement that would formalize the territorial concessions.

At 12 o'clock precisely, on Saturday, the 15th day of May, 1847, the van of the invading army of the North, with the gallant and intrepid Worth at its head, entered in triumph and without opposition the south gate of the city of Puebla, and marched to the Grand Plaza fronting the Cathedral, where they stacked their arms, and supplied themselves with water from the fountain…

I thought I had seen large masses of human beings before, but I never saw a shoreless sea of living, moving, animated matter, composed of crowding thousands of men, women and children, ebbing and flowing like the agitated waves of the ocean. As I cast my eyes round, I almost shuddered for the fate of our little army, although I saw no arms or warlike implements of any kind, nor any thing like a military organization, yet the immense cloud of hostile citizens that hovered round our little band in dark and portentous gloom, was altogether sufficient to have crushed our whole force into utter annihilation, without the aid of any other arms than clubs and rocks… For I afterwards learned that all they wanted was a bold and daring leader who could have given direction and impetus to public feeling, and led the already excited populace in a united and organized body against the heart of the invading foe. Many of the citizens and foreign residents, in speaking afterwards of our entry into the city, acknowledge themselves perfectly astonished at the cool and careless indifference that seemed to characterize every movement of the American army while such imminent danger encompassed them on all sides. They actually stacked their arms in the plaza and marched off to the fountain to get water, and then passed on to the market to buy bread and fruit, while those who remained to guard our arms lay down and went to sleep, and at the same time we were surrounded in every direction by hostile thousands of bloody-minded foes, who were anxiously waiting an opportunity to wreak their vengeance upon the invaders of their soil…

TOWARD MEXICO CITY

[Diary of Lieutenant Daniel Harvey Hill]

Aug. 18th [1847]. Morning, we passed through the singularly picturesque town of Cayahualco. The houses are built of volcanic rock & the most of them thatched with the reed called bagies. Rude walls of stone enclosed the narrow streets on each side and in the yards were lovely & magnificent groves of the thick-foliaged olive. A mile or two beyond Cayahualco, we passed through a smaller town in all respects very like it, called San Gregorio. The Volunteers had been here the night before & had committed the most shameful depredations. For five miles we saw continuous groves of the olive. That road was most horrible & as the train was in front of us, we were much delayed by it & on an average did not advance more than three hundred yards at a time without a halt. The Mexicans had obstructed the road in several places by rolling down immense rocks from the hills & it required much labor to remove these obstacles.

We only marched eight miles but I am more fatigued now than I have been after a march of twenty-five. The road was truly horrible, if a man made the least false step he was sure to be plunged over his hips in the mud. To make the matter worse, a piercingly cold rain poured down in torrents upon us for hours & being without shelter we of course got thoroughly drenched to the skin. We at length reached… to Xochimilco… We learned to our great surprise on arriving here that the works on this side of Mexico [City] are represented to be excessively strong and can only be taken with heavy loss…

Scott left Puebla on August 7 with four divisions: one commanded by Worth, another by Twiggs, a third by Pillow, and the last by Quitman. Pictured above is the cover of the sheet music for the song "Gen. Worth's Quick Step." The title alludes both to the pace of the march and the popular American dance.

In this view of the Valley of Mexico, the city and its lakes can be seen in the background.

U.S. ARMY
ON THE ROAD TO PADIERNA

Aug. 23d. Pueblo of Coyoacan. The last four days have been full of danger, hardship and suffering. On the morning of the 19th we moved at 8 o'clock from the village of Zochimilco [sic] & about 10 A.M. we reached San Augustine de las Cuevas or Tlálpam [sic]. Here all the wagons of the divisions were halted and we all, officers & men, took each a blanket and one day's rations in our haversacks & then moved off, taking the advance of the whole American Army. Our expedition was looked upon as one of the most forlorn & desperate character and the troops of the other Divisions at San Augustine (Pillow's and Quitman's) came to the roadside & bade us farewell. San Augustine is a large & beautiful town, I do not think that I ever have seen so many fruit trees as were there. The vile Volunteers had committed the usual excesses & the lovely town was in good part deserted. I observed three beautiful girls seated in a window, calmly looking at us as we passed and the sight gratified me no little, though I expected so soon to be on the field of blood.

FIGHTING AT THE PEDREGAL OF PADIERNA

We advanced for several miles over an exceedingly bad road, which in many places had just been made by our pioneers and at length came in sight of a Fort on the heights of Padierna, which completely commanded the road that we were pursuing. Genl. Twiggs here mysteriously disappeared and that consummate fool Genl. Pillow assumed command of our division and detached our brigade (Riley's)…in all (1,100) men to get between the Fort at Padierna and the City of Mexico, whilst he made an attack upon the work in front… Certainly of all the absurd things that the ass Pillow has ever done this was the most silly. Human stupidity can go no farther than this, the ordering of six and twelve pounders to batter a Fort furnished with long sixteens, twenty-fours and heavy mortars!! Sage general, the Army appreciates you if the country does not. Our light batteries were cut to pieces in a short time and some of our best officers & men killed or mortally wounded. In the meanwhile our Brigade crossed over boggy cornfields & deep ravines, clambered over sharp volcanic rock called Pedregal until we reached the main road to Mexico… Soon after a splendid looking body of Cavalry issued from the Fort and from an adjacent height began to taunt our regiment… Whilst Col. Riley appeared to be hesitating whether to accept the taunting challenge or not we saw four long columns of soldiers, Foot & Cavalry, advancing from the City… We moved off seemingly with the intention of attacking the troops which had come out from the City. Our brigade was now halted when just beyond musket range of the Mexicans and we now learned that the whole of Twiggs' division had come up and a portion of Pillow's. A Council of

The capital city, which appears open and welcoming in the illustration on the previous page, was located in a hollow that provided a certain amount of natural protection. It was surrounded on three sides by lakes whose shores were too swampy for moving heavy artillery, and on the fourth by a broad rocky plain of petrified lava (known as the Pedregal) impassable for the animals hauling the artillery. Their horseshoes literally shattered on the porous rocks. Unfavorable as it was for combat, the Pedregal was where the bloody battle took place.

When the Americans realized that they could not move their cannon and horses across the Pedregal, they set to exploring the terrain: amid the boulders they found the outlines of a road which, once reshaped and strengthened by their military engineers, allowed them to launch a surprise attack on General Valencia's rearguard.

War was now held as to the advisability of giving battle to the Mexican troops in front whilst a strong Fort was so near in our rear… We have since learned that the force which came out from the City was 10,000 strong under the command of General Santa Anna in person…We had scarcely got into our position when it began to rain very hard and continued to do so all night. We had no shelter except such as was afforded by the trees & were all soon drenched to the skin.

NIGHTTIME MARCH

Before two o'clock we were aroused & t'was [sic] whispered that a night attack upon the Fort was to take place and as our arms were not to be relied upon in the tremendous rain that it was to be carried by the bayonet alone… The night was so dark that 'twas [sic] scarcely possible to see the hand before the face & the path was muddy & slippery… We wandered about for hours not knowing where we were. At length we got upon the right trail and succeeded in reaching the rendezvous at daylight. Finding it so late our arms were got ready for firing and we moved on to the Fort which was reached about half an hour after sunrise.

THE ASSAULT

The enemy was expecting us though he was taken somewhat by surprise as all his preparations had not still been completed. He therefore threw out an Advance corps to check us until more cannon could be brought to bear on our column. This corps poured a heavy fire into us before we had completed our deployment. Riley's brigade constituted the entire storming column and our regiment led the column. We returned the fire of the advance Corps with deadly effect & then marched forward… Cannon now opened upon us, charged with grape & canister [sic], but owing to the fright of the gunners did but little injury.

In the foreground of this lithograph, three American regiments can be seen heading from the lower left corner toward the center of the picture to attack General Valencia, whose artillery can be seen at the edge of a gorge lined with trenches. On the right, the Americans open fire to distract the Mexican forces from the main assault. In the distance on the left is a gray mass—Santa Anna's army. If he had decided to attack, his enemy would have been pinned between two lines of fire, from the north and the south, and perhaps the outcome of the battle would have been different. But Santa Anna retreated.

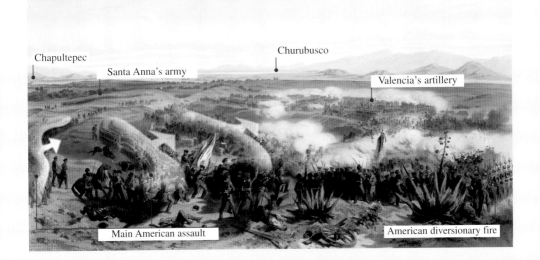

Chapultepec

Santa Anna's army

Churubusco

Valencia's artillery

Main American assault

American diversionary fire

My company carried the colors and in consequence suffered more severely than any other as the standard drew the enemy's fire… This morning, the tassel carried off by a cannon shot and soon after the color bearer was killed.

Our advance was steady under a heavy but far from destructive fire as the Mexicans took no aim. After fighting for half an hour we discovered that the enemy's Infantry & Cavalry were in full retreat leaving the artillerists still at their guns…

Capt. Drum of our Regt. captured two guns, which proved to be the very guns that Lt. O'Brien of our Regt. lost at Buena Vista… The enemy was now completely routed & was retreating in disorder towards Mexico [City].

CHASING THE MEXICANS TOWARD CHURUBUSCO

[Letter of Captain Ephraim Kirby Smith to his wife]

Tacubaya, August 22, 1847

I hardly know how to commence a description of the events of the last three days. My brain is whirling from the long continued excitement and my body sore with bruises and fatigue—but I will try to… record things as they happened…

As soon as the result [of the Battle of Contreras] was known to General Worth, the Second Brigade of this division with our battalion were put in motion to endeavor to turn the position at San Antonio. For two hours we ran over the rocks moving by a flank, the enemy in a heavy column marching parallel to us and almost in gun shot, until the head of the Fifth Infantry pierced their line and the fight began… We soon reached the road and turned in hot pursuit…

It was soon seen as we rushed along the road that the enemy was only retreating to a fortified position, which constituted their second line of defenses at Churubusco…

THE DIN OF BATTLE

We had advanced on the road less than a mile when we were ordered into the fields to assault the right of the enemy's position… At this time the battle was fiercely contested on our left and front…

It must have been about half past twelve. Immediately in front of us, at perhaps five hundred yards, the roll of the Mexican fire exceeded anything I have ever heard. The din was most horrible, the roar of cannon and musketry, the screams of the wounded, the awful cry of terrified horses and mules, and the yells of the fierce combatants all combined in a sound as hellish as can be conceived…

We could not tell what was before us… all was hidden by the tall corn.

After capturing the convent at Churubusco, the American troops set up camp in Tacubaya. From there Captain Ephraim Kirby Smith wrote this long letter recounting the battle to his wife. Smith would die in the very next battle he fought, that of Molino del Rey.

The convent at Churubusco was surrounded by cornfields. The corn was as tall as a man and provided the Americans with easy cover.

The bridge and convent at Churubusco were the most important fortified positions on the southern approach to Mexico City. In this lithograph, Nebel portrays General Worth's troops scaling the tête du pont, the fortified bulwark at the entrance to the bridge, which featured loopholes, cannon and a moat. At the center of the picture, the back of the convent can be seen.

At Churubusco, Worth Attacks the Bridge and Twiggs the Convent

We soon came out of it into a crossroad near some small houses, where we were exposed to a dreadful cross fire... Many had fallen and the battalion was...broken. The grape round shot and musketry were sweeping over the ground in a storm which strewed it with the dead and dying. I found it extremely difficult to make the men stand or form, but finally succeeded with my own company which was at once ordered to charge... My men were just formed and I had ordered the charge which I was about to lead, when the dreadful cry came from the left and rear that we were repulsed. A rush of men and officers in a panic followed, running over and again breaking my little command... I shouted that we were not repulsed—to charge—and the day would be ours...

…We now learned that Twiggs and others were pressing them [Mexicans] on the left and had been fighting them an hour or more. Before this we had discovered we were under the fire of two forts, one a bastion front *tête du pont* flanking, and being flanked by a larger work, built round an extensive convent. Now as the whole army shouted and rushed to the assault, the enemy gave way, retreating as best they could to Mexico. They were pursued by all, hundreds being shot down in the retreat pursued them…

As soon as the battle terminated and the pursuit ceased, I went back, tired and sore as I was, to collect the dead and dying of our battalion and did not return until night. The field presented an awful spectacle—the dead and the wounded were thickly sprinkled over the ground—the mangled bodies of the artillery horses and mules actually blocking up the road and filling the ditches…

While Worth's troops assaulted the bastion of the bridge, Twiggs directed a frontal attack on the convent. This lithograph allows us to appreciate the defensive features of the building, especially its thick walls with buttresses. There is an interesting detail on the left: two Mexican horsemen are using a lasso to catch an American infantryman. Lassos were certainly employed by guerrillas, but there is little evidence they were used by regular troops.

Following the defeats at Padierna and Churubusco, the Mexican government accepted a cease-fire and entered into peace talks with the U.S. envoy. But on September 6, the truce was broken and hostilities began anew. Two days later, the U.S. Army advanced from Tacubaya to Chapultepec Woods, near Molino del Rey, where the next battle took place.

In this lithograph, General Worth's troops can be seen attacking Molino del Rey. The roofs of the long buildings in the background are lined with snipers, and camouflaged Mexican batteries can be seen among the maguey cactuses. Grapeshot from these guns surprised the Americans.

The illustration shows the position of the fortifications at Molino del Rey relative to Chapultepec Castle (surrounded by woods), which would become the next target.

STRATEGIC DESCRIPTION
OF MOLINO DEL REY AND CASA MATA

[Lt. Raphael Semmes, "The Campaign of General Scott in the Valley of Mexico"]

The reconnaissance of the engineers showed that the enemy's left rested on a group of strong stone buildings (El Molino), at the western slope of Chapultepec and about half a mile from the base of the hill; that the right of his line rested on another stone building, called Casa-Mata...; that these two buildings were more or less connected by irregular dikes, planted with the maguey, affording excellent cover for infantry; and that the enemy's field-battery occupied a position, midway between the two buildings, supported by infantry on either flank, lying perdue [sic] behind the dikes. Both Molino del Rey and Casa Mata were filled with infantry, the long azotea of the Molino; in particular, affording them an excellent position from which to pick off our troops as they advanced...

THE BATTLE OF MOLINO DEL REY

We were astir, at headquarters, at half-past two A. M. on the morning of the memorable 8th [of September]... We of the staff rode along in silence... We seemed to have a sort of presentiment of the bloody tragedy which was to be enacted. The night was perfectly clear, but without moon, and the sun afterward rose in all his glory, over the battle field to light up the work of carnage and death.

At the earliest appearance of dawn in the east, Huger opened with his heavy pieces, which, for a while, gave forth the only sounds that broke in upon the perfect silence for the field. Chapultepec seemed fast asleep, and it was some minutes before it could be aroused into returning our fire... Wright, with his storming party... rushed gallantly forward to assault and pierce the enemy's center. He was met by a most appalling fire of musketry, and grape and canister, which at

Mexican soldiers crowd the rooftops on Molino del Rey.

General Winfield Scott never thought that the fighting at Molino del Rey and Casa Mata would be so fierce. Having heard rumors that those buildings were being used as forges to make cannon, Scott decided to send General Worth to capture and destroy them. Worth found only a few munitions and several molds, which he blew up, p. 140.

During the assault on Molino del Rey, General Worth sent Colonel McIntosh to attack Casa Mata, a building contiguous with the Molino which was protected by trenches and a strip of maguey cactuses. General Pérez's troops hid among the cactuses, rendering themselves invisible to the Americans. The assault, although victorious in the end, turned into a disaster for the Americans, who suffered many losses, among them Colonel McIntosh himself. At the center of the lithograph on the opposite page he can be seen falling from his horse.
To this day, the battle remains a matter of some controversy among U.S. historians, who debate whether such a price was inevitable. They wonder if the Americans should have ignored this bastion, as they had the Ciudadela in Monterrey and San Juan de Ulúa Castle in Veracruz.

once revealed to General Worth the formidable numbers he had opposed to him. Nothing daunted, however, he rushed on, driving infantry and artillerymen, at the point of the bayonet, but at terrible loss. The ground…formed a gradual slope down the enemy's lines…; our brave fellows were compelled to march without so much as a twig to shelter them; while the enemy lay concealed behind the dikes and maguey plants, or was protected by the walls and parapets (around the azotea) of the Molino…

ASSAULT ON CASA MATA

While these operations were progressing on the enemy's left and center…the 2d brigade under McIntosh…moved steadily on to the assault of the Casa Mata, which instead of being an ordinary stone house, as had been supposed by the engineers, proved to be a citadel, surrounded with bastion intrench-ments [sic] and impassable ditches—an old Spanish work, recently repaired and enlarged....

While McIntosh was moving forward to assault this formi-dable work, a large body of cavalry (it afterward appeared from the official reports of the enemy, that there were four thousand of them, under Alvarez) was seen approaching us on our extreme left, as with a view of charging us on that flank, or endeavoring to turn and envelop that position. As soon as Duncan's battery was masked… [McIntosh] was ordered to change front, to hold the enemy's cavalry in check, which he did rapidly, moving a little farther to the left… In taking up this position, the gallant major, in order to avoid some ditches which impeded his march, was forced to pass within pistol shot of the Casa Mata when [sic, where] his command suffered considerably; the enemy knocking several of his dragoons from the saddle, and the affrighted and wounded horses career-ing wildly over the field. One of the enemy's brigades... moved boldly forward (Duncan purposely withholding his fire to invite it) until it had come within good canister range,

when the gallant lieutenant-colonel opened upon it one of those exceedingly rapid and terrible fires for which his battery was so celebrated. The enemy could not withstand the shock… and then thrown into confusion…and whole four thousand horse disappeared from the field…

Let us now return to McIntosh, whom we left advancing upon the Casa Mata...

McIntosh was a man whom danger never daunted, and he moved on amid this storm of balls until he was cut down mortally wounded. The brigade, under the lead of the gallant Martin Scott, continued on, however, until it reached the very slope of the parapet that surrounded the citadel. By this time Scott himself was shot dead; his next in command, Major Waite, was knocked down, badly wounded and a large proportion of the gallant fellows were destroyed... and the remainder of the brigade now fell back for support upon Duncan's battery... Duncan being now at liberty to renew his fire opened again upon the Casa-Mata… and in a few minutes thereafter we had the satisfaction of seeing the enemy abandoned his stronghold… Upon reaching the Molino, which was no Molino-mill at all, no vestige could be found of furnace, tools, or any other apparatus for the casting of cannon…

In the battle of Casa Mata, the Americans suffered so many casualties that one of their officers admitted bitterly, "A few more such victories and this army would be destroyed." The battle also ended the close personal friendship between Generals Scott and Worth. In 1840 Worth had named his only son Winfield Scott Worth; after the war he changed it to William Worth.

At the time of the American invasion, the old Spanish viceroyal palace on the summit of Chapultepec Hill was a military college. This illustration shows the hill in all its unassailable grandeur. To take it, Scott chose a simultaneous assault on two sides. This view portrays General Quitman's assault from the southwest. On the extreme right, near the arches of the aqueduct, the Americans are hauling an artillery battery uphill. In the center, parapets can be seen lining the lower flanks of the hill, and behind them Mexican riflemen. In the foreground on the left, American troops flee under heavy fire. Among them is one with his arm in a sling—General Shields, p. 271.

Chapultepec: The Greatest Challenge

[Diary of Lieutenant Daniel Harvey Hill]

We are now in the City of Mexico after a hard day's fight on yesterday. On the evening of the 11th... I got a quiet night's rest. We heard that night that Chapultepec was to be the real point of attack and that a feint was to be made on the Niño Perdido causeway... It proved to be a most abortive diversion indeed...

We all felt satisfied that the building [of Chapultepec] was rendered untenable but knew that there was too much shelter behind the walls that encircled the hill and under the projection of the hill itself for the enemy to have sustained much injury. Affairs now looked dark and gloomy in the extreme. Chapultepec was regarded to be impregnable... There was deep depression among us also, the fruitless victory of the 8th, attended with the loss of so many of our best officers and men had a very dispiriting influence upon us all and in a great degree destroyed our confidence in our Commanders.

That evening a call was made for a storming party from our Division... This body was to cooperate with a similar corps selected from Genl. Worth's Division. These parties to be sustained by several Regiments of Volunteers and raw levies under the command of Genls. Pillow, Quitman & Shields. As the leading storming party "the forlorn hope" was expected to suffer very much and strong incentives were held out to induce us to volunteer... I volunteered... We were supplied with pickaxes and scaling ladders...

Military College in the Crossfire

Early on the morning of the 13th, we advanced down the main road to attack the Fortress in front whilst the storming party from Genrl Worth's Division attacked it in rear. A very strong building used as a Military College placed upon a very rugged, steep hill surrounded by two thick walls twelve

General Pillow attacked Chapultepec Hill on the western flank, from Molino del Rey. Riflemen cleared the way for the infantry, who advanced taking cover behind boulders and in clefts in the rock. To climb the hill they had to use crowbars and pickaxes. The fighting was vicious: Pillow himself was wounded in the groin.

feet high and defended by strong works in front constituted the famous Fortress of Chapultpec. Our column of attack had moved but a short distance down the main road when we were exposed to a heavy fire of Artillery & escopotery…. We then dashed forward along the road and drove the Mexicans before us with great slaughter. The other storming party had in the meanwhile gained the height from the opposite side and when we entered the enemy's advanced works, the Stars and Stripes were flying from the highest point of the Castle.

No Mexican Asks for Clemency

The havoc among the Mexicans was now horrible in the extreme. Pent up between two fires they had but one way to escape and all crowded toward it like a flock of sheep. I saw dozens hanging from the walls and creeping through holes made for the passage of water & whilst in this position were shot down without making the least resistance. Our men were shouting give no quarters "to the treacherous scoundrels" and as far as I could observe none were asked by the Mexicans. I collected my little party and for more than a mile was far in advance of all our troops in the chase of the enemy... Twas a sublime and exalted feeling that which we experienced whilst chasing some five thousand men with but little more than a dozen…

A Spectacular Victory Determines the Outcome of the War

The storming of Chapultepec is looked upon as the most brilliant operation of the whole war. The enemy was in the strongest position he has ever occupied and was twelve thousand strong with ten pieces of cannon, the whole force being under command of Santa Anna in person…

War correspondent George W. Kendall decided to portray the two lines of attack—Quitman's and Pillow's—perhaps to avoid wounding either general's pride, since both of them claimed to have won the battle. Victories were a source of discord among commanding officers, with everyone wanting to take the credit. Quitman and Pillow quarreled over the victory at Chapultepec. After the war Pillow also took General Scott to military court over who had won the victories at Padierna and Churubusco. In this cartoon, which appeared at the time of that trial, Scott drives his sword into a pillow being inflated by General Pillow.

SELF-INFLATING PILLOW.

The whole of our Army I understand as well as the whole of the Mexican not engaged in the fight were looking on with almost breathless interest during the hour & a half that the bloody struggle lasted. All felt that upon its issue depended the triumph or defeat of the American arms, the fate of the campaign & the gain or loss of the grand City of Mexico...

For his depiction of General Scott's entrance into Mexico City, Carl Nebel used the same view as in the painting for his album Viaje pintoresco y arqueológico sobre la parte más interesante de la República Mexicana, ✍ *p. 168.*

THE OCCUPATION FACES RESISTANCE
FROM MEXICO CITY RESIDENTS

[George W. Kendall, correspondence of the *New Orleans Picayune*]

October 14, 1847

At 7 o'clock this morning Gen. Scott, with his staff, rode in and took quarters in the national palace, on the top of which the regimental flag of the gallant rifles and the stars and

stripes were already flying, and an immense crowd of blanketed leperos, the scum of the capital, were congregated in the plaza as the commander-in-chief entered it. They pressed our soldiers, and eyed them as though they were beings of another world. So much were they in the way, and with such eagerness did they press around, that Gen. Scott was compelled to order our Dragoons to clear the plaza… About five minutes after this, and while Gen. Worth was returning to his division near the Alameda, he was fired upon from a house near the convent of San Francisco. Some of the cowardly Polkas [sic], who had fled the day previous without discharging their guns, now commenced the assassin game of shooting at every one of our men they saw, from windows, as well as from behind the parapets on the azoteas or tops of the houses. In half an hour's time our good friends, the leperos, in the neighborhood of the hospital of San Andres and the church of Santa Clara, also commenced discharging muskets and throwing bottles and rocks from the azoteas…

For several hours this cowardly war upon our men continued, and during this time many were killed or wounded… Orders were given to shoot every man in all the houses from which the firing came, while the guns of the different light batteries swept the streets in all directions. As the assassins were driven from one house they would take refuge on another; but by the middle of the afternoon they were all forced back to the barriers and suburbs. Many innocent persons have doubtless been killed during the day, but this could not be avoided. Had orders been given at the outset to blow up and demolish every house or church from which one man was fired upon, the disturbances would have been at once quelled…

Journalist George W. Kendall was in the main plaza when Scott took control of the capital city. Here are his impressions and his summary of the facts. In the lithograph above, which he requested of Carl Nebel, U.S. troops can been seen in front of the Cathedral, and the Stars and Stripes flies over the National Palace. The entrance of General Scott into the city's main square as depicted in the lithograph on the opposite page seems ceremonial and peaceful. But a close look at the roof of the house on the corner reveals snipers lying in wait. A leper in front of the wine store is picking up a stone. He will throw it a moment later as the signal to attack the invaders, and again blood would flow.

GOING TO AND RETURNING FROM MEXICO.

This cartoon entitled "Going to and Returning from Mexico" calls attention to the price paid by the soldiers who went off to war, many of whom came back permanently disfigured, p.118.

The U.S. Army fielded a total of 48,000 soldiers in the war against Mexico. During the fighting, 22,259 were killed or wounded (1,548 died in combat, 10,970 died from disease or injuries of some sort, and 9,749 were sent home due to maiming, wounds, disease or injuries). In addition, the Americans lost some 3,000 soldiers to desertions.

XI

The Treaty of Guadalupe Hidalgo

*W*hen President Polk heard the news that Veracruz had fallen in the spring of 1847, he sent a peace envoy, Nicholas P. Trist, to see if a negotiated settlement could be reached. Trist brought with him to Mexico a list of unconditional demands, among them establishing the Rio Grande as the border of Texas, ceding New Mexico and Upper California, and setting the 32nd parallel as the border between Mexico and the United States from El Paso to the Pacific. Trist was also ordered to insist that Mexico cede Baja California, although he was given some flexibility on that point. The U.S. also demanded free transit through the Isthmus of Tehuantepec. Finally, Trist was authorized to offer payment of up to $30 million in compensation, depending on how much territory Mexico was prepared to give up. Polk himself conceded that any amount would surely be less than the cost of another year of war.

On November 16, 1847, Trist received the order to return to Washington, but he decided to stay on to try to strike a deal. A few days later, the Mexican government offered to renew negotiations in the city of Querétaro, and on February 2, a peace treaty was signed in the town of Guadalupe Hidalgo. The U.S. Senate approved it on March 10, 1848, and on May 30, following a ratification ceremony held in Querétaro, the U.S. Army began pulling out of that portion of Mexico's territory that still belonged to Mexico.

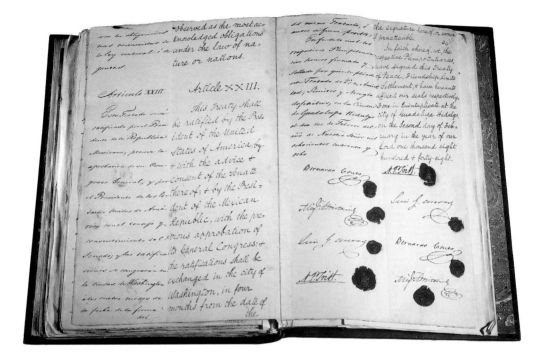

*T*he road to peace was long. Envoy Nicholas P. Trist arrived in Veracruz on May 6, 1847. He first made indirect contact with Mexican officials during the American occupation of Puebla, but not until the cease-fire following the Battle of Churubusco did the first negotiations take place. During those talks, the invasion was termed "an unnatural war." At the meetings on September 11 and 12, several of Mexico's demands were agreed to: not giving up Baja California, defining the border with Texas as the Nueces River, and making the border west of El Paso the 33rd parallel (the latitude of El Paso) rather than the 32nd, thereby keeping San Diego in Mexican territory. However, a final accord was not reached. Following the American occupation of Mexico City, circumstances were less favorable to the curbing of U.S. territorial demands, and some American newspapers even began campaigning for "all Mexico" to be annexed to the United States, an opinion shared by several members of the U.S. Congress.

On October 6, 1847, Polk decided to revoke Trist's appointment. However, upon receiving that order six weeks later and seeing the willingness of the new Mexican government to negotiate, Trist remained to conclude the negotiations.

POLK ORDERS NICHOLAS TRIST RECALLED

[James Buchanan, Secretary of State, to Nicholas Trist]

Nicholas P. Trist was selected to negotiate peace with Mexico due to his diplomatic experience, his knowledge of Spanish and his loyalty to the Democratic Party.

Washington D.C., October 6, 1847

Your original instructions were framed in the spirit of forbearance and moderation. It was hoped that after the surrender of Vera Cruz and the Castle of San Juan de Ullúa, the Mexican Government would be willing to listen to the counsels of peace. The terms, therefore, to which you were authorized to accede were of the most liberal character considering our just claims on Mexico and our success in the war. New Mexico, the Californias, several of the Northern States and most of the important ports of Mexico were then in our possession: and yet we were at that time willing freely to surrender most of these conquests and even to make an ample compensation for those which we retained. Circumstances have entirely changed since the date of your original instructions. A vast amount of treasury has since been expended, and what is of infinitely more value, the lives of a great number of our most valuable citizens have been sacrificed in the prosecution of the war…

After a series of brilliant victories, when our troops were at the gates of the capital and it was completely in our power, the Mexican government have not only rejected your liberal offers, but have insulted our country by proposing terms the acceptance of which would degrade us in the eyes of the world and be justly condemned by the whole American people…

In this state of affairs, the President, believing that your continued presence with the army can be productive of no good, but may do much harm by encouraging the delusive hopes and false impressions of the Mexicans, has directed me to recall you from your mission and to instruct you to return to the United States by the first safe opportunity. He has determined not to make another offer to treat with the Mexican government…

Virginia Randolph Trist, wife of Nicholas Trist and granddaughter of Thomas Jefferson, revealed in this letter what her husband said about his feelings during the signing ceremony. Trist's attitude helps explain why the Mexican negotiators said they held but "favorable and honorable memories [of him] in Mexico."

The signature of Nicholas P. Trist on the treaty.

I'll Sign, but Shamefully

[Letter of Virginia Randolph Trist to Tuckerman]

July 8, 1864

Just as they were about to sign the treaty in the "sanctuary" [church of Guadalupe] to which they had repaired for the purpose, one of the Mexicans, Don Bernardo Couto, remarked to him [Trist], "this must be a proud moment for you; no less proud for you than it is humiliating for us". To this Mr. Trist replied, "we are making peace, let that be our only thought".
—But, said he to us in relating it, "Could those Mexicans have seen into my heart at that moment, they would have known that my feeling of shame as an American was far stronger than theirs could be as Mexicans. For though it would not have done for me to say so there that was a thing for every right-minded American to be ashamed of, and I was ashamed of it, most cordially and intensely ashamed of it. This had been my feeling at all our conferences and especially at moments when I had felt it necessary to insist upon things which they were averse to. Had my curse at such moments been governed by my conscience as a man, and my sense of justice as an individual American, I should have yielded in every instance. Nothing prevented my doing so but the conviction that the treaty would then be one which there would be no chance for the acceptance of by our government. My object throughout was, not to obtain all I could, but on the contrary to make the treaty as little exacting as possible from Mexico, as was compatible with its being accepted at home. In this I was governed by two considerations; one was the iniquity of the war, as an abuse of power on our part; the other was that the more disadvantageous the treaty was made to Mexico, the stronger would be the ground of opposition to it in the Mexican Congress by the party who had boasted of its ability to frustrate any peace measures.

The Impact of the War

A good number of prominent Americans opposed what became known as "Mr. Polk's War." Some questioned the justification and the "fairness" of the war, and others the impact it would have on United States society and government.

The opinion of experienced politicians was particularly relevant. As unwavering patriots and great defenders of the regions they represented, they were quick to embrace the notion of territorial expansion, but they balked at achieving it by means of armed conquest in defiance of the law.

The fundamental concern of Americans opposed to the war was that territorial expansion might lead to the breakup of the Union. And they were right: the war against Mexico bestowed a large and valuable piece of property on the United States, but it also sowed divisions that with time would erode the ties that bound the states together.

Among the opponents of the war were several prominent writers: Henry David Thoreau, whose essay "On Civil Disobedience" encouraged popular resistance to an unjust war; Charles Sumner, who pointed out that the war would extend slavery into a territory where the Mexicans had done away with "that odious institution;" and Abraham Lincoln, who denounced the illegality of the war.

PLUCKED:

OR,

THE MEXICAN EAGLE BEFORE THE WAR!   THE MEXICAN EAGLE AFTER THE WAR!

This cartoon, which appeared in May 1847, before the war ended, shows the Mexican eagle before and after the American intervention, summing up the transformation with a single word: "Plucked." The texts in this chapter demonstrate that not all American leaders shared this point of view.

EFFECTS OF AN UNNATURAL WAR

[Henry Clay, "Speech in Lexington, KY"]

November 13, 1847

The day is dark and gloomy, unsettled and uncertain, like the condition of our country, in regard to the unnatural war with Mexico. The public mind is agitated and anxious, and is filled with serious apprehensions as to its indefinite continuance, and especially as to the consequences which its termination may bring forth, menacing the harmony, if not the existence, of our Union…

We are informed by a statement which is apparently correct, that, the number of our countrymen slain in this lamentable Mexican war, although it has yet been of only 18 months existence, is equal to one half of the whole of the American loss during the seven years war of the Revolution!

THE WAR WE STARTED WAS UNJUST

How did we unhappily get involved in this war? It was predicted as the consequence of the annexation of Texas to the United States. If we had not Texas, we should have no war. The people were told that if that event happened, war would ensue. They were told that the war between Texas and Mexico had not been terminated by a treaty of peace; that Mexico still claimed Texas as a revolted province and that, if we received Texas in our Union, we took along with her, the war existing between her and Mexico. And the Minister of Mexico [Juan N. Almonte] formally announced to the Government at Washington, that his nation would consider the annexation of Texas to the United States as producing a state of war. But all this was denied by the partizans [sic] of annexation… But, notwithstanding a state of virtual war necessarily resulted from the fact of annexation of one of the belligerents to the United States, actual hostilities might have been probably averted by prudence, moderation and wise statesmanship.

Henry Clay, who had been Congressman, Senator, Secretary of State, and twice presidential candidate, warned that the war against Mexico and the manner in which Polk waged it set a dangerous precedent for the abuse of presidential authority, manipulation of the legislative branch, and thus subversion of the constitutional order, the very foundation of the American nation. He saw in this war the seeds of the eventual breakup of the United States. The war affected him personally, as he lost one of his sons, ☞ p. 240.

If General [Zachary] Taylor had been permitted to remain, where his own good sense prompted him to believe he ought to remain. At the point of Corpus Christi, and, if a negotiation had been opened with Mexico, in a true spirit of amity and conciliation, war possibly might have been prevented. But, instead of this pacific and moderate course, whilst Mr. [John] Slidell was bending [sic, wending] his way to Mexico with his diplomatic credentials, General Taylor was ordered to transport his cannon, and to plant them, in a warlike attitude, opposite to Matamoras [sic] on the east bank of the Río Bravo [Río Grande]; within the very disputed territory, the adjustment of which was to be the object of Mr. Slidell's mission…

Thus the war commenced, and the President [James K. Polk] after having produced it, appealed to Congress. A bill was proposed to raise 50,000 volunteers, and in order to commit all who should vote for it, a preamble was inserted falsely attributing the commencement of the war to the act of Mexico… This is no war of defense, but one unnecessary and of offensive aggression. It is Mexico that is defending her fire-sides, her castles and her altars, not we…

THE COST OF CONQUERING ALL MEXICO

Shall this war be prosecuted for the purpose of conquering and annexing Mexico, in all its boundless extent, to the United States?… Does any considerate man believe it possible that two such immense countries, with territories of nearly equal extent, with populations so incongruous, so different in race, in language, in religion and in laws, could be blended together in one harmonious mass, and happily governed by one common authority? Murmurs, discontent, insurrections, rebellion, would inevitably ensue, until the incompatible parts would be broken asunder, and possibly, in the frightful struggle, our present glorious Union itself would be dissevered or dissolved…

THE UNITED STATES PROVOKED THE WAR

[Albert Gallatin, *Peace with Mexico*]

…The annexation of Texas, then at war with Mexico, was tantamount to a declaration of war, and that the comparative weakness of Mexico alone prevented its government from considering it as such.

Mexico had resorted, as a substitute for war, to the harmless suspension of the ordinary diplomatic… The attempt to make it retract that measure, before any negotiations for the restoration of harmony between the two countries should be entered, into, was neither countenanced by the acknowledged law of nations, nor necessary for any useful purpose.

But that the refusal of Mexico to submit to that additional contumely should have been considered as an insult to the United States betrays the pride of power, rather than a just sense of what is due to the true dignity and honor of this nation.

It has been demonstrated that the republic of Texas had not a shadow of right to the territory adjacent to the left bank of the lower portion of the Rio Norte; that, though she claimed, she never had actually exercised jurisdiction over any portion of it; that the Mexicans were the sole inhabitants and in actual possession of that district; that, therefore, its forcible occupation by the army of the United States was, according to the acknowledged law of nations, as well as in fact, an act of open hostility and war; that the resistance of the Mexicans to that invasion was legitimate; and that therefore the war was unprovoked by them, and commenced by the United States.

Abraham Alfonse Albert Gallatin was a Congressman, then a Senator from Pennsylvania. He held the post of Secretary of the Treasury during the presidency of Thomas Jefferson, as well as ambassador to Russia, Great Britain and France. In retirement, and only two years before his death, he wrote this essay to sway public opinion against the war.

THE UNITED STATES ABANDONED ITS TRUE PURPOSE

In their external relations the United States, before this unfortunate war, had, whilst sustaining their just rights, ever acted in strict conformity with the dictates of justice, and displayed the utmost moderation. They never had voluntarily injured any other nation. Every acquisition of territory from foreign powers was honestly made, the result of treaties not imposed, but freely assented to by the other party. The preservation of peace was ever a primary object.

At present all these principles would seem to have been abandoned.

RACISM AS JUSTIFICATION FOR WAR: WHAT EVER HAPPENED TO DEMOCRACY?

In the total absence of any argument that can justify the war in which we are now involved, resort has been had to a most extraordinary assertion. It is said that the people of the United States have an hereditary superiority of race over the Mexicans, which gives them the right to subjugate and keep in bondage the inferior nation. This, it is also alleged, will be the means of enlightening the degraded Mexicans, of improving their social state, and of ultimately increasing the happiness of the masses. Is it compatible with the principle of democracy, which rejects every hereditary claim of individuals, to admit an hereditary superiority of races?

Although he was the foremost defender of Southern slave interests and a supporter of annexing Texas, John Caldwell Calhoun, ⚙ p. 195, opposed the war against Mexico. He believed that the acquisition of more territory would deepen the conflict between the North and the South, and would put the Union at risk.

MEXICO: FORBIDDEN FRUIT

[John C. Calhoun, Speech on the Three Million Project]

February 9, 1847

The course of policy which we ought to purse in regard to Mexico is one of the greatest problems in our foreign relations. Our true policy, in my opinion, is not to weaken or humble her; on the contrary, it is our interest to see her strong, and respectable and capable of sustaining all the relations that ought to exist between independent nations. Mexico is to us the forbidden fruit; the penalty of eating it would be to subject our Institutions to political death.

OUR HERO'S OF 1848 AND 1865.

President Polk would leave office satisfied with the astonishing expansion of the United States under his leadership. Nevertheless, making good on the promise to offer Oregon to the North and Texas to the South did not put an end to the conflicts between the two, and in 1861 civil war broke out. Many of those who fought the Civil War had gained military experience in the war against Mexico. This illustration depicts the two generals considered heroes of the wars of 1846-1848 and 1861-1865: Scott (right) who made an unsuccessful bid for the presidency; and Ulysses Grant (left) who became president in 1868.

TO THE HONORED MEMORY
OF 750 AMERICANS
KNOWN BUT TO GOD
WHOSE BONES COLLECTED BY
THEIR COUNTRY'S ORDER
ARE HERE BURIED

In 1851, the U.S. government bought a piece of land in Mexico City near the San Cosme guard-house, where the last fighting took place. There, in a common grave, they buried the remains of 750 soldiers who died during the capture and occupation of the city. Today an additional 813 people are buried in the cemetery, most of them veterans of the war and their descendants.

Sources
Illustrations
Index

SOURCES

MEXICAN VOICES

I. Americans Viewed by a Liberal
▪ Lorenzo de Zavala, "Viaje a los Estados Unidos del Norte de América," in *Obras. Viaje a los Estados Unidos del Norte de América. La cuestión de Texas,* prologue, compilation and notes by Manuel González Ramírez, México, Porrúa, 1976.

II. Cultural Conflict during the Colonization of Texas
▪ Lorenzo de Zavala, *Viaje a los Estados Unidos...,* op. cit.
▪ Report of General Manuel Mier y Terán to the president of the Republic Guadalupe Victoria, 1828, in Vito Alessio Robles, *Coahuila y Texas, desde la consumación de la Independencia hasta el Tratado de Paz Guadalupe Hidalgo,* 2nd ed., México, Porrúa, 1979, vol. I.
▪ Report of Colonel Juan Nepomuceno Almonte, 1834, in Celia Gutiérrez Ibarra, *Cómo México perdió Texas. Análisis y trascripción del "Informe secreto" (1834) de Juan Nepomuceno Almonte,* México, INAH, 1987.

III. A Star is Born
▪ Ramón Alcaraz, Alejo Barreiro, Manuel Payno, Guillermo Prieto, Ignacio Ramírez et al., *Apuntes para la historia de la guerra entre México y los Estados Unidos,* prologue by Josefina Zoraida Vázquez [1st ed., 1848], México, Conaculta, 1991 (Col. Cien de México).
▪ José María Roa Bárcena, *Recuerdos de la invasión norteamericana (1846–1848), por un joven de entonces,* prologue by Gastón García Cantú [1st ed., 1883], Jalapa, Universidad Veracruzana, 1986.
▪ Letter from President Santa Anna to General D. Vicente Filisola, Battlefield of San Jacinto, April 22, 1836, in Lorenzo de Zavala, *Obras. Viaje a los Estados Unidos...,* op. cit.
▪ Letter from General D. Vicente Filisola to the Secretary of War and Navy

Office, Guadalupe Victoria, May 14, 1836, ibid.
▪ Letter from General D. Vicente Filisola to the Secretary of War and Navy Office, Field on the right bank of the Nueces River, May 31, 1836, ibid.

IV. The Scar of Texas
▪ Letter from José María Bocanegra to Waddy Thompson, August 23, 1843, in Carlos Bosch García, *El endeudamiento de México (abril de 1836–noviembre de 1843),* México, UNAM—Instituto de Investigaciones Históricas, 1984, vol. III (Documentos de la relación de México con los Estados Unidos).
▪ Note from José María Bocanegra to Benjamin E. Green, chargé d'affaires of the United States, May 30, 1844, in Carlos Bosch García, *De las reclamaciones, la guerra y la paz (1 de diciembre de 1843-22 de diciembre de 1848),* México, UNAM-Instituto de Investigaciones Históricas, 1985, vol. IV (Documentos de la relación de México con los Estados Unidos).
▪ Ramón Alcaraz et al., *Apuntes para la historia de la guerra...,* op. cit.

V. The Debate on the American Threat
▪ "Nuestra profesión de fe," *El Tiempo,* no. 19, February 12, 1846, in Gastón García Cantú (ed.), *Lecturas Universitarias, Antología. El pensamiento de la reacción mexicana (1810–1859),* México, UNAM, 1986, vol. I.
▪ "Al Tiempo," *El Republicano,* March 28, 1846.

VI. The Inevitable Conflagration
▪ Ramón Alcaraz et al., *Apuntes para la historia de la guerra...,* op. cit.
▪ José María Roa Bárcena, *Recuerdos de la invasion...,* op. cit.
▪ Manifesto of General Paredes, in Josefina Zoraida Vázquez (ed.), *Planes en la Nación Mexicana (1841–1854),* México, Senado de la República/El Colegio de México, 1987, vol. IV.

▪ Decree of the Mexican Congress, July 2, 1846, in Josefina Zoraida Vázquez (ed.), *Planes en la Nación Mexicana (1841–1854),* ibid.

VII. The Abyss of War
▪ Ramón Alcaraz et al., *Apuntes para la historia de la guerra...,* op. cit.
▪ Manuel Balbontín, "La invasión americana 1846–1848. Apuntes del subteniente de artillería Manuel Balbontín," in *Memorias del coronel Manuel Balbontín,* México, Elede, 1958.
▪ José María Roa Bárcena, *Recuerdos de la invasión...,* op. cit.

VIII. The Invasion of the Northwest
▪ José María Roa Bárcena, ibid.
▪ Ramón Alcaraz et al., *Apuntes para la historia de la guerra...,* op. cit.

IX. Defense of the Californias
▪ Ramón Alcaraz et al., ibid.

X. Invasion from the East
▪ Ramón Alcaraz et al., ibid.
▪ José María Roa Bárcena, *Recuerdos de la invasión...,* op. cit.
▪ Carlos María de Bustamante, *El nuevo Bernal Díaz del Castillo, o sea, historia de la invasión de los angloamericanos en México,* México, Conaculta, 1990.
▪ Abraham López, *La Revolución de los polkos o la cruzada de México en el siglo XIX,* en *Décimo calendario de Abraham López para el año de 1848* Imprenta tipográfica y litográfica, México, 1848.
▪ Letter from Guillermo Prieto, in Guillermo Prieto, *Memorias de mis tiempos. Obras completas,* prologue by Fernando Curiel, introduction and notes by Boris Rosen, México, Conaculta, 1992.

XI. The Price of Peace
▪ "Exposición dirigida al Supremo Gobierno por los Comisionados que firmaron el tratado de paz

con los Estados Unidos," Secretaría de Relaciones Exteriores, Querétaro, Imprenta de José M. Lara, 1848.

▩ Ramón Alcaraz et al., *Apuntes para la historia...*, op. cit.

XII. The Consequences of the War
▩ "Frutos de la guerra," *El Monitor Republicano*, July 7, 1848.

AMERICAN VOICES

I. Mexico in the Eyes of the U.S. Minister Plenipotentiary
▩ Joel R. Poinsett, Minister of the United States in Mexico, to Martin Van Buren, Secretary of State, Mexico, March 1, 1829, *Department of State*, vol. 4, doc. 196, National Archives, Washington, D.C.

II. The First American Settlers in Texas
▩ Stephen Austin, "Apuntes relativos a la Colonia de Texas," in Eugene C. Baker, ed., *The Austin Papers, The Annual Report of the American Historical Association for the Year of 1919*, Washington, D.C., Government Printing Office, 1924.

III. Texas Secedes
▩ Message of Samuel Houston, Washington-on-the-Brazos, Texas, December 12, 1835, in Donald Day and Harry Herbert Ullom (ed.), *The Autobiography of Sam Houston*, Norman, University of Oklahoma Press, 1947.

▩ "Declaration of Independence made by the Delegates of the People of Texas in General Convention," in William Carey Crane, *Life and Select Literary Remains of Sam Houston of Texas*, Freeport, New York, Books for Libraries Press, 1884.

IV. Annexation
▩ Instructions of John C. Calhoun,

Secretary of State, to William Shannon, Minister of the United States in Mexico, Washington, D.C., September 10, 1844, *Instructions, Department of State*, vol. 15, doc. 6, National Archives, Washington, D.C.

▩ Joint Resolution of Congress annexing Texas to the United States, March 1, 1845, in Henry Steele Commager, ed., *Documents of American History*, Englewood Cliffs, New Jersey, Prentice-Hall, 1973.

V. The "Manifest Destiny" of American Expansionism
▩ John L. O'Sullivan, "The Great Nation of Futurity," *Democratic Review*, November 1839, in Thomas G. Paterson, ed., *Major Problems in American Foreign Policy, Documents and Essays*, Lexington, Mass., D.C. Heath, 1984.

▩ John L. O'Sullivan, "Annexation," *United States Magazine and Democratic Review*, July 1845, in *The Annals of America*, vol. 7, Chicago, Encyclopedia Britannica, 1976.

VI. Declaration of War
▩ James Knox Polk, Message to Congress on War with Mexico, May 11, 1846, in Henry Steele Commager, ed., *Documents of American History*, op. cit.

VII. Taylor's Campaign
▩ Letter from Lieutenant Edmund Kirby Smith to Frances K. Smith, Matamoros, May 20, 1846, in George Winston Smith and Charles Judah, eds., *Chronicles of the Gringos, The U.S. Army in the Mexican War, 1846–1848. Accounts of Eyewitnesses and Combatants*, Albuquerque, New Mexico, The University of New Mexico Press, 1968.

▩ Report of Lieutenant Jeremiah Mason Scarnitt to Colonel Joseph G. Totten, May 12, 1846, ibid.

▩ Letter of Lieutenant Jenks Beaman to C.R. Mallory, Matamoros, May 29, 1846, ibid.

▩ John R. Kenly, "The Maryland Volunteer," ibid.

▩ Letter of Lieutenant Edmund Bradford to Caroline Bradford, Monterrey, September 27, 1846, ibid.

▩ "Touching Incidents," *Louisville Journal*, September 19, 1846, ibid.

▩ Letter of General Brigadier John E. Wool to Mayor W.W.S. Bliss, Agua Nueva, Coahuila, March 4, 1847, ibid.

VIII. The Conquest of New Mexico
▩ Letter of Andrew T. MacClure to his wife, Río Viguita, August 22, 1846, ibid.

▩ Dispatch of Colonel Sterling Price to General Roger Jones, Taos, February 15, 1847, ibid.

IX. The Conquest of California
▩ Letter of Lieutenant Archibald McRae to John McRae, San Francisco, California, October 25, 1846, ibid.

▩ Letter of John M. Stanley to *St. Louis Reveille*, San Diego, January 19, 1847, ibid.

▩ Mayor William H. Emory, "Notes of a Military Reconnaissance from Fort Leavenworth, Missouri, to San Diego, California, ibid.

X. Scott's Campaign
▩ Letter of Lieutenant Colonel Ethan A. Hitchcock to Elizabeth Nicolls, Veracruz, March 27, 1847, ibid.

▩ Letter of Lieutenant Peter V. Hagner to Mary M. Hagner, Veracruz, March 30, 1847, ibid.

▩ Anonymous letter, Jalapa, Veracruz, June 7, 1847, ibid.

▩ H. Judge Moore, "Scott's Campaign in Mexico," 1849, ibid.

▩ Diary of Lieutenant Daniel Harvey Hill, ibid.

▩ Letter of Captain Ephraim Kirby Smith to his wife, Tacubaya, August 22, 1847, ibid.

▩ Lieutenant Raphael Semmes, "The Campaign of General Scott in the Valley of Mexico, 1852, ibid.

▩ George W. Kendall, correspondence of the *New Orleans Picayune*, October 1847, ibid.

XI. The Treaty of Guadalupe Hidalgo

■ James Buchanan, Secretary of State, to Nicholas Trist, Washington, D.C., October 6, 1847, Instructions, Department of State, vol. 16, doc. 5, National Archives, Washington, D.C.

■ Letter of Virginia Randolph Trist to Tuckerman, July 8, 1864, in Robert W. Drexler, *Guilty of Making Peace. A Biography of Nicholas P. Trist*, Lanham, Maryland, University Press of America, 1991.

XII. The Impact of War

■ Henry Clay, Speech in Lexington, KY, November 13, 1847, in Melba Porter Hay and Carol Reardon, eds., *The Papers of Henry Clay*, Lexington, KY, The University Press of Kentucky, 1991.

■ Albert Gallatin, *Peace with Mexico*, New York, Bartlett & Welford, 1847.

■ John C. Calhoun, Speech on the Three Million Project, February 9, 1847, Washington, D.C., *The Congressional Globe*, Appendix, 29th Congress, 2nd Session.

COVER "General Wool's army marches toward Monclova in Mexico," watercolor by Samuel Chamberlain, 1846, The San Jacinto Museum of History, Houston.

2 Migrant at the border, Tijuana, 1990. Photo: Eniac Martínez Ulloa.

3 Recycling, New York, 2004. Photo: Andrés Stebelski.

4 Two Flags, Thanksgiving Day celebration, El Paso, Texas, 2004. Photo: Eniac Martínez Ulloa.

5 Virgin and Flags, Tortugas, New Mexico, 2001. Photo: Eniac Martínez Ulloa

8–9 "Battle of Buena Vista—Fought February 23rd, 1847—The American Army under Gen. Taylor were completely victorious," lithograph, hand-colored, James S, Baillie, 1847, Library of Congress, Prints and Photographs Division, LC-USZC4-6127.

10 "Battle of Cerro Gordo, April 18, 1847 (detail), lithograph, Nathaniel Currier, 1847, Library of Congress, Prints and Photographs Division, LC-USZC2-656.

12 "Territories of the United States and Mexico at the Beginning of the Nineteenth Century," map by Iván Ávalos.

14 "View of New York, Brooklyn, and the Navy Yard, from the Heights near Williamsburg," Nicolino V. Calyo, gouache, c. 1835–1840, Museum of the City of New York.

15 TOP "City Hall Park and Chambers Street from Broadway," Arthur J. Stansbury, watercolor, c. 1825, Museum of the City of New York.

15 B. "Auction in Chatham Square," E. Didier, oil on canvas, c. 1843, Museum of the City of New York.

17 "The Ladder of Fortune," Currier & Ives, lithograph, 1875, Museum of the City of New York.

18 "Boston," lithograph, in *Revista Científica y Literaria*, 1847, Hemeroteca Nacional de México.

20 "Colonies in Texas at the Beginning of the Nineteenth Century," map by Iván Ávalos, based on an 1836 map by Stephen Austin.

21 "El colono norteamericano," in *Décimo calendario*, Ignacio Cumplido, 1849, Biblioteca Nacional de México, Fondo Reservado.

22 Mapa que localiza las provincias de Texas, Nuevo México, Nueva Vizcaya, parte de los reinos de nueva Galicia y Nueva España, s/f, Archivo General de la Nación, Mapoteca. Photo: Janusz Polom.

24 "San Antonio de Béjar," in George Wurtz Hughes, *Memoir Descriptive of the March of a Division of the United States Army, under the Command of Brigadier General John E. Wool, from San Antonio de Bexar, in Texas, to Saltillo, in Mexico*, Washington D.C., 1850, private collection.

25 "Galveston," lithograph, in *Revista Científica y Literaria*, 1847, Hemeroteca Nacional de México.

26 TOP "Juan Nepomuceno Almonte," in Vicente Riva Palacio, *México a través de los siglos*, facsimile edition, vol. IV, México, 1971.

26 B. "Indígenas a caballo," in Th. Armin, *Das hentige Mexico*, Leipzig, 1865, private collection. Photo: Adrián Bodek.

28 "The War against the Texas Insurrection," map by Iván Ávalos.

29 Title page from Ramón Alcaraz et al., *Apuntes para la historia de la guerra entre México y los Estados Unidos*, México, 1848, private collection. Photo: Adrián Bodek.

30 "El Álamo," interior, in George Wurtz Hughes, op.cit., private collection.

31 TOP "Fall of the Alamo," in John Frost, *Pictorial History of Mexico and the Mexican War*, Philadelphia, 1849, private collection. Photo: Adrián Bodek.

31 B. "Plano de la Ciudad de San Antonio de Béjar y fortificación del Alamo, levantado y labado por el Cor.

Ignacio de Labastida, Comandante de Ingenieros del ejército del Norte, quien lo dedica al E. S. General D. Vicente Filisola," Center for American History, University of Texas, Austin.

32 TOP "El Álamo," exterior, in George Wurtz Hughes, op. cit., private collection.

32 B. "Santa Anna defeated at San Jacinto, 1836," playing card from deck illustrating scenes from the life of Santa Anna, 19th century, private collection. Photo: Adrián Bodek.

34 "La guerra de Texas," cartoon in *El Calavera*, January 19, 1847, México, Archivo General de la Nación. Photo: Janusz Polom.

35 "Houston, Santa Anna and Cos," lithograph, Henry R. Robinson after Edward Williams Clay, 1836, New York, Library of Congress, Prints and Photographs Division, LC-USZ62-1273.

36–37 Playing cards from deck illustrating scenes from the life of Santa Anna, 19th century, private collection. Photo: Adrián Bodek.

38 TOP "Samuel Houston," daguerrotype, c. 1844–1860, Library of Congress, Prints and Photographs Division, LC-USZ62-110113.

38 B. "Houston, Capital of Texas," lithograph, in *Revista Científica y Literaria*, 1847, Hemeroteca Nacional de México.

40 "The United States Following the Annexation of Texas," map by Iván Ávalos.

43 TOP "José Joaquín de Herrera," in Vicente Riva Palacio, op. cit.

43 B. "Santa Anna es arrojado de la presidencia y destruido, 1844" (Santa Anna is booted out of the presidency and destroyed, 1844), playing card from deck illustrating scenes from the life of Santa Anna, nineteenth century, private collection. Photo: Adrián Bodek.

44 "Guerra a Texas y a los Estados Unidos," cartoon, in *La Voz del Pueblo*, March 26, 1845, México,

Archivo General de la Nación. Photo: Janusz Polom.

46 "The Expansion of the United States," map by Iván Ávalos.

48 "Lucás Alamán," portrait, Museo Nacional de las Intervenciones, INAH, CNCA, MEX. Photo: Yanet Margarita Cruz Aceves.

49 "República Mexicana," cartoon, in *El Calavera*, February 2, 1847, private collection. Photo: Adrián Bodek.

52 "Deployment of U.S. Military Forces at the Beginning of the War," map by Iván Ávalos.

54 "Corpus Christi," lithograph, in *Revista Científica y Literaria*, 1847, Hemeroteca Nacional de México.

55 "Mariano Paredes y Arrillaga," in Vicente Riva Palacio, op. cit.

56 TOP "Troops landing at Point Isabel," in John Frost, *Pictorial History of Mexico and the Mexican War,* Philadelphia, 1849, private collection.

56 B. "Fort Brown," ibid.

57 "Mariano Arista," oil, Edouard Pingret, Secretaría de Relaciones Exteriores, Fototeca del Acervo Histórico Diplomático, Photo: Elsa Chabaud.

58 "Matamoros," hand-colored lithograph, in John Phillips and Alfred Rider, *Mexico Illustrated in Twenty-Six Views*, London, 1848, private collection. Photo: Adrián Bodek.

60 "Lt. Abraham Buford Scouting out a Report of the Enemy, watercolor, Samuel Chamberlain, 1846, The San Jacinto Museum of History, Houston.

62 "The Taylor–Wool Campaign," map by Iván Ávalos.

63 "Mexican Lancer," in John Frost, *op. cit.,* private collection. Photo: Adrián Bodek.

64–65 "Battle of Palo Alto, May 8th, 1846," lithograph, Emil Klauprecht after Angelo Paldí, 1847, Library

of Congress, Prints and Photographs Division, LC-USZ62-125.

65 B. "The night after the battle: burying the dead," hand-colored lithograph, Currier & Ives, c. 1846, Library of Congress, Prints and Photographs Division, LC-USZC2-2884.

66–67 "Battle of Resaca de la Palma, May 9th, 1846," lithograph, Emil Klauprecht after Angelo Paldí, 1847, Library of Congress, Prints and Photographs Division, LC-USZ62-125.

67 B. "Capture of Genl. La Vega by the gallant Capt. May, at the Battle of Resaca de la Palma," lithograph, Nathaniel Currier, c. 1846, Library of Congress, Prints and Photographs Division, LC-USZC4-2958.

68 TOP "A correct map of the Seat of War in Mexico, being a copy of General Arista's Map, taken of Resaca de la Palma, with editions and corrections," New York, 1847, private collection. Photo: Adrián Bodek.

68 B. "American entering Arista's camp," in John Frost, *op. cit.,* private collection. Photo: Adrián Bodek.

69 "Colonel Haney's Dragoons Cross the Rio Grande into Mexico," watercolor, Samuel Chamberlain, 1846, The San Jacinto Museum of History, Houston.

70 "General Ampudia," in Vicente Riva Palacio, op. cit.

71 "Heroica defensa de la ciudad de Monterrey contra el ejército norteamericano, el 23 de septiembre, 1846," (detail) lithograph, in Julio Michaud y Thomas, *México Álbum Pintoresco de la República Mexicana,* c. 1850, private collection. Photo: Adrián Bodek.

72–73 "View of the Battle of Monterrey, Sept. 21, 1846," lithograph, after Stephen G. Hill, Amon Carter Museum, Fort Worth, Texas, 79.87.

74 "Heroica defensa de la ciudad de Monterrey contra el ejército norteamericano, el 23 de septiembre, 1846," lithograph, in Julio Michaud

y Thomas, op. cit., private collection.
Photo: Adrián Botek.

75 "Genl. Ampudia treating for
the capitulation of Monterey with Genl.
Taylor, 24th Sept. 1846," hand-colored
lithograph, Sarony & Major, 1846,
Library of Congress, Prints and
Photographs graphs Division,
LC-USZC4-6211.

76 "Tampico," in John Frost,
op. cit., private collection.
Photo: Adrián Bodek.

77 "U.S. steam frigate
Mississippi, in the Gulf of Mexico,
March 1847," hand-colored lithograph,
Nathaniel Currier after Henry Walke,
Library of Congress, Prints and
Photographs Division, LC-USZC2-3129.

78 TOP "Santa Anna," miniature.
Photo: Elsa Chabaud.

78 B. Left: "Santa Anna vuelve
a la república, 1846." Right: "Santa
Anna se retira del campo de la
Angostura, 1847," playing cards from
deck illustrating scenes from the
life of Santa Anna, 19th century,
private colletion.
Photos: Adrián Bodek.

79 "Pass in the Sierra Madre—
near Monterrey," in John Phillips
and Alfred Rider, op. cit., private
collection. Photo: Adrián Bodek.

80 "Soldados mexicanos,"
sepia, Francisco Castro, 1847, private
collection. Photo: Adrián Bodek.

81 TOP "A Camp Kitchen,"
in John Frost, op cit., private collection.
Photo: Adrián Bodek.

81 B. "Camp at Agua Nueva,"
watercolor, Samuel Chamberlain, 1846,
The San Jacinto Museum of History,
Houston.

82 TOP "General Wool Encounters
a Bursting Shell," watercolor, Samuel
Chamberlain, 1846, The San Jacinto
Museum of History, Houston.

82 B. "McCulloch examining
a Mexican deserter," in John Frost,
op. cit., private collection.
Photo: Adrián Bodek.

83 "On the battlefield the night
after the battle," watercolor, Samuel
Chamberlain, 1846, The San Jacinto
Museum of History, Houston.

84 "El buitre sobre un soldado
muerto," in John Frost, op. cit., private
collection. Photo: Adrián Bodek.

85 "Massacre of the Big Train,"
watercolor, Samuel Chamberlain, 1846,
The San Jacinto Museum of History,
Houston.

86 "Pass in the Sierra Madre —
near Monterrey," (detail) in John Phillips
and Alfred Rider, op. cit., private collection. Photo: Adrián Bodek.

88 "The Kearny–Doniphan
Campaign," map by Iván Ávalos.

89 "General Wool's Army
Marching into Mexico toward
Monclova," watercolor, Samuel
Chamberlain, 1846, The San Jacinto
Museum of History, Houston.

90 "Texas Indians," watercolor,
Samuel Chamberlain, 1846, The San
Jacinto Museum of History, Houston.

91 "El Paso, in John Frost, op,
cit., private collection. Photo: Adrián
Bodek.

92 "Batalla del Sacramento,
terrible carga de los lanceros mexicanos,
contra el ejercito norteamericano,
el 28 de febrero 1847," (detail) lithograph, in Julio Michaud y Thomas, op.
cit., private collection. Photo: Adrián
Bodek.

93 "Batalla del Sacramento,"
lithograph, ibid.

96 "The Deployment of Forces
in the Conquest of California," map by
Iván Ávalos.

97 TOP "Caravanas de los Estados
Unidos en el territorio mexicano," lithograph, in *Revista Científica y Literaria,*
1847, Hemeroteca Nacional de México.

97 B. Document promoting Irish
immigration to California, Archivo
General de la Nación. Photo: Janusz
Polom.

98 "Col. Fremont Planting the
American Standard on the Rocky

Mountains," wood engraving, 1856,
Library of Congress, Prints and
Photographs Division, LC-USZ62-49597.

99 The original flag of the Bear
Republic, photograph, c. 1864, The
Society of California Pioneers.

100 LEFT "Una casa en la América
Rusa," lithograph, in *Revista Científica
y Literaria,* 1847, Hemeroteca Nacional
de México.

100 RIGHT "Establecimiento ruso,"
lithograph, ibid.

101 TOP "Puerto de Monterey,"
lithograph, ibid.

101 B. "U.S. Squadron at Anchor.
Peace at Monterey," watercolor, in
William H. Meyers, *Naval Sketches of
the War in California,* Franklin D.
Roosevelt Library.

103 "Typical lancer of the
Mexican troops that opposed the
American naval forces in California,
watercolor, ibid.

104 "Battle of the Plains of Mesa,
January 9th, 1847," (detail) watercolor,
ibid.

105 "Un californiano,"
in John Frost, op. cit., private collection.
Photo: Adrián Bodek.

106 "Battle of Santa Clara,
January 2nd, 1947," watercolor, in
William H. Meyers, *Naval Sketches of
the War in California,* op. cit.

108 "Scott's Campaign," map by
Iván Ávalos.

109 "Veracruz," lithograph,
Archivo General de la Nación, Centro de
Información Gráfica. Photo: Janusz Polom.

110 TOP "La Profesa," illuminated
lithograph, A. López, in *Col. de vistas
tomadas en la revolución llamada de los
Polkos, en México el año de 1847.* No. 1,
private collection. Photo: Adrián Bodek.

110 B. "La trinchera ambulante,"
in *Décimo calendario,* Abraham López,
1848, Biblioteca Nacional de México,
Fondo Reservado.

111 "Bombardment of Vera Cruz,
March 25, 1847," hand-colored
lithograph, Nathaniel Currier, c. 1847,

Library of Congress, Prints and Photograph Division, LC-USZC2-1753.

112 "Scene from the Bombardment of Vera Cruz, March 25, 1847," illuminated lithograph, Nathaniel Currier, 1847, private collection. Photo: Adrián Bodek.

114 "Mexicans killing the wounded at Buena Vista," in John Frost, op. cit., private collection. Photo: Adrián Bodek.

115 "View of Cerro Gordo with Genl. Twiggs' Division Storming the Main Heights, April 18, 1847," hand-colored lithograph, H. Méndez, 1847, Amon Carter Museum, Fort Worth, Texas, 119.72.

116 "Battle of Cerro Gordo, April 18, 1847," hand-colored lithograph, Nathaniel Currier, 1847, Library of Congress, Prints and Photographs Division, LC-USZC2-656.

117 TOP "Flight of Santa Anna at the Battle of Cerro Gordo," hand-colored lithograph, Richard Maggy, 1847, Library of Congress, Prints and Photographs Division, LC-USZC4-6209.

117 B. "The Capture of Santa Anna's Leg," lithograph, contemporary U.S. newspaper, private collection.

118 "Amputation of the Leg of Sergeant Antonio Bustos," daguerrotype, 1847, CONACULTA-SINAFO-FOTOTECA DE INAH.

119 TOP "Jalapa," hand-colored lithograph, in John Phillips and Alfred Rider. op. cit. Photo: Adrián Bodek.

119 B. "A New Rule in Algebra," lithograph, E. Jones and G.W. Newman, 1846, Library of Congress, Prints and Photographs Division, LC-USZ62-9915.

120 TOP "American Soldier with a Street Vendor," in John Frost, *The Mexican War and its Warriors*, Philadelphia, 1848, private collection. Photo: Adrián Bodek.

120 B. "Mexican Inn, between Jalapa and Puebla," in John Frost, *Pictorial History of Mexico and the Mexican War* op. cit., private collection. Photo: Adrián Bodek.

121 "U.S. Dragoons Cutting their Way through a Mexican Ambuscade," hand-colored lithograph, Currier & Ives, 1846, Library of Congress, Prints and Photographs Division, LC-USZC2-3117.

122 "Puebla," in John Phillips and Alfred Rider, op. cit., private collection. Photo: Adrián Bodek.

124 "Río Frío," ibid.

125 "Map of the Operations of the Mexico Army in the Valley of Mexico, in August and September," lithograph, E. Schieble, 1847, private collection. Photo: Adrián Bodek.

127 "Fortificación del Peñon," lithograph, in *Décimo calendario*, A. López, 1848, Biblioteca Nacional de México, Fondo Reservado.

128 "Grand Mass before Buena Vista," watercolor, Samuel Chamberlain, 1846, The San Jacinto Museum of History, Houston.

129 "Battle of Contreras, Mexico, August 19 and 20, 1847," (detail: Valencia's positions) lithograph, Joaquín Heredia, 1847, Amon Carter Museum, Fort Worth, Texas, 31.75.

130 "Santa Anna abandona a Valencia y se retira a México," (Santa Anna abandons Valencia and returns to Mexico City), playing card from deck illustrating scenes from the life of Santa Anna, 19th century, private collection. Photo: Adrián Bodek.

131 "Battle of Contreras, Mexico, August 19 and 20, 1847," lithograph, Joaquín Heredia, 1847, Amon Carter Museum, Fort Worth, Texas.

132 "Sitio del Convento de Churubusco por los norteamericanos, al 20 de agosto de 1847," oil signed by Solís, 1893, Museo Nacional de las Intervenciones, INAH, CNCA, MEX. Photo: Yanet Margarita Cruz Aceves.

133 "Ataque de Churubusco, por la division del general Worth, el dia 20 de Agosto de 1847," (Attack at Churu-busco, by the division of General Worth, August 20, 1847) lithograph, Ignacio Cumplido, 1848, Amon Carter Museum, Fort Worth, Texas, 32.75.

134 "Cartas histórico-geográficas mexicanas formadas bajo la dirección de Lic. Victoriano Pimentel: La invasión norteamericana 1846–1848," (detail of Generals Anaya and Twiggs) Archivo General de la Nación. Photo: Janusz Polom.

135 Front and back of the St. Patrick's Battalion Commemorative Medal, 1847, Museo Nacional de las Intervenciones, INAH, CNCA, MEX. Photo: Yanet Margarita Cruz Aceves.

136 "The San Patricio Execution at Mixcoac," watercolor, Samuel Chamberlain, 1846, The San Jacinto Museum of History, Houston.

138 "El pueblo apedrea los carros," in *Noveno calendario*, A. López, 1847, Biblioteca Nacional de México, Fondo Reservado.

140 "Map of the operations of the Mexico Army in the Valley of Mexico, in August and September," (detail) lithograph, E. Schieble, 1847, private collection. Photo: Adrián Bodek.

141 "Vista de Chapultepec y Molino del Rey," in Julio Michaud y Thomas, op. cit., private collection. Photo: Adrián Bodek.

142 TOP "Nicolás Bravo," oil, Carlos Tejada, twentieth century, Secretaría de Relaciones Exteriores, Fototeca del Acervo Histórico Diplomático, Photo: Elsa Chabaud.

142 B. "Chapultepec," lithograph, Reinaldo after an unknown artist, Amon Carter Museum, Fort Worth, Texas, 33.75.

143 "Recuerdo de la guerra con los Estados Unidos. Trofeos y monumentos existentes en México," in Vicente Riva Palacio, op. cit.

144 "Castillo de Chapultepec," in Julio Michaud y Thomas, op. cit., private collection. Photo: Adrián Bodek.

145 "Gate of Belen: Mexico, the 13th September, 1847," illuminated lithograph, Currier & Ives, 1847, Library of Congress, Prints and Photographs Division, LC-USZC2-2398.

147 "Entierro de los americanos," in *Undécimo calendario*, A. López, México, 1849, private collection. Photo: Adrián Bodek.

148 "Siege of Puebla, began Sept. 13, ended Oct. 12th, 1847," chromolithograph, Sarony & Mayor, New York, from a drawing on the spot by James T. Shannon, 1850, private collection. Photo: Adrián Bodek.

149 "San Ángel," lithograph, 1847, private collection. Photo: Adrián Bodek.

150 "Margaritas, calendario," A. López, Biblioteca Nacional, Fondo Reservado.

151 "Americanos comerciando en la Ciudad de México," lithograph, Rocha, 19th century, Museo Nacional de las Intervenciones, INAH, CNCA, MEX. Photo: Yanet Margarita Cruz Aceves.

152 TOP "Los azotes dados por los Americanos," in *Undécimo calendario*, A. López, México, 1849, private collection. Photo: Adrián Bodek.

152 B. "Santa Anna sale de la República, 1847," (Santa Anna leaves the country, 1847), playing card from deck illustrating scenes from the life of Santa Anna, 19th century, private collection. Photo: Adrián Bodek.

154 "The Territory under Negotiation," map by Iván Ávalos.

155 Map comparing the territories of the United States and Mexico after the war, Iván Ávalos.

156 "Mexican Family," daguerreotype, c. 1847. Amon Carter Museum, Fort Worth, Texas, 81.65/18.

157 "Group of Apaches," in John Russell Bartlett, *Personal Narrative of Explorations and Incidents in Texas, New Mexico, California, Sonora and Chihuahua,* New York, 1854, private collection. Photo: Adrián Bodek.

160 "Military Operations, 1846–1847," map by Iván Ávalos.

163 "Enarbolan el pabellón mexicano," in *Undécimo calendario,* A. López, México, 1849, private collection. Photo: Adrián Bodek.

164–165 "Battle of Buena Vista— Fought February 23rd, 1847—The American Army under General Taylor were completely victorious," hand-colored lithograph, James S. Baillie, 1847, Library of Congress, Prints and Photographs Division, LC-USZC4-6127.

166 "An available candidate. The one quaification of a Whig president," lithograph, Currier & Ives, 1848, Library of Congress, Prints and Photographs Division, LC-USZ62-5220.

168 "Plaza Mayor de México," hand-colored lithograph, in Carl Nebel, *Voyage pittoresque et archéologique dans la partie la plus intéressante du Mexique,* París, 1836, private collection. Photo: Adrián Bodek.

169 "Senator Joel Roberts Poinsett," lithograph, Charles Ferderich, 1838, National Portrait Gallery, Smithsonian Institution.

170 "Procession in Santo Domingo Plaza," hand-colored lithograph, in John Phillips and Alfred Rider, op. cit., private collection. Photo: Adrián Bodek.

171 "Escenas de mestizaje," Luis de Mena, Museo de América, Madrid.

172 "Valley of Mexico," (detail) Conrad Wise Chapman. Collection of the Banco de México.

174 "Mapa de la Sierra Gorda y costa del Golfo Mexicano," 1792, Archivo General de la Nación, Mapoteca, 977/0207.

176 "Unidentified Mason," colored daguerreotype, c. 1847, Amon Carter Museum, Fort Worth, Texas, 83.9/2.

178 "Stephen Fuller Austin," oil, William Howard, 1833, Center for American History, UT-Austin, CT 0008.

182 "Stampede of the Train by Wild Horses," in John Frost, *The Mexican War and its Warriors,* op. cit., private collection. Photo: Adrián Bodek.

183 "The Attack on an Emigrant Train," oil, Charles Wimar, 1856, Bequest of Henry C. Lewis, 1895.80.

185 TOP "The Old Plantation," unknown, c. 1800, Abby Aldrich Rockefeller Folk Art Museum, Colonial Williamsburg Foundation, Williamsburg, Virginia, 1935.301.3.

185 M. "Virginian Luxuries," unknown, c. 1815, Abby Aldrich Rockefeller Folk Art Museum, Colonial Williamsburg Foundation, Williamsburg, Virginia, 91993.1

185 B. "United States Slave Trade," etching, 1830, Library of Congress, Prints and Photographs Division, LC, USZ62-89701.

188 Title page from *Texas in 1840, or the Emigrant's Guide,* New York, 1840, Dorothy Sloan, Rare Books, Inc.

189 "Sam Houston," in John M. Nieles, *South America and Mexico,* Hartford, 1837, private collection. Photo: Adrián Bodek.

191 TOP "Battle of the Alamo," ibid.

191 B. "Battle of San Jacinto," ibid.

194 "The Polk and Dallas Banner," courtesy Dallas Historical Society.

195 "Matty Meeting the Texas Question," lithograph, H. Bucholzer, 1844, Library of Congress, Prints and Photographs Division, LC-USZ62-791.

197 "Texas Coming In," lithograph, H. Bucholzer, 1844, Library of Congress, Prints and Photographs Division, LC-SZ62-10802.

200 "American Progress," oil, John Gast, 1872, Autry Museum of Western Heritage, Los Angeles.

203 "Hunting Indians in Florida with Bloodhounds," lithograph, James Baillie, 1848, Library of Congress, Prints and Photographs Division, LC–USZ62-89725.

205 "Westward the Course of Empire Takes Its Way," oil, Emmanuel Gottlieb Leutze, 1861, Smithsonian American Art Museum, Washington, DC / Art Resource, New York.

208 "Birds-eye View of the Camp of the Army of Occupation, Commanded by Genl. Taylor, near Corpus Christi Texas (from the North), Oct. 1845," hand-colored lithograph, Charles Parsons after Daniel Powers Whiting, 1847, Amon Carter Museum, Fort Worth, Texas, 2.74/1.

209 "James Knox Polk," daguerrotype, c. 1847–1849, Amon Carter Museum, Fort Worth, Texas, 81.65/12.

210 TOP "Irish Soldier Presenting Arms to General Wool," watercolor, Samuel Chamberlain, 1846, The San Jacinto Museum of History, Houston.

210 B. "Drilling Raw Recruits," in John Frost, *Pictorial History of Mexico and the Mexican War*, op. cit., private collection. Photo: Adrián Bodek.

211 "Volunteers for Texas, As You Were," lithograph, Frances Palmer, 1846, Library of Congress, Prints and Photographs Division, LC–USZ62-1272.

212 "Map of Mexico and Texas," private collection. Photo: Adrián Bodek.

213 "Exeter, N.H. Volunteers," daguerrotype, c. 1846, Amon Carter Museum, Fort Worth, Texas, 79.33.

214 "General Taylor writing to the War Department," in John Frost, *Pictorial History of Mexico and the Mexican War*, op. cit., private collection. Photo: Adrián Bodek.

216 "Zachary Taylor," oil, William Garl Browne, Jr., 1847, National Portrait Gallery, Smithsonian Institution, NGP, 71.57.

217 "Death of Mayor Ringgold, of the Flying artillery, At the Battle of Palo Alto, Texas, May 8th, 1846," lithograph, Nathaniel Currier, Amon Carter Museum, Fort Worth, Texas, 67/71.

218 "Battle of Palo Alto," (detail) hand-colored lithograph, Adolphe-Jean-Baptiste Bayot after Carl Nebel, in George Wilkins Kendall, *The War Between the United States and Mexico Illustrated*, New York, D. Appleton & Company, 1851, private collection. Photo: Adrián Bodek.

219 Twelve lithographs by Adolphe-Jean-Baptist Bayot after Carl Nebel, from George Wilkins Kendall, op. cit., private collection. Photo: Ádrian Bodek.

220 Explanation of "Bataile de Palo Alto," hand-colored lithograph, Adolphe-Jean-Baptist Bayot after Carl Nebel, ibid.

221 "Battle of Palo Alto," ibid.

222 "News from Mexico," etching, A. Jones after an oil by Richard Caton Woodville, 1851, Library of Congress, Prints and Photographs Division, LC–USZC4-4559.

224 TOP "Soldiers Drinking," in John Frost, *Pictorial History of Mexico and the Mexican War*, op. cit., private collection. Photo: Adrián Bodek.

224 B. "Gran Plaza Camargo," ibid.

225 Explanation of "Capture of Monterrey," hand-colored lithograph, Adolphe-Jean-Baptist Bayot after Carl Nebel, in George Wilkins Kendall, op. cit., private collection. Photo: Ádrian Bodek.

226–227 "Capture of Monterrey," ibid.

228 "Heights of Monterrey, from the Saltillo Road looking toward the City (from the West)," (detail: retreat of the Mexican cavalry), hand-colored lithograph, F. Swinton after Daniel Powers Whiting, 1847, private collection. Photo: Adrián Bodek.

229 "Heights of Monterrey, from the Saltillo Road looking toward the City (from the West)," ibid.

230 "Storming of the Bishop's Palace: at the siege of Monterrey, Sept. 22nd, 1846," hand-colored lithograph, Nathaniel Currier, 1847, Library of Congress, Prints and Photographs Division, LC-USZC2-3037.

231 "Monterrey, from Independence Hill, in the rear of the Bishop's Palace. As it appeared on 23rd September, 1846, (looking East)," hand-colored lithograph, F. Swinton after Daniel Powers Whiting, 1847, private collection. Photo: Adrián Bodek.

232 "Monterrey, As seen from a House-Top in the Main Plaza (to the West) October 1846," toned lithograph, F. Swinton after Daniel Powers Whiting, 1847, private collection. Photo: Adrián Bodek.

233 "Distinguished military operations with a hasty bowl of soup," lithograph, Edward Williams Clay, 1846, Library of Congress, Prints and Photographs Division, LC-USZ62-62676.

234 "Una mexicana atendiendo al herido," in John Frost, *Pictorial History of Mexico and the Mexican War*, op. cit., private collection. Photo: Adrián Bodek.

235 "General Wool and Staff, calle Real, to South," daguerrotype, Amon Carter Museum, Fort Worth, Texas, 81.65/22.

236–237 "Battle of Buena Vista, View of the Battleground of The Angostura, Fought Near Buena Vista, Mexico, February 23rd, 1847 (Looking S. West)," hand-colored lithograph, Frances Flora Bond (Fanny) Palmer after Joseph Horace Eaton, 1847, Amon Carter Museum, Fort Worth, Texas, 48.71.

238 TOP "Major General Zachary Taylor," woodcarving, W.M. & J.T. Howland after S. Wallin, 1847, Library of Congress, Prints and Photographs Division, LC-USZ62-90658.

238 B. "Robo al soldado muerto," in John Frost, *Pictorial History of Mexico and the Mexican War*, op. cit., private collection. Photo: Adrián Bodek.

239 Explanation of "Battle of Buena Vista, View of the Battleground of The Angostura, Fought Near Buena Vista, Mexico, February 23rd, 1847 (looking S. West)," op. cit., Amon Carter Museum, Fort Worth, Texas, 48.71.

240 TOP "Death of Col. Henry Clay," illuminated lithograph, Kellogg, Library of Congress, Prints and Photographs Division, LC-USZC4-6197.

240 B. "Burial site of Lieutenant Colonel Henry Clay," daguerrotype, c. 1847, Amon Carter Museum, Fort Worth, Texas, 81.65/41.

241 Explanation of "Battle of Buena Vista," hand-colored lithograph, Adolphe-Jean-Baptist Bayot after Carl Nebel, in George Wilkins Kendall, op. cit., private collection. Photo: Adrián Bodek.

242 "Battle of Buena Vista," hand-colored lithograph, Adolphe-Jean-Baptist Bayot after Carl Nebel, ibid.

243 TOP "Camp Followers. Two carrying Soldier on Litter," watercolor, Samuel Chamberlain, 1846, The San Jacinto Museum of History, Houston.

243 B. "The night after the battle: burying the dead," hand-colored lithograph, Nathaniel Currier, 1847, Library of Congress, Prints and Photographs Division, LC-USZC2-2885.

244 "Rackensackers on the Rampage," watercolor, Samuel Chamberlain, 1846, The San Jacinto Museum of History, Houston.

246 "Santa Fe," engraving and etching, in W. Abert, *Report of Lieut. J. W. Abert, of His Examination of New Mexico, in the Years 1846–1847,* 1848, Amon Carter Museum, Fort Worth, Texas, 65.75/1.

247 "General Stephen W. Kearny," in John Frost, *The Mexican War and its Warriors,* op. cit., private collecton. Photo: Adrián Bodek.

248 "Rout of the Mexicans," ibid.

250 "Mexican Guerrillas," watercolor, Samuel Chamberlain, 1846, The San Jacinto Museum of History, Houston.

251 "Ruins of the Casas Grandes in Chihuahua," in John Russell Bartlett, *Personal narrative of Explorations and incidents in Texas, New Mexico, California, Sonora and Chihuahua,* New York, 1854.

252 "Battle of Sacramento," hand-colored lithograph, Nathaniel Currier, 1847, Library of Congress, Prints and Photographs Division, LC-USZC2-3544.

254 "The *Dale*'s 32 pounders aid their shipmates ashore, 17 Nov. 1847," watercolor, in William H. Meyers, op. cit., Franklin D. Roosevelt Library.

255 "La bahía de San Francisco," in William Milvaine, Jr., *Sketches of Scenery and Notes of Personal Adventures in California and Mexico,* Philadelphia, 1850, private collection. Photo: Adrián Bodek.

257 "The Battle of San Pascual. General Kearny reinforced by sailors and California volunteers fighting his way to San Diego," watercolor, in William H. Meyers, op. cit., Franklin D. Roosevelt Library.

258 "Crossing the San Gabriel River. Commodore Stockton's first encounter on the final march to Los Angeles. 8 Jan. 1847," ibid.

259 "The American encampment on the San Gabriel Battle. 8 Jan. 1847," ibid.

260 "The decisive battle for Los Angeles. The repulse of the Mexicans on the plains of La Mesa. 9 Jan. 1847," ibid.

262 "The Dale's armed launch in action on detach service. 11 Nov. 1847," ibid.

264 TOP "Winfield Scott," oil, Robert Walter Weir, 1855, National Portrait Gallery, Smithsonian Institution, NPG. 95.52.

264 B. "A bad egg: Fuss and feathers," lithograph, probably Nathaniel Currier, 1852, Library of Congress, Prints and Photographs Division, LC-USZ62-50949.

265 "Landing of the U.S. Army under general Scott, on the beach near Vera Cruz March 9th 1847," lithograph, Henry Dacre after Charles Crillon Barton, 1847, Library of Congress, Prints and Photographs Division.

266 "Bombardment of Vera Cruz, March, 1847, Attack of the Gun Boats upon the City, and Castle of San Juan de Ulloa," hand-colored lithograph, Nathaniel Currier, 1847, Library of Congress, Prints and Photographs Division, LC-USZC2-1753.

267 "Bombardment of Vera Cruz," lithograph, Adolphe-Jean-Baptist Bayot after Carl Nebel, in George Wilkins Kendall, op. cit., private collection. Photo: Adrián Bodek.

268 "Capitulation of Vera Cruz: The Mexican soldiers marching out, and surrendering their arms to Genl. Scott, March 29, 1847," hand-colored lithograph, Nathaniel Currier, 1847, Library of Congress, Prints and Photographs Division, LC-USZC2-2034.

269 "Battle of Cerro Gordo," lithograph, Adolphe-Jean-Baptist Bayot after Carl Nebel, in George Wilkins Kendall, op. cit., private collection. Photo: Adrián Bodek.

270 "Defensa de Cerro Gordo contra el ejército americano, el 18 de abril 1847," lithograph, Ed. Bastin after an unknown artist, in Julio Michaud y Thomas, op. cit., private collection. Photo: Adrián Bodek.

271 "Scott visiting General Shields wounded," in Edward D. Mansfield, *The Mexican War, a History of its Origin,* New York, 1848, private collection. Photo: Adrián Bodek.

272 "The First Division Volunteers encamped in Elencerro, Mexico, under command of Maj. Gen. Robert Patterson," toned lithograph, M.H. Traubel after Jason D. L. Polhemus, c. 1848. Amon Carter Museum, Fort Worth, Texas, 49.74.

273 "Castillo de Perote, México," lithograph, after James T. Shannon, 1847, private collection. Photo: Adrián Bodek.

274 "Vista General de Puebla," Illuminated lithograph, N. Gonzalez Madrid.

275 "Gen. [Wm. Jenkins] Worth's Quick Step; music cover showing U.S. troops in battle in the Mexican war," lithograph, Bufford & Co., c. 1846, Library of Congress, Prints and Photographs Division, LC-USZ62-62427.

276 "Valle de México," Conrad Wise Chapman, collection of the Banco de México.

277 "Tambor," in John Frost, *Pictorial History of Mexico and the Mexican War,* op.cit., private collection. Photo: Adrián Bodek.

278 "Soldados en la lluvia," in John Frost, *The Mexican War and its Warriors,* op. cit., private collection. Photo: Adrián Bodek.

279 "Assault at Contreras," lithograph, Adolphe-Jean-Baptist Bayot after Carl Nebel, in George Wilkins Kendall, op. cit., private collection. Photo: Adrián Bodek.

280 "Pursuit of the Mexicans by the U.S. Dragoons: under the intrepid Col. Harney, at the Battle of Churubusco," hand-colored lithograph, Nathaniel Currier, 1847, Library of Congress, Prints and Photographs Division, LC-USZC2-2939.

281 "Battle at Churubusco," (detail) lithograph, Adolphe-Jean-Baptist Bayot after Carl Nebel, in George Wilkins Kendall, op. cit., private collection. Photo: Adrián Bodek.

282 "Battle at Churubusco," ibid.

283 "Churubusco, 1847," lithograph, Pierre-Frédéric Lehnert, in Julio Michaud y Thomas, op. cit., private collection. Photo: Adrián Bodek.

284 "Molino del Rey—Attack upon the Molino," lithograph, Adolphe-Jean-Baptist Bayot after Carl Nebel, in George Wilkins Kendall, op. cit., private collection. Photo: Adrián Bodek.

286 "Molino del Rey—Attack upon the Casa Mata," (detail), ibid.

287 "Molino del Rey—Attack upon the Casa Mata," ibid.

288 "Storming of Chapultepec—Quitman's Attack," ibid.

289 "Storming of Chapultepec—Pillow's Attack," (detail), ibid.

290 "Storming of Chapultepec—Pillow's Attack," ibid.

291 "Self-inflating pillow," lithograph, Peter Smith [Nathaniel Currier], 1848, Library of Congress, Prints and Photographs Division, LC-USZ62-11404.

292 "Genl. Scott entrance into Mexico," lithograph, Adolphe-Jean-Baptist Bayot after Carl Nebel, in George Wilkins Kendall, op. cit., private collection. Photo: Adrián Bodek.

294 "Going to and returning from Mexico," in *Yankee Doodle,* 1847, p. 71, Library of Congress, Prints and Photographs Division, LC-USZ62-84833.

296 Treaty of Guadalupe Hidalgo, page with negotiators' signatures, 1848, Secretaría de Relaciones Exteriores, Fototeca del Acervo Histórico Diplomático. Photo: Elsa Chabaud.

298 Signature of Nicholas P. Trist, 1848, Secretaría de Relaciones Exteriores. Photo: Elsa Chabaud.

300 "Plucked or The Mexican eagle before the war! The Mexican eagle after the war!," illustration in *Yankee Doodle,* v. 2, no. 32 (May 15, 1847), Library of Congress, Prints and Photographs Division, LC-USZ62-130816.

301 "Henry Clay," daguerrotype, 1850–1852, Library of Congress, Prints and Photographs Division, LC-USZ62-109953.

303 "Albert Gallatin," daguerrotype, private collection.

304 "Daniel Webster, Henry Clay, John Caldwell Calhuan," cut-out of John Caldwell Calhuan, drawing by Clifford Kennedy Berryman, 1931, Library of Congress, Prints and Photographs

División, CD-1– Berryman (C.K.), no. 1148.

305 "Our heroes of 1848 and 1865," lithograph Kimmel & Forster, 1865, Library of Congress, Prints and Photographs Division, LC-USZ62-115109.

306 American cemetery, Mexico City, June 7, 2004. Photo: Andrés Stebelski.